The Isles of the
Many Gods

Published by Avalonia

BM Avalonia
London
WC1N 3XX
England, UK

www.avaloniabooks.co.uk

THE ISLES OF THE MANY GODS

ISBN 1-905297-10-6

First Edition 2007
Design by Avalonia
Cover Image © Phil Bartlett
Copyright © David Rankine, Sorita D'Este

All rights reserved. No part of this publication may be reproduced or utilized in any form or by any means, electronic or mechanical, including photocopying, microfilm, recording, or by any information storage and retrieval system, or used in another book, without written permission from the authors.

The Isles of the Many Gods

David Rankine & Sorita D'Este

Dedicated to MLTM

May you continue to create unsurpassable Greatness,
Love and Happiness in all that you do.

Table of Contents

About the Authors 14
Author's Foreword 15
    Author's Notes 17
    1. Evidence for Inclusion 17
    2. The Argument for Divinity 19

MANY GODS
The Origins of the Gods 24
Literary Evidence 33
    Literature Timeline 36
The Unnamed Gods 40
The Christian Influence 45

A –Z LISTING : Gods & Goddesses of Pagan Britain
    Key to understanding A-Z entries: 50

A
    Abandinus 51
    Abraxas 51
    Aegil 52
    Aeron 52
    Aesculapius 53
    Agroná 54
    Áine 54
    Alaisagae 56
    Alator 56
    Amaethon 57
    Ammon 58
    Ancasta 58
    Andescociuoucus 59
    Andraste 59

Anextiomarus 60
Angus Mac Og 60
Anicetus 61
Antenocitus 62
Anubis 62
Aoibheall 63
Apollo 64
Arawn 65
Arecurius 66
Arianrhod 66
Arimanius 68
Arnemetia 68
Astarte 68
Atargatis 69
Attis 69

B

Badb 71
Bacchus 72
Baldur 73
Balor 74
Banba 75
Barrecis 76
Bastet 76
Bé Chuille 76
Belatucadros 77
Belenus 78
Beli 78
Belisama 79
Bellona 80
Bé Néit 80
Bes 81
Bilé 81
Black Annis 82
Blodeuwedd 83
Boann 85

Bona Dea 86
Bonus Eventus 87
Braciaca 88
Bran 88
Branwen 90
Bregans 91
Bres 92
Brian 93
Brigantia 94
Brigit 95
Britannia 96
Búanann 96

C

Caelestis 98
Cailleach 98
Callirius 104
Camulos 104
Carman 105
Cautes 105
Cautopates 106
Ceres 106
Ceridwen 107
Cernunnos 109
Clídna 110
Cocidius 111
Concordia 112
Condatis 112
Contrebis 113
Corotiacus 113
Coventina 114
Creidhne 115
Cuda 115
Cunobelinus 116
Cupid 116
Cybele 117

D

- Daghda 118
- Danu 120
- Deo Qui Vias et Semitas Commentus Est 122
- Diana 122
- Dian Cecht 123
- Disciplina 124
- Dolichenus 124
- Don 125
- Donn 126
- Dylan 127

E

- Edeyrn 129
- Eostra 130
- Epona 130
- Erce 131
- Ériu 132
- Ernmas 134
- Étaín 135

F

- Fates 136
- Faunus 136
- Fea 137
- Fedelm 137
- Fergus 139
- Flidais 140
- Fortuna 141
- Fotla 142
- Frigg/Freya 143

G

- Garmangabi 145
- Geat 145
- Gilvaethwy 146
- Gobannos 147

Goibniu 147
Govannon 148
Grannos 149
Grián 149
Gwenwynwyn 150
Gwydion 151
Gwyn ap Nudd 153

H

Harimella 156
Harpocrates 156
Helioserapis 157
Helith 157
Hercules 157
Herne 158
Hiccafrith 160
Horus 161
Hreda 161
Hu Gadarn 162
Hygiaea 164

I

Ialonus 165
Ing 165
Isis 166
Iuchar 167
Iucharba 168

J

Juno 169
Jupiter 169

K

Kymideu Kymeinvoll 171

L

Latis 173

Lenus 173
Lir 174
Lleu Llaw Gyffes 174
Llyr 177
Loki 177
London Hunter God 178
Loucetius 178
Luchta 178
Ludd 179
Lugh 180

M

Mabon 183
Macha 184
Manannán MacLir 187
Manawyddan 189
Maponus 190
Mars 191
Math Mathonwy 192
Matunus 193
Medb 193
Medigenus 195
Medocius 196
Mercury 196
Methe 197
Midir 198
Minerva 199
Mithras 200
Modron 201
Mogons 202
Morrígan 202

N

Nantosuelta 206
Nechtan 206
Néit 207
Neith 208

Nemain	208
Nemesis	209
Nemetius	210
Nemetona	210
Neptune	211
Nerthus	212
Nodens	213
Nuada	215
Nudd	216
Nyx	216

O

Oceanus	217
Ocelus	217
Ogma	218
Olloudius	219
Olwen	219
Onirus	220

P

Pan	221
Panakeia	221
Pax	222
Penarddun	222
Priapus	223
Pryderi	223
Pwyll	224

R

Rata	226
Rhiannon	226
Ricagumbeda	227
Rider God	228
Rigisamus	228
Rigonemetis	229
Roma	229
Rosmerta	230

S

- Sabrina ... 232
- Saitada ... 232
- Salus ... 233
- Saturn ... 233
- Scáthach ... 234
- Seaxnéat ... 235
- Segomo ... 235
- Serapis ... 235
- Setlocenia ... 236
- Silvanus ... 236
- Sionna ... 237
- Sol Invictus ... 238
- Soter ... 238
- Spes ... 239
- Sucellos ... 239
- Sulis ... 240

T

- Tailtiu ... 241
- Taranis ... 241
- Tethys ... 242
- Terminus ... 243
- Teutates ... 243
- Thoth ... 244
- Thunor ... 244
- Tiw ... 245
- Tridamus ... 246
- Tyche ... 246

V

- Vanuntus ... 247
- Venus ... 247
- Verbeia ... 248
- Vernostonus ... 248
- Victoria ... 248
- Vinotonus ... 249

Viradecthis 249
Viridios 250
Vitiris 250
Vulcan 251

W
Weland 252
Wheel God 253
Woden 254

APPENDIX
Genealogies 258
    The Welsh Pantheon 259
    The Irish Pantheon 261
Timelines 263
    Historical Timeline 263
The Return of the Pagan Gods 266

Bibliography 268

Index 284

About the Authors

Sorita D'Este and David Rankine are internationally recognized for their research and writing on mythology, spirituality and magickal practices of both ancient and modern times. They have collaborated on a number of projects in the past, including *"The Guises of the Morrigan"* and *"Circle of Fire"*. Between them they have authored more than a dozen books, sometimes working with other authors with expertise in a particular area. In addition to books, Sorita and David have also contributed many articles to magazines, journals and websites over the years. Notably they were major contributors to the very successful D'Agostini *"Enhancing Your Mind Body Spirit"* partwork. They live and work in Wales (UK).

For more information visit: www.avalonia.co.uk

Their published works include:

- *Climbing the Tree of Life*, David Rankine, Avalonia, 2006
- *Heka (Ancient Egyptian Magic & Ritual)*, David Rankine, Avalonia, 2006
- *Artemis – Virgin Goddess of the Sun & Moon*, Sorita D'Este, Avalonia, 2005
- *Circle of Fire*, Sorita D'Este & David Rankine, Avalonia, 2005
- *The Guises of the Morrigan – Irish Goddess of Sex & Battle*, David Rankine & Sorita D'Este, Avalonia, 2005
- *Becoming Magick*, David Rankine, Mandrake of Oxford, 2004
- *Crystals Healing & Folklore*, David Rankine, Capall Bann, 2002

If you wish to contact the authors, please write to:

Sorita D'Este & David Rankine
c/o BM Avalonia
London
WC1N 3XX
United Kingdom

Author's Foreword

This book was a labour of love – both in that we felt the need for such a book for use by those interested in the Gods and Goddesses worshiped and celebrated by our ancestors in Ancient Britain, but also because we enjoyed doing the research so much! In fact, though this is true to a certain extent for all projects we work on, we found it very difficult to stop adding new information and rewriting parts of this volume more than we have ever done with any book we have worked on in the past. So much so that it was more than six months late in going to print and contains around 30 more deities than it did when we first thought it was "all done"!

This book looks at the deities which were worshipped in the British Isles during the first millennium through to the Middle Ages. These include indigenous Gods and Goddesses, as well as many foreign ones which immigrated to these isles with waves of invading cultures. It is also worth considering that though we think of Christianity as being a religion which has been the dominant European religion for fifteen hundred years now it was slow at taking root in these isles and existed for many centuries alongside the older Pagan religions and practices.

Many of the Gods and Goddesses included in this book are immigrant deities who came to the British Isles from other parts of the world. This book is concerned only with the known evidence for their worship in the British Isles and as such we have not included details of their worship or the way in which they were viewed other than this. This should be kept in mind when reading through the entries of deities that originate in other parts of the world.

It is our hope that the information we have brought together in this volume will help provide inspiration for those readers who are interested in exploring the historical spiritual traditions of the British Isles in more depth. Throughout you will find footnotes and at the end a complete bibliography of all the materials we consulted whilst compiling this volume. We hope that this will help provide points of reference for those wishing to explore a particular subject in further depth.

We would like to express our special thanks for help with the research of this project to the staff at the *British Library* (London), for their patience and assistance. Also the staff at *Abergavenny Public Library* for their help during the final stages of our research, for providing assistance in finding specific works and a haven of quiet during the chaos during our house move in the Autumn of 2006. Thank you.

Thank you also to Phil and Tracy Bartlett from *Stagman Creations* for their kind permission to use their image "Lord of the Greenwood" for the cover of this book. To find out more about their work and to purchase prints of *"Lord of the Greenwood"* visit their website www.stagmancreations.co.uk

We hope that you find the information here interesting and that it will in turn inspire others to continue the work of looking at the spiritual heritage of these magical isles.

Sorita D'Este & David Rankine
Monmouthshire, Wales
December 2006

Author's Notes

1. Evidence for Inclusion

The source material available defines the scope of any work. When writing this book we drew from two distinct categories of material, archaeological and literary.

The archaeological evidence can be described as follows:

- Roman inscriptions found throughout Britain (the RIB),
- Stonework, including statues, friezes and sculptures,
- Jewellery, including amulets and talismans
- Curse tablets (defixiones),
- Votive offerings,
- Military equipment such as swords, shields and helmets,
- Currency (coins),
- Miscellaneous items depicting deities such as caskets or sceptres,
- Place names, including the names of rivers and towns.

The literary evidence covers a period of around seventeen hundred years and comes from a number of different cultural groups. Much of this literature was written by the dominant military and religious powers and so a cultural bias is inevitable in such writings, which must therefore be seen as representative evidence rather than absolute fact.

The literature can be categorised as follows:

- Early classical writings by Roman and Greek writers from the period first century BCE to the third century CE, which ranged from neutral reports such as Ptolemy's Geography to hostile bias such as in Julius Caesar's Gallic Wars.

- Saxon Christian writings from the seventh to the eleventh century CE. These range from religious texts to biographies to leech-books (books of charms and herbals).
- Celtic Christian writings from the fifth to the seventeenth century CE, from Ireland and Wales. This is the broadest corpus of material, which is largely recording of myths and folk tales, and also includes genealogies. The style of these works ranges from favourable to hostile and belittling.
- Icelandic writings on the Germanic gods, i.e. the thirteenth century CE Eddas.

2. The Argument for Divinity

When considering deities it is inevitable that one must consider their origins in order to understand both their existence and purpose. This then leads to questions in regards to the different types of deity, as well as criteria for when a god becomes a god. In some pantheons this is easier to distinguish than in others.

The Roman inscriptions of the early indigenous gods refer to the gods using the term *"deus"* or *"deae"*, indicating whether they are a god or goddess, so this is not a problem. Likewise the level of information regarding the deities brought to Britain by the Romans makes determination of the origins of a deity and whether it fits the criteria for inclusion a simple matter. The northern European gods are specifically referred to as deities, and for these pantheons there is no issue as to who is divine.

We have not included deified figures who were humans, such as the Roman emperors, or hero figures from myths who did not have at least one divine parent. Hercules is included due to his divine parentage, whereas Digenis, born of mortal parents, is not. For the gods brought by the Romans, it is a case of, if born a god they are included, but if made into a god they are not.

The most challenging area when considering the origins of deity is that of the Welsh gods. The characters in the Welsh literary myths found in works such as the *White Book of Rhydderch* are not specifically referred to as deities. Considering the Christian filter put on the tales by the monks who recorded the tales, modern pagan perception declares many of these figures as gods and goddesses, but where is the line drawn? As criteria we have chosen to consider the descriptions of characters and descriptions of their qualities and abilities, and also their relationships.

This can best be illustrated by example. In the tale of Taliesin, none of the characters are described as deities. Why then have we included Ceridwen and none of the others? Ceridwen's husband Tegid Voel is described in passing as a man, with no other reference. Ceridwen herself gives birth to

Creirwy, *"the fairest maiden in the world"*, and also has the ability to produce the cauldron of inspiration and shape-shift into a range of animal forms. These facts suggest a more than human character, hence her divinity. This line of argument could then be used to argue that Taliesin is also a god. However he starts off as a mortal, Gwion Bach, is transformed by Ceridwen's potion, and then reborn as Taliesin. This could be considered an apotheosis, which then puts him into the category of transformed mortal.

It could be argued that Cú Chulainn should be included in this work as he is the son of Lugh. However in the Irish tales the emphasis is entirely on his heroism and not on his divinity, and we decided to exclude him on this basis.

The Isles of the Many Gods

Many Gods

The Origins of the Gods

Through the first millennium CE until the Middle Ages a wide range of gods and goddesses were worshipped in the British Isles. Some of these were local gods, others were brought to these islands by the many waves of invaders, conquerors and travellers throughout the centuries. It is also likely that there were many more deities than those recorded in this book, for which evidence of their existence is lacking or currently inconclusive.

The British Isles became home to the peoples, practices and gods of many different cultures during its history; and through the merging of old and new, it is clear that Britain has long been a spiritual centre in which diversity was accepted.

Let us now consider the origins of the gods and goddesses who played a role in the shaping of both the landscape and culture of Britain:

From the eighth century BCE onwards tribes from Europe were travelling to Britain and settling, often inter-marrying with the indigenous tribes. These tribes are sometimes referred to as Celtic, and this emigration may have resulted in the introduction of gods from Europe. Later waves of European tribes, such as the Belgae from Gaul, probably brought some of their Gallic gods with them, resulting in the introduction of non-indigenous gods who were already being worshipped in Britain when the Romans invaded.

The peoples in Britain prior to the Roman invasion did not build in stone, and had an oral culture. The result of this is that very little evidence of indigenous gods from pre-Roman times has survived, and never with associated names to enable identification. What is clear is that these deities were usually local deities, worshipped by individual tribes in the area where they lived, and sometimes associated with particular places because of landscape features such as rivers and wells or springs. Where there is no obvious parallel in Europe, we can conjecture that deities may have been native rather than being introduced from Europe, though this is almost impossible to prove either way.

The gods we are defining with the label *"indigenous"* are those whose names were first recorded by the Romans in inscriptions on altars and statues, for whom the earliest evidence is found in Britain. These are gods who were being worshipped in Britain before the Roman invasion of 43CE, and because the indigenous tribes were oral cultures, the names of these deities were Latinized by the Romans who recorded them, so we cannot even be sure their names are accurate survivals of those they were worshipped by. This translation of oral native cultures into the literary Roman culture resulted in variations in the recording of names, even within localized areas. Thus we see, for example, fifteen different variant spellings of the name of the god Vitiris on the forty Roman altars with his name on that have been discovered in northern England and Scotland.

When we look at the early indigenous and imported British gods, we see that little is known about them, and what is known is by comparison with the qualities of the Roman gods equated with them. The Romans, whose gods were very specific in their roles, often merged their deities with the native deities, by comparison of roles and qualities. Thus Mars would have been merged with warrior gods, Apollo with solar or healing gods, Silvanus with woodland gods, etc. From this perspective it is interesting to note that sometimes several of the indigenous gods were associated with one Roman god, whilst sometimes more than one Roman god was associated with the same indigenous god, indicating a number of roles.

The word Celt has been incredibly misused and abused. It is derived from the ancient Greek word *keltoi*, meaning *"barbarian"* or *"uncivilized"*. It first appears in the writings of the Greek historian Hecataeus in 517 BCE when he referred to a Germanic tribe. The Greek historian Herodotus in his *Histories* (431-425 BCE) also referred to the Keltoi, with regard to Germanic tribes. The Romans used the latinised version of this term, *Celta*, applying it to the tribes of Gaul and the surrounding areas.

Celtic as a term is now usually accepted as representing a large group of European tribes starting from around 1200 BCE. Initially these tribes were centred on Hallstatt in Austria and are known as the Hallstatt culture. From the late Bronze Age through to the Iron Age, during the time period 1200 - 475

BCE, these tribes expanded and their territories extended east as far as Croatia, Slovenia, Slovakia, and Western Hungary; and west and south to Eastern France, Southern Germany, Bohemia, Northern Italy and Switzerland.

A second phase of development of the *"Celtic"* tribes was the La Tene culture, named after the place in Switzerland where evidence was first discovered. The La Tene period was from 500 - 15 BCE, and seems to have had a greater military focus than the previous Hallstatt culture. The La Tene tribes were originally found between Eastern France and Bohemia. However they expanded rapidly, settling in Spain around 450 BCE and Northern Italy around 400 BCE. They also invaded and pillaged various other cultures successfully, including Rome in 390 BCE and Greece in 279 BCE. By 200 BCE they had spread through France, Belgium, Germany, Holland, Switzerland and Britain.

Although there were many areas of commonality, each tribe also had unique practices, and this is also reflected in their deities. Many Celtic gods and goddesses were localized deities, often tutelary gods of tribes, with links to the sacred landscape, particularly water features.

Any consideration of the Celtic religious and spiritual worldview is of necessity reconstructed from external evidence of the time recording their oral culture, beliefs and practices. In the case of the Celts this information is largely archaeological and also literary evidence written by classical observers who were not themselves Celts. The result of this is that the conclusions reached are hypotheses which are usually possible and sometimes probable representations of the Celtic beliefs.

Prior to the Roman influence, the Celts did not have the same tendency to anthropomorphise their gods, and this is probably why the evidence for some of the deities is confined to Romano-Celtic dedicatory inscriptions. Indeed, when the Celts overran the shrine at Delphi in 279 BCE, the Celtic leader Brennus laughed at the Greek anthropomorphic images of their gods.[1] The Celts seem to have associated their deities very strongly with nature, through

---

1 The Library of History, XXII.9.4, Diodorus Siculus.

the landscape and the animals which inhabited it. A result of this is the importance attached to cult animals attributed to particular deities, such as the bear, boar, bull, horse, raven and serpent.

The Celts did not worship in buildings in the manner of the classical cultures, preferring to work within the landscape, in sacred groves and at sacred waterways. This animistic worldview may also be why many of the representations that do exist of the Celtic gods are simple and roughly hewn carvings in stone, as it would have been easy enough for artisans as skilled as the Celts to produce much finer images if they chose to.

Sacrifice was a significant factor in the Celtic religious practices. We know that animal sacrifice was frequently practiced at specific festivals, such as bull sacrifice at Lughnasadh (1st August), and conversely also purification, such as the driving of cattle between two fires at Beltane (1st May). In addition to animal sacrifice, the predominance of votive offerings of (frequently broken) metal tools and weapons in sacred waterways also indicates propitiation or requests for divine assistance.

The Celts were head-hunters, frequently gathering the heads of their slain enemies. Diodorus Siculus commented on this,[2] but the religious significance of this act was ignored by the Romans, who considered it a sign of barbarism and endeavoured to stamp the practice out. However as the Celts believed the soul resided in the head, in addition to demonstrating their own martial prowess they may also have seen this as a way of preventing their enemies from reincarnating. That the Celts believed in the transmigration of souls is recorded by Caesar, Lucan and Diodorus,[3] and is a significant element of the Celtic spiritual worldview.

---

2 "When the enemies fall, the Gauls cut off their heads and fasten them to the necks of their horses ... They nail up the heads in their houses. They embalm in cedar oil the heads of the most distinguished of their enemies and keep them carefully in a chest: hey display them with pride to strangers. They refuse to accept for them a large sum of money or even the weight of the head in gold", The Library of History, V.29.4-5.
3 The Gallic Wars VI.14, Caesar; Pharsalia 1.446, Lucan; The Library of History V.28.6, Diodorus.

Although Rome was founded in 625 BCE, it would be centuries before it became the powerful Empire that was to conquer much of Europe and Britain. The early Roman culture was significantly influenced by external forces, both through conquest and trade. The Etruscans from northern Italy were early rulers of Rome, and the ancient Greeks had a significant cultural impact on the development of Rome. This is particularly seen in the way the Romans adopted many of the Greek gods and equated them with their own pantheon.

The Romans left a huge amount of literature and archaeology behind them which has provided a great volume of clear details of the development of their religious and spiritual worldview. The Romans were polytheistic and inclusive when it came to deities. As well as their own gods, they also adopted a large number of foreign gods, based on the twin factors of expansion of and immigration into the empire.

The most significant Roman gods were the Capitoline Triad of Jupiter, Juno and Minerva, who were the deities of state. The original triad was Jupiter, Mars and the Etruscan god Quirinus. It is interesting to consider that the triad changed in form from three gods to a god and two goddesses, though Jupiter retained his supreme position.

In the cities the deities were worshipped both in their temples and in private households. Every deity had a specific festival during the year when their worship was emphasised, each lasting anything from one day to a week or more. Dedicated priesthoods maintained the temples and conducted the ceremonies of worship of their gods.

The apotheosis of Roman emperors to divine status followed by the growth of Christianity with its adoption as the state religion caused a decline in the worship of the gods. It was deities who were popular amongst the rural population, such as Silvanus, Diana, Mercury and Hercules, whose worship continued on for longer.

It is interesting to note that it was during the period of state worship of the family of native and adopted deities that the term pagan came into popular use. The word pagan is derived from the Latin "*paganus*", meaning "*country dweller*" or "*villager*", and was used in a derogatory context of the "*country bumpkins*" who did not live in the more "*civilized*" cities. The term would not have been initially used in regards to the urban city dwellers worshipping such gods as Jupiter, Isis or Mithras.

When the Romans invaded Britain in 43 CE they brought with them a whole host of gods from conquered cultures, who had been absorbed into the religious spectrum of the Roman Empire. Information about these gods has been recorded in far more detail in Roman writings, and the worship of these gods goes back to the founding of Rome or earlier. The information provided in this work looks specifically at the evidence for their worship in the British Isles, and does not explore the wealth of information about the deities to be found in Roman writings, a task which would require many volumes to do.

What is necessary however is to explore the way some of these gods came to be worshipped by the Romans and brought with them to Britain to further spread their influence. A whole host of gods from conquered cultures, including the Egyptians, Greeks, Persians, Syrians and Phoenicians were absorbed into the religious spectrum of the Roman Empire. Of these gods, the most evidence of worship found in Britain is for the Greco-Egyptian gods.

In 332 BCE the Greek ruler Alexander the Great entered Egypt as a liberator, but soon showed himself to be a conqueror, adding the country to his empire. After his death the country was ruled for several centuries by the Greeks, who adopted many Egyptian customs and names. The Greek ruler Ptolemy I began the thirty-second Dynasty, the final Dynasty in Egypt's long history, which is commonly known as the Ptolemaic Dynasty. This Dynasty survived until the Romans made Egypt a Roman province in 31 BCE, with their rule continuing until 395 CE.

The Greeks of Ptolemaic Egypt adapted many of the Egyptian gods into a form that would better fit into their own culture, so for example the Egyptian god Osiris became transformed into the Greek god Serapis, who still retained the same role of husband of the goddess Isis; and her child Horus became Harpokrates (Horus the child).

When the Romans took over Egypt from the Greeks, they continued the process of integrating the local gods into their own system of deities. The Romans with their love of Greek culture adopted the Greco-Egyptian deities and many of these deities gained popularity in Rome and throughout the Roman Empire.

There is evidence for the worship of some of the Greco-Egyptian deities such as Ammon, Isis and Serapis in the British Isles. When we consider that there is firm evidence to show that the original forms of many of the ancient Egyptian deities were being worshipped in Egypt before 3000 BCE, these gods represent the most ancient deities whose worship can be proven in the British Isles.

Before the annexation of Ptolemaic Egypt, Rome had already conquered Greece and made it part of the Roman Empire by 146 BCE. Many of the Greek gods were adopted by the Romans, and some were Romanised into popular forms. Thus we see, for example, Apollo and Nemesis were adopted as they were by the Romans; whereas Herakles became Hercules, and Panakeia became Panacea.

The Romans also brought to Britain the worship of other gods they had assimilated from Middle Eastern countries they had conquered. This included deities such as the Syrian god Dolichenus, the Phoenician goddess Caelestis and the Persian god Mithras.

The Roman technique of incorporating warriors from conquered tribes into their army and then sending them to another part of the Empire resulted in other deities being brought to Britain with those warriors. Notably this included deities from Gaul (France), and what is now Belgium and Germany, such as Epona, Nantosuelta and Sucellos, Gobannos, the Alaisagae and others.

In 410 CE, as the Roman Empire fell apart, the Romans pulled the last of their troops out of Britain. The Romans had already been contending with marauding tribes of Angles, Jutes and Saxons from Germany for over a century. The remaining British tribes held off the bulk of the Saxons and other tribes until around 450 CE, when they started settling in southern England. The main influx of Saxons was from around 500 CE, though the Battle of Mount Badon in 496 CE staved the Saxon expansion through England for about fifty years.

The gods worshipped by these tribes were versions of those that were worshipped by the Scandinavian Norse culture, with the same qualities and legends and being mainly distinguished by variations in name. Thus we see for example Woden rather than Odin, Thunor rather than Thor. Nevertheless their qualities are largely the same, and they played a major role in daily life as protectors and providers of good weather and crops, to be propitiated and appealed to for help.

Like the Celts, the Saxons had a very animistic and vital spiritual and religious worldview. It was heavily populated with non-human creatures like elves and other spirits. As with the Celts, there is much less recorded documentation of the Saxon spiritual practices, and what there is must be viewed through the Christian filter of those who recorded it.

The Saxon kings claimed direct descent from Woden, and he is listed in some early royal genealogies as the progenitor of some of the lines of English kings. Thus Bede recorded, *"Woden, from whose stock the royal race of many provinces deduce their original."*[4] Seaxnéat, like Woden, was described as being the ancestor of royal lines, in the genealogies of Essex. Geat is the third Saxon ancestor god, mentioned by Asser, the biographer of Alfred the Great, as being a divine ancestor of Alfred's.

Due to the paucity of information on the Saxon deities, much of what is known about them has been derived from Norse sources based on their counterparts. Hence the lore contained in the *Eddas* and *Skaldic Verses* has been used over the centuries to flesh out the hints and references found in Saxon poetry and the works of contemporary writers like Bede.

---

[4] The Ecclesiastical History of the English Nation, ch. 15.36.

That the worship of the Saxon gods was a significant part of British religious development cannot be doubted, as evidenced by the traces they have left behind, in the names of the days of the week from Tuesday to Friday, and in many place names across England. As with the Saxons themselves, their deities became firmly a part of the British Isles.

The figures viewed today as Welsh gods are known only from literature recorded by Christian monks. Books such as the *Black Book of Carmarthen* and *White Book of Rhydderch* are full of references to mythic feats. A number of the names of characters in these works seem to be clearly derived from earlier gods worshipped in Britain, and so they are included in this work.

As with Wales, the volume of Irish literature recorded by Christian monks details myth cycles. However in the Irish tales there are references to specific groups of Irish deities who ruled Ireland after various invasions. These groups include the Fir Bolgs, the Túatha dé Danann, the Fomorians and the Milesians.

We have also included figures from British folklore, who which is reasonable evidence that they may be the survival of older gods or developments of imported gods. An example of this is Hiccafrith, who survived in the tales of the Giant Tom Hickathrift. In the stories the giant is said to be carrying a giant wheel and club and is the case with Black Annis, the tales have degenerated over the years, giving him a cannibalistic bent. There is some evidence to suggest that he was a Fenland version of the Wheel God. For this reason we have included him.

Whilst the gigantic size of some characters from folklore and myth may be an indication of godly status it is usually a matter of speculation, rather than evidence. For this reason we have omitted characters for which evidence of deity status was lacking, thus only including those for which there is reasonable evidence.

Literary Evidence

A number of Roman writers recorded details of Celtic practices, albeit with a certain level of propaganda. These writers include Julius Caesar in the mid first century BCE, Strabo around 40-25 BCE, Diodorus Siculus in 60-30 BCE, Lucan in 60-65 CE, Tacitus in 98-117 CE and Dio Cassius from 155-230 CE.

The first Celtic literary evidence comes from when the Irish Celts started recording their oral tradition from the sixth century CE. Much of the surviving material was recorded by Christian monks during the twelfth century CE, referring back to tales that stem from at least the previous six hundred years, possibly earlier. These tales divide into three groups, the first of which is the Mythological Cycle, which includes the *Book of Invasions (Lebor Gabála Érenn)* and the *History of Places (Dinshenchas)*. The deities are most prominent in the tales of this cycle.

The other two groups are the Ulster Cycle and the Fionn Cycle. The Ulster Cycle includes the *Cattle Raid of Cooley (Táin Bó Cúailnge)*, and focuses more on the heroes, though there is interaction with many of the deities. The Fionn Cycle focuses on the adventures of the hero Finn, again with reference to supernatural interactions. Other pertinent works from the twelfth century include *The Book of the Dun Cow (Lebar na nUidre)* and *The Book of Leinster (Leabhar na h-Uidhri)*, as well as later works such as *The Book of Fermoy (Leabhar Fhear MaÃ)*, *The Book of Lismore*, *The Great Book of Lecan (Leabhar Mór Leacain*, more commonly known as the *Book of Lecan)* and *The Yellow Book of Lecan (Leabhar Buidhe Lecain)*

It has been commented that the Irish myths survived as *"mythology refracted through literature."*[5] If this is true of the Irish gods, it is even more so for the Welsh ones.

The Welsh myths suffered from very poor documentation. The material now known as *The Mabinogion* comes from two sources, the *White Book of*

---

5 Mythology in Táin Bó Cúailnge, T. Ó'Cathasaigh, 1993, p128.

Rhydderch[6](*Llyfyr Gwyn Rhydderch*, c. 1300 CE) and the *Red Book of Hergest*[7] (*Llyfr Coch Hergest*, late fourteenth century CE). Some of the stories may date back some centuries earlier than this, such as the tale of *Kilhwch and Olwen*, which is found in both these works and is thought to be tenth century CE. All the material in the *White Book of Rhydderch* is also found in the *Red Book of Hergest*, including a version of the *Welsh Triads* (*Trioedd Ynys Prydein*), and with the addition of *The Dream of Rhonabwy*. The Book of Taliesin is also to be found in the *Red Book of Hergest*. There are also some references in the thirteenth century *Black Book of Carmarthen (Llyfr Du Caerfyrddin)*.

The material of prime interest in these works is the *Four Branches* and the tale of *Kilhwch and Olwen*. A number of other stories from the two primary works were added into the collection collated by Lady Charlotte Guest as *The Mabinogion*, which are much more Arthurian and continental in their flavour.

The major information on the Saxon gods comes from three major sources. These are the Anglo-Saxon works, the *Eddas* and the *Skaldic Verses*. The former of these, the Anglo-Saxon literature, is the only directly relevant corpus of material, as it was recorded in Britain, albeit sometimes with a mixture of Christian and pagan themes. These works include the *Beowulf* manuscript, which contains both *Beowulf* and *Judith*, the *Exeter Book*, the *Junius Manuscript*, and the *Vercelli Book*, which contains *The Dream of the Rood*, *Andreas* and *Elene*.

The Saxon gods were also mentioned in some Anglo-Saxon leech books (books of healing charms). Thus we see direct and indirect references in such texts as *The Lacnunga* (circa 1000 CE),[8] *Bald's Leechbook*[9] (circa 950 CE) and *The Old English Herbarium* (already in circulation in the ninth century CE).

The second source, the *Eddas*, are largely Icelandic in origin and refer to the Norse versions of these gods. The main Eddas are the *Prose Edda* of Snorri Sturluson (circa 1220 CE) and the *Poetic Edda* also known as the *Elder Edda*

---

6 MSS Peniarth 4, 5 and parts of 12.
7 Jesus MS111.
8 MS Harley 585 in the British Library.
9 MS Royal 12.D xvii in the British Library.

(circa 1270 CE). This information is of interest contextually as it provides details of the myths and gods of the Vikings who invaded from Scandinavia, and thus gives us clues about the Saxon tribes like the Angles, Saxons and Jutes.

The Skaldic verses were Scandinavian court poetry, and were recorded from the ninth century CE through to the Middle Ages. As with the Irish and Welsh literature, this is largely seen through a Christian gloss. Like the *Eddas*, it refers to the Norse gods and so is only relevant as giving contextual hints.

In the case of written works, for the Celtic Christian literature it should be noted that the dates are of surviving manuscripts. Many of the works may be older than this, by up to several centuries, e.g. although the *Táin Bó Cúailnge* is given as eleventh century, it is now thought likely to be at least ninth century, if not seventh century CE.

Literature Timeline

Time period	Story or Book
5th century BCE	Histories – Herodotus
1st century BCE	The Gallic Wars - Caesar
	The Library of History - Siculus
	The Annals - Tacitus
	The Histories - Tacitus
	Germania - Tacitus
1st century CE	Pharsalia - Lucan
	Geography - Strabo
2nd century CE	History of Rome - Cassius
	Geography - Ptolemy
	Apologeticum - Tertullian
3rd century CE	Against All Heresies - Tertullian
	History of the Empire after Marcus - Herodian
5th century CE	Niall Noigíallach (Niall of the Nine Hostages)
7th century CE	Codex Durmachensis (The Book of Durrow)
	Immram Brain (The Voyage of Bran)
	Widsith
	Y Gododdin (Gododin Poems)
8th century CE	Aislinge Oenguso (The Dream of Angus)
	Bretha Déin Chécht (The Judgments of Dian Cecht)
	Ecclesiastical History of the English Nation - Bede
	Mesca Ulad (The Intoxication of the Ulstermen)
	Moí coire coir goiriath (The Hawk of Achill)
	Tochmarc Étaíne (The Wooing of Étaín)
	Waldere

9th century CE	Aithbe Dam Bés Mora (The Lament of the Old Woman of Beara)
	Berne Scholiasts
	Cath Muighe Tuireadh (The First Battle of Moytura)
	Cath Maige Tuired (The Second Battle of Moytura)
	Historia Britonum (The History of Britain) - Nennius
	Liber Ardmachanus (The Book of Armagh)
	Life of King Arthur - Asser
	Life of Saint Samson of Dol
	Noínden Ulad 7 Emuin Macha (The Debility of the Ulstermen and the Twins of Macha)
	Old English Herbarium
	Reicne Fothaid Canainne (Song of Fothad Canainne)
	Sanais Cormac (Cormac's Glossary)
	The Dream of the Rood
10th century CE	Æcerbot (Field Blessing)
	Bald's Leechbook
	Beowulf
	Exeter Book
	Kilhwch and Olwen
	Tochmarc Émire (The Wooing of Emer)
	Uath Beinne Etair (The Hiding in the Hill of Howth)
	Vercelli Book
11th century CE	Baile in Scáile (The Frenzy of the Phantom)
	Codex Sangallensis (Codex of St Gall)
	Lacnunga
	Medicina de Quadrupedibus (Medicines from Animals)
	Táin Bó Cúailnge (The Driving of the Cattle of Cuailnge)
	Waldere

12th century CE	Banshenchus (The Lore of Women) Cath Magh Mucrama (The Battle of Mag Mucrama) Cath Muighe Rath (The Battle of Mag Rath) Cogadh Gaedhel re Gallaibh (The War of the Gaedhil with the Gaill) Cóir Anman (Fitness of Names) Compert Mongán (The Conception of Mongán) De Gabáil in t-Sída (The Taking of the Fairy Mound) Dinshenchas (History of Places) Dunaire Finn (The Poem Book of Finn) Leabhar na h-Uidhri (The Book of Leinster) Lebar na nUidre (The Book of the Dun Cow) Lebor Gabála Érenn (The Book of Invasions) Longes mac nUsnig (The Exile of the Sons of Usnech) Oidheadh Chloinne Tuireann (The Fate of the Children of Tuirenn) Scéla Conchobair maic Nessa (The Tidings of Conchobar son of Ness) Serglige Con Culainn (The Wasting Sickness of Cú Chulainn) Táin Bó Flidais (The Driving of the Cattle of Flidais) Táin Bó Fraích (The Driving of the Cattle of Fraích) Tochmarch Ferbae (The Courtship of Ferb) Togail Bruidne Da Derga (The Destruction of Da Derga's Hostel)

13th century CE		Annála Locha Cé (Annals of Lough Cé)
		Canu Taliesin (Book of Taliesin)
		Llyfr Du Caerfyrddin (Black Book of Carmarthen)
		Preiddeu Annwn (The Spoils of Annwn)
		Trioedd Ynys Prydein (The Welsh Triads)
		Prose Edda
		Poetic (Elder) Edda
		Englynion y Beddau (The Stanzas of the Graves)
14th century CE		Echtra Mac Echach Muigmeddóin (The Adventure of the Sons of Eochaid Muigmedón)
		Leabhar Bhaile an Mhóta (The Book of Ballymote)
		Leabhar Buidhe Lecain (The Yellow Book of Lecan)
		Leabhar Fhear MaÃ (The Book of Fermoy)
		Leabhar Méig Shamhradháin (The Book of Magauran)
		Leabhar Ui Mainu (The Book of Hy Many)
		Llyfr Coch Hergest (The Red Book of Hergest)
		Llyfyr Gwyn Rhydderch (The White Book of Rhydderch)
		Llyfr Taliesin (The Book of Taliesin)
		Oidhe Chloinne Lir (The Fate of the Children of Lir)
15th century CE		Aithed Gráinne re Diarmait ua nDuibne (The Pursuit of Diarmud and Grainne)
		Bruiden Da Chocae (The Destruction of Da Choca's Hostel)
		Leabhar Mór Leacain (The Great Book of Lecan)
		Uath Beinne Etair (The Hiding of the Hill of Howth)
16th century CE		Bonedd yr Arwyr in Peniarth MS 127
		The Book of Lismore (Book of the Dean of Lismore)
		O'Davoren's Glossary
17th century CE		Cad Goddeu (The Battle of the Trees, short later version in Peniarth MS 98b)
19th century CE		The Mabinogion published by Lady Charlotte Guest

The Unnamed Gods

As well as named individual gods, the Romans often referred to types of unnamed gods. These include the Conservatores, Cultores, Custodes, different types of Genius, Hospitales and Penates.

The Conservatores are the *"Preservers of Welfare"*. An inscription to them was found at South Shields (Co. Durham).[10] The Cultores are akin to Genius Loci, being *"Gods of this Place"*. Reference to them is made at Risingham (Cambridgeshire).11 The Custodes fulfill a similar function, being *"Guardian Gods"*. An inscription to them was found at Vindolanda (Northumberland).[12]

Another type of gods is the Hospitales, or *"Gods of Hospitality"*. Three dedications to them have been found, at Colchester (Essex), York and Newcastle-upon-Tyne (Tyne & Wear).[13] The Penates were the *"Gods of the Storeroom"*, household gods responsible for the protection of provisions. An inscription to them has been found on an altar at York.[14]

The Genius, or Spirit, is a common type of Roman protective being which took on different names, depending on whether they protected places, objects or organisations. These names include Genius Centuriae (*"Spirit of the Century"*, a military unit) at Carlisle (Cumbria),[15] Genius Cohortis (*"Spirit of the Cohort"*, another military unit) at Gloucester,[16] Lanchester (Co. Durham)[17] and High Rochester (Northumberland),[18] Genius Collegi (*"Spirit of the Guild"*) at High Rochester,[19] Genius Praetori (*"Spirit of the Commandant's House"*) at

---

10 RIB 1054.
11 RIB 1208.
12 RIB 1687.
13 RIB 193, 649, 1317.
14 RIB 649.
15 RIB 446-47, 944.
16 RIB 119.
17 RIB 1083.
18 RIB 1263.
19 RIB 1268.

Lanchester (Co. Durham) and Chesterholm (Northumberland),[20] and Genius Terrae Britannicae (*"Spirit of the Britannic land"*) at Auchendavy (East Dunbartonshire).[21]

Twenty-three inscriptions were also simply to the Genius without any clarifying addition of type.[22] Six engraved gems depicting a Genius have also been found all across Britain. Of these, all bear a cornucopia and patera (offering plate), and four are standing next to an altar with flame on top.[23]

Best known of the Genii is the Genius Loci, or *"Spirit of Place"*, which guarded a specific location. Inscriptions to Genii Loci were often combined with the deities worshipped at a place, and have been found at Maryport (Cumbria), Carlisle (Cumbria), Binchester (Co. Durham), three at Carrawburgh (Northumberland), Chesterholm (Northumberland), and Castlesteads (Cumbria).[24] There is also an inscription to the Genius Loci of York.[25]

Another popular type of Genius is the Genius Cucullatus, which means *"Hooded One"*. This name refers to a whole range of Celtic images found in Britain and Europe, of small figures wearing a large hooded cape known as a *cucullus*.[26] These figures date to the period from 1st-5th century CE.

They were commonly found in triple form (*genii cucullati*), particularly in north and western England. Thus we see reliefs from Lower Slaughter (Gloucestershire) showing three genii cucullati with a warrior and a raven, and another showing three genii cucullati; a relief from Bath showing a horned god with seated goddess, three genii cucullati and a ram; a relief of triple genii cucullati of indeterminate gender from Housesteads (Northumberland), another triple relief from Maryport (Cumbria) and a single genius cucullatus at Birdoswald (Cumbria).

---

20 RIB 1075, 1685-86.
21 RIB 2175.
22 RIB 90, 101, 102, 119, 130, 139, 246, 444a, 446-51, 611, 646-47, 657, 662, 706d, 706e, 712, 792.
23 A Corpus of Roman Engraved Gemstones from the British Isles, Henig, p198-9.
24 RIB 812, 945, 1032, 1538, 1547, 1563a, 1722d, 1984.
25 RIB 657.
26 For evidence of such figures see e.g. RIB 102, 130, 139, 246, 450, 646-7, 712, 792, 812, 945, 1032, 1538, 1583, 1687, 1984.

Genii cucullati were usually male images, but some examples exist where it is difficult to determine gender (e.g. the Housesteads relief) and it has been suggested they were female. Irrespective of gender they usually occur in relation to prosperity and fertility, depicted occasionally carrying eggs. A Cirencester relief shows three genii cucullati with a seated goddess, with two of them bearing swords, which may indicate a martial quality to them as well, supported by the Lower Slaughter relief with warrior and raven.

There are a large number of inscriptions from across Britain to the Deae Matres or *"Mother Goddesses"*.[27] As they were called Mother Goddesses they must also be considered in the context of the mother goddess. These unnamed figures were commonly represented in the potent triple form so popular amongst the Celts. Commonly the figures all bear fruits or bread in their hands, indicating their bountiful nature. Their motherly function is indicated on some images where an infant is also shown.[28]

In Gloucestershire the Mothers seem to have been particularly associated with the Genii Cucullati, as they are frequently found together. Two altars have been found with inscriptions connecting the Three Mothers to the Fates, under the Roman name of Parcae.[29] A second century CE ring from Backworth (Northumberland) bears an unusual inscription, to *"the Matres Coccae"* (Red Mothers), and though suggestive the context is unclear.

That the Matres were a class of goddess is clear when considering the range of inscriptions to Matres of different countries that have been found in Britain. There is an inscription to Matres Germaniae (*"German Mothers"*) at Hadrian's Wall,30 six inscriptions to Matres Tramarinae (*"Mothers from Overseas"*),[31] an inscription at Winchester to Matres Italae Germanae Gal[lae] Brit[annae],

---

27 See e.g. RIB 2, 65, 88, 130, 192, 455, 456, 574, 586, 618, 629, 652-54, 708, 729, 881, 901, 919, 920, 951, 1030-34, 1224, 1265, 1318, 1334, 1421, 1424, 1453, 1539-41, 1598, 1692, 1785, 1791, 1902, 1988, 1989, 2025, 2050, 2055, 2059, 2064, 2135,2141, 2147, 2335.
28 Six examples were found in London showing a suckling infant, and one at Cirencester with the central figure holding an infant. See The British Celts and their Gods under Rome, Graham Webster, p65.
29 RIB 881, 951.
30 RIB 2064.
31 RIB 919-20, 1030, 1224, 1318,1989.

("*Mothers of Italy, Germany, Gaul, and Britain*"),[32] and at York to Mat[res] Af[rae] Ita[lae] Ga[llae] ("*Mothers of Africa, Italy and Gaul*").[33]

This theme is continued in four inscriptions to Matres Ollototae ("*Mothers from other peoples*"),[34] and an inscription at Castlesteads (Cumbria) to Matres Omnium Gentium ("*Mothers of all races*").[35] In keeping with this worship of the Matres wherever a person might be, an inscription to the Matres Brittiae ("*British Mothers*") has been found at Xanten in Germany.[36]

There have also been five inscriptions to the Matres Domesticae ("*Household Mothers*") found, all in northern England.[37] This role may be akin to that of the Lares (Household Gods), as protectors of the individual family living within a dwelling.

The Mothers are the main figure represented in British jewellery, with inscriptions to them being found in rings. This does not occur significantly for any other British figures. The Backworth (Tyne-and-Wear) hoard contained a skillet with a gold engraving to the Mothers, and a hollow gold ring with a dedication to the Mothers in the bezel.[38] Another northern inscription to the Mothers was found on a silver ring found at Carrawburgh (Northumberland).[39]

An interesting relief depicting four Mothers was found at Blackfriars (London), though one of the figures is clearly a Dea Nutrix, whilst the others bear foodstuffs.[40]

A final category of Mother was the Campestres, or Matres Campestris, who were the Roman "*Mothers of the Camp Ground*", to whom the army parade

---

32 RIB 88.
33 RIB 653.
34 RIB 574, 1030-32.
35 RIB 1988.
36 ILS 4789.
37 RIB 237, 339, 652, 2025, 2050.
38 The Jewellery of Roman Britain, Jones, 1996, p212.
39 The Jewellery of Roman Britain, Jones, 1996, p60.
40 Museum of London.

ground was sacred. Six inscriptions to them have been found, all at army bases centred around Hadrian's Wall.[41]

Another type of mother goddess was the Dea Nutrix or *"Nursing Goddess"*. She was an unnamed domestic goddess depicted bearing one or two children, reminiscent of the Lares (household gods) of the Romans. Clay figures of such seated goddesses have been found across Europe in graves, temples and domestic sites.[42]

The figures were mass produced in Gaul and on the Rhine in the second century CE and distributed across Western Europe. Examples were found in Bath (Somerset), Caerwent (Monmouthshire), London, and Springhead; and a bronze figurine of a goddess nurturing two infants was found at Culver Hole Cave (Gower).

There were also a large number of unnamed nymph goddesses depicted in inscriptions and reliefs. Whilst some of these may be representations of named deities, such as Brigantia and Coventina who were both referred to as nymphae (nymphs) in inscriptions,[43] it is also likely that many of them may have been other goddesses whose names have been lost.[44]

Nymphs were shown both in the singular, in triplicities, and with other deities. A relief from High Rochester (Northumberland) shows a trio of nymphs, one of whom carries an amphora and another bearing what appears to be a cornucopia. Adjacent to the Coventina well at Carrawburgh (Northumberland) was a Nymph well, and also an altar, dedicated to the nymphs and genius loci.[45]

---

41 RIB 1206, 1334, 2121, 2135, 2177, 2195.
42 Fine examples have been found e.g. in London, and Arrington (Cambridgeshire) and a bronze in Culver Hole Cave (Gower).
43 RIB 2066 & RIB 1526-27.
44 RIB 460, 744, 1228, 1547, 1789, 2160.
45 RIB 1547.

The Christian Influence

Although the scope of this work is what are commonly called "pagan" deities, by which is meant non-Christian deities, the influence of Christianity cannot be ignored. After a couple of centuries of slowly spreading and being persecuted, the early fourth century saw Christianity extend its influence in the Roman Empire. Despite a Christian presence in Britain from the mid-second century CE, this influence was not really felt in a significant way in Britain until centuries later.

Following the Edict of Milan in 313 CE, Christianity was tolerated in the Roman Empire. After this were eighty or so years of religious power struggles, with Christianity becoming the religion of the Roman Empire officially in 394 CE, and sixteen years later the Romans pulled out of Britain.

The Christian influence in Ireland is first seen with Saint Palladius, who was sent there in 431 CE and established Christianity in the province of Leinster. When Saint Patrick arrived in 447 CE, he seemed to focus his attention on the still pagan provinces of Connaught and Ulster. From Ireland, Celtic Christianity spread to Scotland, with Saint Columba founding a monastery on Iona in 563 CE and subsequently almost single-handedly converting the Picts of Scotland.

The earliest influence of Christianity in England was in the most Romanised southern areas. Saint Albanus of Verulamium (St Albans) was martyred in 209 CE; indicating persecution of Christians was going on at this time. A group representing the British Church went to the Council of Arles in 314 CE, showing there was already a degree of organization by this time.

With the Roman departure in 410 CE, the majority of the Christians in England fled to the west to Wales. These Welsh Christians incorporated indigenous pagan elements into their faith creating the unique strand of Welsh Christianity.

The Christian influence in England really began to take hold when King Aethelbert was baptized and became the first Anglo-Saxon Christian king. Aethelbert was married to Bertha, a Frankish princess, who was a Christian. When Saint Augustine arrived in Britain in 597 CE, his first major success was the conversion of Aethelbert. The date of his baptism is in question however, and some sources suggest this baptism may have taken place up to four years later.

However Aethelbert did not insist on his subjects becoming Christians, so at this stage the worship of other deities was still openly tolerated. As the King of Kent, the centre for the Christian church in England at the time was inevitably going to be in his territory, and was established at his capital of Canterbury. Even today the Archbishop of Canterbury remains the highest ranking archbishop in Britain.

The spread of Christianity through Britain took several centuries until a substantial dominance was established. In the early days of Christian attempts to spread the word by converting kings, there were no guarantees of lasting success. Thus although Saint Mellitus converted King Sabert in 604 CE and established Christian worship in London, on the king's death in 616 CE his pagan sons banished the bishop and re-established the worship of the pagan gods.

The Synod of Whitby in 664 CE marked the meeting of the two major strands of Christianity in Britain at the time. The Celtic Christians met with the Roman Christians to discuss differences in worship, and King Oswys of Northumberland, a Celtic Christian, gave way to the Roman view, ensuring the spread of Catholicism through Britain. This may have been a political as well as a spiritual decision, as the power of the Irish Church was waning at the time, and that of the Roman Church was waxing.

Although the pagan kings had been tolerant of Christianity, the same was not the case when Christianity gained the ascendancy. Thus we see such draconian rules for heathens who turn away from the Church from around 690 CE as:

> "If anyone, in ignorance, eats or drinks by a heathen shrine they are to promise never to do so again and to do forty days penance on bread and water. If it is deliberately done again, that is, after a priest has declared that it is a sacrilege and the place of demons, the offender shall do penance on bread and water for thrice forty days. But if it is done to glorify the idol the penance shall be for three years."[46]

In 738 CE the Welsh Christian Church was also brought back into the fold, and a (fairly) unified Christianity dominated the religious landscape of Britain for the first time. With the spread of Monasticism from the fifth century onwards, Christian influence subtly increased, and this form of worship was a major factor in the development of British Christianity.

When King Alfred the Great defeated the Vikings at the Battle of Edington in 878 CE, he forced the Viking king Guthrum to be baptized. Alfred also subsequently encouraged church schools, ensuring the spread of learning amongst the higher social classes was intimately connected to the Christian church.

From the tenth century CE onwards, the Christian dominance of the religious landscape was such that the dwindling worship of pagan deities was of necessity a secret endeavour practiced away from prying eyes. However despite the Christian persecution of the pagan deities, it was also the Christian monks who recorded the old tales, and have given us the written legacy of Celtic myths, specifically of the Irish and Welsh gods.

---

46 Anglo-Saxon Mythology, Migration & Magic, Linsell, 1994, p159.

A –Z

Of Pagan Gods & Goddesses worshipped in the British Isles

The First Millenium to the Middle Ages

Key to understanding A-Z entries:

At the beginning of most entries you will find a table with various entries. For clarity of understanding we felt we should elaborate on these tables.

- Name - this is the translation into English of the deity name.
- Place of Origin - in many cases the deities did not originate in Britain, and so the original place of worship is given.
- Place of Worship - places specifically in the British Isles where evidence has been found for the worship of the deity.
- Period of Worship - the probable time frame within which worship of the deity was conducted within Britain. Obviously for deities brought here from abroad the period of worship would be far greater, e.g. for Egyptian gods which may have been worshipped pre-3000 BCE.
- Other Names - alternative names by which the deity was worshipped.
- Literary References - books and manuscripts in which references to the deity can be found.

A

Abandinus

Name	Defender of the River?
Known Period of Worship	2nd-4th century CE
Place of Origin	Cambridgeshire?
Place of Worship	Godmanchester

Abandinus is an obscure god whose presence is marked by a single altar stone at Godmanchester (Cambridgeshire).[47] A group of bronze votive feathers were also found at the site, one of which was dedicated to Abandinus, which may suggests some sort of avian connection.[48] His name may be connected to the river Abona, and as there was also a well near to the shrine it is possible he was a local water god. Alternatively it has been suggested that his name comes from the words *abon* meaning *"river"* and *din* or *dun* meaning *"fortification"*, giving a meaning of something like *"Defender of the River"*.

Abraxas

Name	Composite word
Known Period of Worship	2nd-13th century CE
Place of Origin	Egypt
Other Names	Abrasax

The Gnostic solar god Abraxas was proposed by the Alexandrian Basilides in the early second century CE, as the Supreme Being. The name was created by using the first letters of the Greek names for the visible seven planets, which

---

47 RIB 230.
48 Religious Cults at Roman Godmanchester, H.J.M. Green, 1986, in Pagan Gods and Shrines of the Roman Empire, p29-56.

significantly added to 365, the number of days in the year. He is subsequently referred to by Tertullian in the third century CE in his work *Against All Heresies*.

He is shown with cockerel head and snake legs, bearing a whip in his right hand and shield in the left. He is depicted in this manner on a jasper ring from Thetford (Norfolk) and another from Silchester (Hampshire), both dating to third century CE. The Gnostic word IAO is inscribed on the back of both rings.

Amulets of Abraxas were still being used in Britain during the thirteenth century CE. The name *"Abraxas stone"* eventually came to be incorrectly applied to any stone with a Gnostic image on, including those bearing the word Abracadabra and being used as a protection from plague.

Aegil

Aegil is an archer god who was brother to Weland, the Smith God, depicted fighting off foes on the Franks Casket (a seventh century CE Anglo-Saxon whalebone ivory box in the British Museum). Little has been recorded about Aegil, except that he was associated with the star constellation of Orion.

Aeron

Name	Renowned in Battle
Place of Origin	Wales
Place of Worship	Wales?
Literary References	The Gododin Poems

Aeron is an obscure Welsh god who may be derived from Agroná. He is mentioned in *The Gododin Poems*, where he is referred to as possessing *"desolating spears"*.[49] Aeron was also an old name for the river Avon.

---

49 Y Gododdin.

The town of Aberaeron in Cardiganshire takes its name from Aeron, and is based at the mouth of the river Aeron, hence the prefix *Aber*, meaning *"mouth of the river"*.

Aesculapius

Name	Cut Open
Known Period of Worship	1st-5th century CE
Place of Origin	Greece
Place of Worship	Throughout England
Other Names	Asclepius, Asklepios
Literary References	Medicina de Quadrupedibus

Aesculapius (or Asclepius) is a Roman healer god, the son of Apollo and the mortal Coronis, derived from the Greek healer god Asklepios. His name may mean *"Cut-open"* referring to his role as a healer. He was taught by the centaur healer Chiron, and sailed on the Argo on the quest for the Golden Fleece. Six inscriptions to him have been found in Britain, two of which are in Greek.[50] The inscriptions are spread across northern and southern England, indicating widespread worship rather than to a localized area.

Aesculapius is one Roman god who was remembered and survived through the centuries after the Romans left Britain. This is evidenced by the image of him in the eleventh century medical manuscript *Medicina de Quadrupedibus*.[51] It is also worth noting that some of the Aesculapius sanctuaries used for dream incubation (healing and/or prophetic dreams) were integrated into the Christian church as sanctuaries to Saint Martin of Tours used for the same purpose.[52]

---

50 RIB 445, 609, 808, 1028, 1052, 1072.
51 MS Cotton Vitellius C.iii folio 76.
52 The Rise of Magic in Early Medieval Europe, Flint, 1991, p259.

Agroná

Name	Slaughter
Place of Origin	Cardiganshire
Place of Worship	Cardiganshire

Agroná is a speculative goddess whose name means *"Slaughter"*, suggesting she may have been a battle goddess. The river Aeron in Cardiganshire is said to be named after her. Despite many writers referring to her, we have not been able to find any evidence to substantiate the existence of this goddess.

Áine

Name	Brightness, Heat or Speed
Known Period of Worship	Pre-8th century CE
Place of Origin	Munster
Place of Worship	Ireland
Other Names	Áine Clí, Ainge, Lair Derg, Leanan Sídhe
Literary References	Cath Magh Mucrama, Lebor Gabála Érenn

Áine is an Irish earth goddess subsequently portrayed as a Faery Queen. Her name means *"brightness"*, *"heat"* or *"speed"*, and she has been connected with the Morrígan by some writers. *"And as to Áine, that some said was a daughter of Manannán, but some said was the Morrigu herself."*[53] However the Book of Invasions gives her family as being a daughter of the Daghda, and sister to Brigid.[54]

Áine was particularly associated with Co. Limerick, and there is a well in Tyrone called Tobar Áine which may imply a connection with healing waters. Áine was said to reside in Cnoc Áine (Knockainey), a hill rising above the Munster plain. The combination of earth and water are classic indicators of her originally being an earth goddess.

---

53 Irish Myths and Legends, Lady Gregory, 1904, p98
54 Lebor Gabála Érenn.

She gave the gifts of poetry and music, and was known as Lair Derg meaning "Red Mare", suggesting she may have been a horse goddess as well. She was also known as Leanan Sídhe, (*"The Sweetheart of the Sidhe"*), demonstrating her links to the faery folk.

The warrior Ferchess and Ailill the king of Munster killed her father and raped Áine, who sucked all the flesh off his ear whilst he did so, causing him to be known as Ailill Bare-Ear. She also cursed him with her magick, causing the battle of Magh Mucrama.[55]

In later tales Áine is referred to as having a son called Gearóid Iarla (Earl Gerald Fitzgerald), who mysteriously disappeared in the form of a goose. By the seventeenth century CE Áine is described in the role of a banshee. As a weeping banshee she brings word of the imminent death of Maurice Fitzgerald in 1642 CE,[56] showing that she had been assimilated into the faery role of the death-messenger. In the nineteenth century Áine was depicted combing her hair on the banks of the Camóg river and at Lough Gur,[57] showing how she was seen as a faery being associated with the banshee.

Áine was one of the early goddesses claimed as a divine ancestor; by the eighth century CE she is already considered the sovereignty bestower for Munster and associated with the dominant line of Eogonacht. This was continued by the Norman Geraldine family, who also claimed Áine as their ancestor in the Middle Ages. She was also claimed by the Corr family of Co. Derry as an ancestor, and their local parish is named after her, Lissan (Lios Áine, or Áine's fort).[58]

---

55 Cath Magh Mucrama.
56 Gearóid Iarla agus an Draíocht, D. Ó hÓgáin, 1979, p240.
57 Popular Tales of Ireland VI: Gearóid Iarla and Áine N'Chliar, D, Fitzgerald, 1879, 4:185-99.
58 Myth, Legend and Romance, D. Ó hÓgáin, 1990, p20-1, 182-3.

Alaisagae

Name	Sending Fears?
Known Period of Worship	2nd-5th century CE
Place of Origin	Germany/Holland
Place of Worship	Northumberland
Other Names	Beda and Fimmilena, Boudihillia and Friagabis

The Alaisagae are Germanic goddesses recorded on three altar stones at a fort at Housesteads (Northumberland) on Hadrian's Wall. Their collective name may be derived from the words *laī-syā* meaning *"sending"* and *agai* meaning *"fears"*, giving a meaning of *"Sending fears"*, which would be highly appropriate for battle goddesses.

On one altar they are called Beda and Fimmilena, and on another Boudihillia and Friagabis.[59] Looking at the meaning of these names, Beda may mean *"burial"*, coming from the root *beddu* meaning *"to bury"*. Boudihillia may come from the roots *boudi* meaning *"victory"* and *hīlījā* meaning *"righteousness"*, which would suggest the name means *"righteousness of victory"*.

The inscriptions also refer to either Mars or the Spirit of the Emperor. There was an ancient German village of Beda, so this might suggest they were tutelary goddesses whose worship was brought to Britain by German soldiers serving in the Roman army, many of whom were based at Hadrian's Wall.

Alator

Name	He who nourishes his People?
Known Period of Worship	2nd-6th century CE
Place of Worship	Hertfordshire, Co. Durham, Kerry
Other Names	Alatto, Allato

---

59 RIB 1576, 1593, 1594.

Alator is a god whose name may mean *"He who nourishes his People"*. Votive silver plates have been found at Barkway (in Hertfordshire) and South Shields (Co. Durham),[60] equating him with the Roman Mars, and suggesting a warrior role.

Two ogham inscriptions from Kerry in Ireland refer to Alatto and Allato, and these may be versions of his name, indicating that his worship also reached Ireland. However these names seem to be derived from the Old Irish root *"alloid"* meaning *"Wild"*.

Amaethon

Name	Ploughman?
Place of Origin	Wales
Place of Worship	Wales
Literary References	Cad Goddeu, Red Book of Hergest, White Book of Rhydderch

Amaethon is an agriculture god who was the son of Don and Beli, and brother to Arianrhod, Penarddun, Gilvaethwy, Govannon, Gwydion and Nudd. His name may be translated as *"Ploughman"*. He is mentioned in the tale of *Kilhwch and Olwen*[61] in regard to ploughing land, showing his agricultural aspect.

Amaethon battles Arawn in a late tale after stealing a white roebuck and a whelp from his realm of Annwn.[62] Amaethon manages to prevail after his brother Gwydion guesses the name of the unnamed warrior fighting for Arawn, who is in fact the god Bran.

---

60 RIB 218, 1055.
61 White Book of Rhydderch.
62 Cad Goddeu, 2nd short version.

Ammon

Name	Invisible, That Which is Concealed
Known Period of Worship	1st-5th century CE
Place of Origin	Egypt
Place of Worship	Kent, Yorkshire
Other Names	Amun

The Egyptian creator god Ammon (or Amun) occurs twice in pottery appliqués at Borough Green (Kent) and Canterbury (Kent). He is combined with the Roman Jupiter as Jupiter-Ammon, bearing ram horns.[63] Two gems depicting him were found in different parts of Yorkshire, one dating to the first century CE and the other now lost, showing his worship was not localized to a single area.[64]

Ancasta

Name	The Sacred One? Or The Very Swift One?
Known Period of Worship	2nd-3rd century CE
Place of Origin	Hampshire
Place of Worship	Hampshire

Evidence for Ancasta has only surfaced in one place in Britain, being an inscription found at Bitterne (Hampshire).[65] It has been suggested that Ancasta was a local goddess associated with the local river Itchen. Her name may mean *"The Sacred One"*, or if it was derived from the root *kast* meaning *"very swift"* it could mean *"The very swift one"*, which is in keeping with the flow of a river.

---

63 The Religions of Civilian Roman Britain, Green, p58.
64 A Corpus of Roman Engraved Gemstones from British Sites (vol 2), Henig, 1974, p50.
65 RIB 97.

Andescociuoucus

Name	Great Impeller or Mover
Known Period of Worship	2nd-5th century CE
Place of Origin	Essex?
Place of Worship	Essex

Andescociuoucus is combined and associated with Mercury, the Roman god of communication in an inscription found in Colchester (Essex).[66] His name can be translated as *"The Great Impeller/Mover"* which would explain the association with the messenger and merchant god Mercury.

Andraste

Name	Victory, Invincible One
Known Period of Worship	1st century CE-?
Place of Origin	Norfolk?
Place of Worship	Norfolk, Suffolk
Literary References	History of Rome

Dio Cassius in his *History of Rome* said that Andraste was the Icenians' name for *"Victory"*, and that she enjoyed their especial reverence. Her name is also translated as *"Invincible One"*. Dio Cassius goes on to say that Boudicca, the Icenian warrior queen, released a hare in honour of Andraste before going into battle as a form of divination, the direction the hare ran indicating victory. This is why the hare is often given as the sacred animal of Andraste.

It is possible that the name Andraste was a title of the Morrígan, used by Boudicca to incite her troops, as we know that she was associated with vocal encouragement before battle as practiced by the Celts.

Due to the similarity in their names it has been suggested there is a connection between Andraste and the Gallic fertility goddess Andarta, though there is no evidence to support this theory.

---

66 RIB 193.

Anextiomarus

Name	The Great Protector
Known Period of Worship	BCE-5th century CE
Place of Origin	Gaul?
Place of Worship	Lincolnshire
Other Names	Anextlomarus

Anextiomarus is a Gallic god, equated by the Romans with Apollo. In Gaul he was called Anextlomarus, which means *"The great protector"*. Inscriptions to him have been found at Nettleton (Lincolnshire) and on a bronze patera at South Shields.[67]

Angus Mac Og

Name	Angus Young Son
Place of Origin	Ireland
Place of Worship	Ireland
Other Names	Aengus, Oengus
Literary References	Aislinge Oenguso, Cath Maige Tuired, De Gabáil in t-Sída, Uath Beinne Etair

Angus (or Oengus) is the son of the goddess Boann and the Daghda. His name of *"Mac Og"* translates as *"Young Son"*, given to him after his mother said, *"Young is the son who was begotten at the break of day and born betwixt it and evening."* Because of this name he is sometimes equated to Mabon and Maponos.

The eighth century Irish tale of *The Dream of Angus*[68] describes his courtship of the fairy maiden Caer Ibormeith (*"Yew Berry"*). She spent alternate years in human or swan form, and to woo her he had to change into a swan at Samhain and fly three times round a lake. Whilst they flew the couple chanted spells to send the other faery to sleep and made good their escape to

---

67 RIB 191, 2415.55.
68 Aislinge Oenguso.

his palace. It was Angus who saved Diarmuid and Grainne when they were about to be betrayed from their hiding place in a cave by an old woman in *The Hiding of the Hill of Howth*.[69]

Angus appears to be a trickster god. It is he who advised the Daghda to put three pieces of gold in the food he gave to Cridenbel the bard, who satirized him to force him to give him the best portions of his food every night. This worked and killed Cridenbel, who choked and died.[70]

Subsequently Angus tricked Elcmar out of his land, on the instructions of the Daghda, and used the same word play when he also tricked his father the Daghda out of the finest of his halls.[71] When the Daghda gave a hall each to his other two sons Lugh and Ogma, he kept two for himself. Angus was not present at the time, and when he returned he was angry at being left out. Mannanan advised him to ask for the hall (called Brugh na Boinne) for a day and a night, and said he would do magick to ensure the Daghda agreed. The hall was given to him, but when the Daghda replied that it was time to return it, Angus said that all time consisted of a day and a night following each other, and gained the hall forever.[72]

Anicetus

Name	Unconquerable
Known Period of Worship	2nd-5th century CE
Place of Origin	Greece
Place of Worship	Gloucestershire, Northumberland
Other Names	Aniketus

Anicetus is a god who was the son of Hercules and Hebe, whose name means *"unconquerable"*. He was originally one of the two gatekeepers of Mount Olympus with his brother Alexiares (*"Warding off War"*). His name and role as a gatekeeper would make him an ideal tutelary god for fortresses.

---

69 Uath Beinne Etair.
70 Cath Maige Tuired.
71 De Gabáil in t-Sída.
72 De Gabáil in t-Sída.

His name appears on two altarstones, both in conjunction with other deities (Apollo, Sol and Mithras where he is conflated with him; and Sulis).[73] When taken in conjunction with the continental inscriptions where he also appears with solar deities like Apollo, Mithras and Sol Invictus, it is possible he may have been seen by the Romans as a solar god.

Antenocitus

Name	Unknown
Known Period of Worship	2nd-5th century CE
Place of Origin	Northumberland
Place of Worship	Northumberland
Other Names	Antocidicus?

Antenocitus is a youthful horned god whose name has been found on three altars at Benwell (Northumberland).[74] The meaning of his name is unknown, but the remains of his statue show a torc and traces of stag horns. There is also reference to a god called Antocidicus at Chesters (Northumberland) who is probably the same deity. The Romans associated Antenocitus with their god of war, Mars.

Anubis

Name	Royal Child
Place of Origin	Egypt
Place of Worship	Anglesey, Wiltshire
Other Names	Anup, Anpu

Anubis is the Egyptian jackal-headed psychopomp and lord of the underworld, who was popular in Rome as the ruler of legions of demons and who was appealed to for help with protection and curses. His name translates as *"Royal Child"*. A carnelian intaglio of him was found in a grave

---

73 RIB 148, 1397.
74 RIB 1327-29.

on the Isle of Anglesey,[75] and one of the figures in the Southbroom hoard (Wiltshire), now lost, was also said to have been an Anubis.[76]

Aoibheall

Name	Bright or Sparkling
Place of Origin	Co. Clare
Place of Worship	Co. Clare, Co. Tipperary
Other Names	Aibheall
Literary References	Cogadh Gaedel re Gallaibh

Aoibheall is another Irish earth goddess who became viewed as a faery queen, whose name means *"Bright"* or *"Sparkling"*. She played the role of the death messenger, in a similar manner to the washer at the ford. Before the battle of Clontarf in 1014 CE, Aoibheall appeared to the Irish high king Brian Boru, forewarning him of his death, and also predicting victory for the Irish. After the battle Aoibheall bestowed sovereignty on one of King Brian's sons, demonstrating the role of the earth goddess as the bestower of sovereignty.[77]

She had previously lent her covering cloak of darkness which made the bearer invisible to her mortal lover Dubhlaing Ua Artigan to protect him. He turned down her offer to spend two hundred years in her company in the otherworld in bliss, to fight with the king's son Murchadh, and died in battle with him the next day at the Battle of Clontarf.[78]

Aoibheall was originally associated with Co. Clare and the northwest of Co. Tipperary, dwelling in Graig Liath (*"Grey Rock"*). Her harp was said to be only heard by members of the UiBriain clan before they died. She was claimed as patroness by the UiBriain clan and ancestor by the Dál gCais family, both of Co. Clare.[79]

---

75 Lexikon, Roscher, ii.416.
76 The Oriental Cults in Roman Britain, Harris, 1965, p81-2.
77 Cogadh Gaedel re Gallaibh, J.H. Todd (trans), 1867, p200-1.
78 Cogadh Gaedel re Gallaibh.
79 Myth, Legend and Romance, D. Ó hÓgáin, 1990, p38.

Apollo

Name	Unknown
Known Period of Worship	1st-5th century CE
Place of Origin	Greece
Place of Worship	Central and Northern England and Scotland

Apollo was originally a Greek god of light, music, poetry, eloquence and healing, who was adopted by the Romans. He is the twin brother of the Greek goddess Artemis, born from a union between the goddess Leto and the Greek father god, Zeus.

There is much debate about the meaning of his name. He was invoked by the Romans as a sun god, as seen by the inscriptions at Rudchester (Northumberland)[80] and Traprain Law (East Lothian) as Apollo Grannus.[81] The native influence can be seen from an altar at Whitley Castle (Northumberland), where Apollo can be seen in a uniquely triple form.[82]

A bronze patera found at South Shields (Co. Durham) was dedicated to Apollo as the great protector (Anextiomarus). Seven gems depicting Apollo have been found dating from 1st-3rd century CE; on three he bears the laurel branch in his right hand.[83]

Thirteen other inscriptions to Apollo have been found,[84] including four to him as Apollo Maponos,[85] identifying him with the young god.

---

80 RIB 1397.
81 RIB 2132.
82 RIB 1198.
83 A Corpus of Roman Engraved Gemstones from British Sites (vol 2), Henig, 1974, p10-11.
84 RIB 93, 633, 965, 1043, 1123, 1665, 2120, 2165, 2174.
85 RIB 583, 1120-2.

Arawn

Name	Silver-Tongue or Silver-Grey?
Place of Origin	Wales
Place of Worship	Wales
Literary References	Cad Goddeu, Preiddeu Annwne, Red Book of Hergest, White Book of Rhydderch

Arawn is the Welsh God of the Underworld, the Lord of Annwn described in the *White Book of Rhydderch*. The meaning of his name is unclear, though it has been suggested as either *"Silver Tongue"* or *"Silver-Grey"*. He is described in the *Triads* as one of the *"Three Wise Counseling Knights"*, whose advice if followed always led to prosperity.[86]

Arawn befriended Pwyll, who stood in for him for a year and a day in his guise. Pwyll fought Arawn's rival Hafgan and slew him, ensuring Arawn's dominion over Annwn. Arawn subsequently gave pigs to Pryderi, Pwyll's son, when he became Lord of Dyved.[87]

Although he is not named, he may well be the father of Modron, who is described in the tale of The Ford of Barking as being the daughter of the King of Annwn. Arawn possessed a magick cauldron embedded with pearls, which King Arthur stole, though it cost him nearly all of the men he took with him (only seven returned from three ships full).[88]

Arawn also appears in the short version of *Cad Goddeu* where he battles Amaethon after he has stolen a white roebuck and a whelp from Annwn.[89]

---

[86] Triad 116.
[87] Referred to in the White Book of Rhydderch, in Math the Son of Mathonwy.
[88] See Preiddeu Annwne in The Book of Taliesin, 30.
[89] Cad Goddeu, short version.

Arecurius

Name	The One who stands before the Tribe
Known Period of Worship	1st-5th century CE
Place of Origin	Northumberland?
Place of Worship	Northumberland, Yorkshire
Other Names	Ariarcon?

Arecurius is an obscure god whose name may mean *"The One who stands before the Tribe"*, who was invoked at Corbridge (Northumberland).[90] The Romans associated him with Apollo. Ariarcon, a name referred to in an inscription at York, may be another name for the same god.[91]

Arianrhod

Name	Silver Wheel
Place of Origin	Wales
Place of Worship	Wales
Literary References	Book of Taliesin, Red Book of Hergest, White Book of Rhydderch

Arianrhod, whose name means *"Silver Wheel"*, is a daughter of the divine couple of Don and Beli, and mother of Dylan and Lleu Llaw Gyffes. She was the sister of Penarddun, Amaethon, Gilvaethwy, Govannon, Gwydion and Nudd. Before giving birth she was one of the *"Three Beautiful Maidens of Britain"*.[92] In *The Tale of Math Son of Mathonwy* she applied to be the virgin in whose lap Math's feet could rest.[93] Unless he was at war Math's feet had to rest in a virgin's lap at all times.

---

[90] RIB 1123.
[91] RIB 640.
[92] Triad 107.
[93] In later versions of the tale she is the virgin whose lap he rests his feet in. Some sources suggest that this is an earlier and truer representation. See e.g. Rhiannon: An Inquiry into the Origins of the First and Third Branches of The Mabinogi, Gruffydd, 1951, p4.

Arianrhod stepped over Math's magick wand, believing herself to be a virgin, but when she did so she gave birth to twins – Dylan and Lleu. Dylan slipped away into the sea, and Gwydion took Lleu into his protection (one source gives Gwydion as the father of Lleu and by implication Dylan, indicating incest with his sister).

Arianrhod cursed Lleu with three curses – he would never bear a name unless he gave it to him, he would never bear arms unless she equipped him, and he would never have a human wife.

Gwydion through his cunning tricked Arianrhod into naming him Lleu Llaw Gyffes, *"Bright One of the Skillful Hand"*, and into arming him. However the third curse of not having a wife required the skill of Gwydion and Math to overcome, which they did by making the flower maiden Blodeuwedd.

The *Triads* refer to a husband and further two sons of Arianrhod.[94] Her husband is Lliaws mab Nwyfre (*"Lord, son of Sky or Firmament"*), and their sons are Gwenwynwyn (*"thrice blessed"*) and Gwanar (*"the knower"*). The tale of *Kilhwch and Olwen* also refers to Gwenwynwyn as the son of Lliaws, though in *Triad 14* he is described as the son of Naf. However Lliaws is derived from Niaws, itself a derivation of Naf, so the references could well be to the same character.

Another reference to Arianrhod is found in the *Chair of Ceridwen*. Here she is refered to as: *"Arianrhod, of laudable aspect, dawn of serenity"*.[95]

---

94 Triad 35.
95 Book of Taliesin, 16.

Arimanius

Name	Unknown
Known Period of Worship	1st-5th century CE
Place of Origin	Persia
Place of Worship	Yorkshire

Arimanius is a Mithraic underworld god, depicted with a lion head. A statue of him has been found at York.[96] It has been suggested that he is derived from the Zoroastrian god of darkness Ahriman, but in the Mithraic sense he did not seem to carry over any negative connotations.

Arnemetia

Name	She Who Dwells over the Sacred Grove
Known Period of Worship	BCE-5th century CE?
Place of Origin	Derbyshire
Place of Worship	Derbyshire

Arnemetia is a goddess whose name means *"She who dwells over the sacred grove"*. She was the goddess ruling the sacred healing waters of Buxton (in Derbyshire). Her name is seen in the Roman name for Buxton, which is Aquae Arnemetiae. The goddess Arnomectae mentioned on an altarstone at Brough-on-Noe (Derbyshire) is probably a variant spelling of Arnemetia.[97]

Astarte

Name	Star
Known Period of Worship	2nd-5th century CE
Place of Origin	Syria
Place of Worship	Northumberland

---

96 RIB 641.
97 RIB 281.

Astarte is the Syrian moon goddess whose worship spread through the Mediterranean. She was associated by the Greeks with Aphrodite and by the Romans with Venus. Her name means *"Star"*, indicating her connection to Venus, the evening star. A single altar dedication to Astarte in Greek has been found at Corbridge (Northumberland).[98]

Atargatis

Name	The Fish Goddess Atar?
Known Period of Worship	2nd-5th century CE
Place of Origin	Syria
Place of Worship	London, Northumberland, Yorkshire
Other Names	Dea Syria, Suria

Atargatis is a Syrian mother goddess associated with the after-life. Her symbols were the fish and the dove, and she was sometimes depicted in a mermaid form. The meaning of her name is unclear, though it may translate as *"The Fish Goddess Atar"*. She was also known as Dea Syria, *"the Syrian Goddess"*, and worshipped by Syrian auxiliaries in the Roman army. Dedications to her have been found at Carvoran (Northumberland) and Catterick (Yorkshire).[99] A small round engraving of her was also found at the London Mithraeum.

Attis

Name	Handsome Youth
Known Period of Worship	2nd-5th century CE
Place of Origin	Phrygia
Place of Worship	London
Other Names	Attes, Attys, Atys

Attis (or Atys) is a Phrygian shepherd god and lover of the goddess Cybele. His rebirth was celebrated each year, and in this he can be seen as a

---

98 RIB 1124.
99 RIB 726, 1791-92, 2335.

vegetation god. He was usually depicted wearing a Phrygian soft cap, and his symbols were the pine cone, bag and syrinx pipes. The meaning of his name as *"Handsome Youth"* could conceivably have seen him linked to Maponos and Mabon, though this is speculation.

The dendrophori (*"Tree-bearer"*) guilds also played a part in his worship, acting as burial associations, which can be seen as highly appropriate for a dying and resurrected god.[100] As his worship seems to have been most focused in London, it is likely that the so-called London Hunter God depicted in the Phrygian soft cap was probably Attis. A seventh century CE Anglo-Saxon gold amulet containing a carnelian cameo of a bearded male head wearing a Phrygian cap may well be an earlier gem which was re-used.[101]

---

100 Religion in Roman Bitain, Henig, 1984, p113.
101 A Corpus of Roman Engraved Gemstones from British Sites (vol 2), Henig, 1974, p274.

B

Badb

Name	Crow or Raven
Place of Origin	Ireland
Place of Worship	Ireland
Other Names	Badbdh, Badbh, Badbh Catha
Literary References	Bruiden Da Chocae, Caithréimm Thoirdhealbhaigh, Cath Muighe Tuireadh, Lebor Gabála Érenn, Tochmarc Émirc, Tochmarch Ferbae, Togail Bruidne Da Derga, Togail na Tebe

Badb, Badbdh or Badbh means *"Crow"* or *"Raven"* and refers to a group of Goddesses, not a single individual. She was often referred to as Badbh Catha, meaning *"the Battle Crow"*, describing the hooded crows that were often seen feasting at the battlefield. Badb usually appeared in crow or hag form.

> *"In the Wood of the Badb, i.e. of the Morrígan. For that is her wood, i.e. the land of Ross, and she is the Badb of battle and is called Bé Néit "'the wife of Néit'."*[102]

Badb was frequently equated with the Morrígan, and is called also the wife of Néit, a battle god, of whom little beyond a name is known. Badb was also a magick goddess, displaying her power when with Macha and the Morrígan she brought down a three day rain of sorcery, fire and blood on the heads of the Fir Bolgs.[103]

Badb is described in *The Book of Invasions* as one of the daughters of Ernmas, which also refers to her as the sister of Macha, Anu, Ériu, Banba and Fotla.[104] Badb is frequently the foreteller of conflict and death. She tells the sleeping

---

102 Tochmarc Émire.
103 Cath Muighe Tuireadh.
104 Lebor Gabála Érenn, 4.63-4.

Queen Medb that her son Mani will die in battle.[105] She also plays a significant part in *Bruiden Da Chocae* as the harbinger of doom.

> *"She put her shoulder against the doorpost and began uttering evil prophecies and words of ill omen to the host, so that she said this: There will be grief in the hostel; there will be mangled bodies in blood; necks will be without heads above the floor of Da Choca's hostel. After that the Badb went from them."*[106]

From around the tenth century CE the name Badb becomes interchangeable in some texts with *fúir* (*"Fury"*) and *bandea* (*"Goddess"*) in connection with the Greek Fury Tesiphone. She becomes seen as representing the classical Greek image of the Fury and is also equated with other war goddesses such as the Roman Bellona in translations of classical texts.[107] By the late fourteenth century CE the word *badb* was being used synonymously with the word *Cailleach*.[108] Tobar na Baidhbe (the Badhbh's Well) in Co. Waterford is named after her.

Bacchus

Name	The Shouter
Known Period of Worship	1st-5th century CE
Place of Origin	Greece
Place of Worship	Throughout England

Bacchus is the Roman god of the vine and Lord of Souls. His name is derived from the Greek word *"iacho"* meaning *"to shout"*, giving a meaning of *"The Shouter"*. There have been more than four hundred finds associated with Bacchus in Britain, including mosaics, coins, inscriptions and pottery, indicating his worship was widespread. Although many of the finds were at wealthy villas or temples, there is also a significant number of finds such as

---

105 Tochmarch Ferbae.
106 Bruiden Da Chocae.
107 Togail na Tebe: The Thebaid of Statius.
108 For an example of this see Caithréimm Thoirdhealbhaigh, 14th century.

helmets with Bacchus images and motifs emphasising his martial nature as well, as the Indian Bacchus.[109]

It is interesting to note that Bacchus is frequently found in connection with other deities, in reliefs or statues at their temple. Thus we see three marble statues of Bacchus found at the London Mithraeum, images of him at the baths at Aquae Sulis and a lead plaque at the temple of Nodens at Lydney (Gloucestershire).

Two engraved gems of Bacchus have been found, one accompanied by a panther dating to 2nd-3rd century CE (Kettering, Northamptonshire) and the other accompanied by Minerva and four Cupids and dating to 1st century CE (Ruxox, Bedfordshire).[110]

Baldur

Name	Lord
Place of Origin	Scandinavia?
Other Names	Baldaeg, Balder
Literary References	The Dream of the Rood

Baldur (or Balder or Baldaeg) is a Germanic god whose name means *"Lord"*. He is Woden's second son, beloved of all and tragically killed by his blind brother with a mistletoe spear by Loki's instigation. The evidence for Baldur is suggestive, being seen by implication from the myths in late poetry. The late tenth century poem *The Dream of the Rood* implies Baldur assimilated with Christ,[111] as well as using terminology more reminiscent of the world-tree Yggdrasill than the sacrificial cross.

---

109 Derived from the Greek tales of the Indian Wars of Dionysus, see Dionysiaca by Nonnos, 5th century CE.
110 A Corpus of Roman Engraved Gemstones from British Sites (vol 2), Henig, 1974, p20.
111 "All creation wept the mourned the king's fall" (1.55-56), The Dream of the Rood, within The Vercelli Book, 980 CE.

Balor

Name	Unknown
Place of Origin	Ireland
Literary References	Banshenchus, Cath Maige Tuired

Balor is the ruler of the Fomorian gods, the primitive raiders who fight the Túatha dé Danann for sovereignty of Ireland. He was also known as Balor of the Evil Eye or Balor of the Piercing Eye due to the ability of his single eye to kill or weaken anything it beheld. He was not born with his evil eye, however; rather it came about through being affected by venomous magickal fumes.

> "It had that poisonous power for this reason: once his father's druids were brewing magic. He came and looked over the window, and the fumes of the concoction affected the eye and the venomous power of the brew settled in it."[112]

Four men lifted his eyelid with a handle which passed through it, and then its power was such that though there were thousands of warriors against him, they would be so weakened that a few warriors could overcome them.[113] This description clearly implies gigantic size, often associated with divinity and with the more primal and chaotic deities.

He was the grandson of Néit, and his daughter Ethne was the mother of Lugh, the grandson who eventually killed him. The *Banshenchus* calls him *Swift-smiting Balor*.[114]

During the Second Battle of Moytura, Lugh cast a sling stone into the eye, knocking it through his head and killing him, as well as twenty-seven Fomorians who were behind him with its gaze.[115]

---

112 Cath Maige Tuired.
113 Cath Maige Tuired.
114 Banshenchus, pt 1.
115 Cath Maige Tuired.

Banba

Place of Origin	Ireland
Place of Worship	Ireland
Other Names	Banbha
Literary References	Banshenchus, Battle of Maige Mucrima, Leabhar Méig Shamhradháin, Lebor Gabála Érenn.

Banba or Banbha was an Irish sovereignty goddess. She was the sister of Ériu and Fotla, with whom she represented the sovereignty of Ireland, and also the sister of Badb, Macha and Anu.[116] They are usually described as daughters of Ernmas, though the *Banshenchus* calls them daughters of Fiachra.

The Irish kings wed the sisters to ensure their position as sovereigns. Tethur MacCecht, one of the sons of the Daghda, was her husband, and she was the mother of Cesair, who led the invasion of Ireland by the Túatha dé Danann.[117] In the battle with the invading Milesians, Banba was killed by the hero Caicher.

Association with Banba was also used to indicate the right to rule. Thus we see references like *"Brian of the Sionann is one of Banba's chiefs."*[118] In the *Banshenchus* she is described as *"ardent Banba"* and *"sweet Banba"*. This text referred to her husband as a man called Etar.[119] In *The Battle of Maige Mucrima*, Banba is referred to as the sovereignty of Ireland, for it says: *"Mac Con seized the land of Banba on every side as far as the bright, clear sea."*[120] There are also a number of references in *Leabhar Méig Shamhradháin* to *"Banba's poets"*, suggesting a possible association with poetry as well as sovereignty. This is reinforced by the reference to *"Banba of wise utterance"* in *The Book of Invasions*.[121]

---

116 Lebor Gabála Érenn 4.63-4.
117 Lebor Gabála Érenn.
118 Leabhar Méig Shamhradháin, II.1.
119 Banshenchus, pt 1.
120 The Battle of Maige Mucrima.
121 Lebor Gabála Érenn, 64.

Barrecis

Name	Supreme
Known Period of Worship	2nd-5th century CE
Place of Origin	Cumbria
Place of Worship	Cumbria

Barrecis (or Barrex) is a mysterious god, as the name means *"Supreme"*, and is found on only one inscription, at Carlisle (Cumbria). The inscription reads *"M[arti] Barrex"*,[122] linking him to Mars.

Bastet

Name	She of the Perfume Jar or She Who Devours
Place of Origin	Egypt

Bastet is the cat-headed Egyptian goddess representing the protective mother and also pleasure and sensuality. Her name may mean *"She of the Perfume Jar"* or *"She Who Devours"*. An amulet depicting her was found at Gloucester.[123]

Bé Chuille

Place of Origin	Ireland
Place of Worship	Ireland
Literary References	Banshenchus, Cath Maige Tuired, Cath Muighe Tuireadh

Bé Chuille is one of the foster-mothers of the Morrígna, who is described as *"a sorceress of the north country"*[124] and seems to be a magick goddess. This is reinforced by her description of what she will do against the Fomorians, where she says she *"will enchant the trees and the stones and the sods of the earth,*

---

122 RIB 947.
123 See The Religions of Civilian Roman Britain, Green, 1976, p58, p172.
124 Banshenchus, pt 1, Cath Maige Tuired.

so that they shall become a host under arms against them, and shall rout them in flight with horror and affliction."[125]

Belatucadros

Name	Bright Beautiful One or Fair Shining One
Known Period of Worship	1st-5th century CE
Place of Origin	Cumbria or Germany?
Place of Worship	Cumbria
Other Names	Belatocadrus, Balatocadrus, Belatucairus, Belatocairus, Balatucairus, Belatucaurus, Baliticaurus, Belleticaurus, Belatucabrus, Belatugagrus, Blatucadrus and Blatucairus

Belatucadros is a god whose name means *"Bright Beautiful One"* or *"Fair Shining One"*. At least twenty-eight altars bearing inscriptions to him have been found, almost all in northern Cumbria, so he may have been a patron to the Carvetii tribe who ruled there.[126] It has been suggested that his origins are with the Germanic Celts.

The Romans associated him with Mars, and the coincidences of inscriptions to him with ram horned god figures (sometimes armed), suggests he was a horned god. He was also referred to in seven inscriptions as the holy or blessed god Belatucadros. Only five of the inscriptions to him equate him with Mars, suggesting he was worshipped in his own right as a deity. Two altars to him use the phrase *"pro se et suis"*, i.e. *"For himself and his own"*, suggesting a role of protective deity.

---

125 Cath Muighe Tuireadh.
126 RIB 759, 772-7, 809, 887-9, 914, 918, 942, 948, 970, 1521, 1775, 1776, 1784, 1976, 1977, 2038, 2039, 2044, 2045, 2056, 2335.

Belenus

Name	Bright or Brilliant
Known Period of Worship	2nd-5th century CE
Place of Origin	Uncertain
Place of Worship	Across Britain
Other Names	Bel

Belenus or Bellinus is a solar god associated with healing whose name means "Bright" or "Brilliant". He was also known as Bel, and the festival of Beltane (Bel's fire) on May 1st was sacred to him. The Romans associated him with Apollo.[127] His worship was widespread, as indicated by evidence from both Gaul and northern Italy. The Roman poet Ausonius refers to sanctuaries of Belenus in Aquitania in the late fourth century CE. Tertullian in the late second century (197 CE) refers to his worship by the Norici tribe in the Alps in his work *Apologeticum*, and Herodian also refers to his worship in northern Italy in his third century CE work *History of the Empire after Marcus*.[128]

The image of a stylised head found at the Roman baths in Bath and mistakenly called a gorgon's head is actually Belenus, suggesting a possible link with Sulis. He is also identified with the Welsh Beli and the Irish Bilé.

Beli

Name	Shining
Place of Origin	Wales
Place of Worship	Wales
Other Names	Beli Mawr
Literary References	Book of Taliesin, Harley MSS 3859, Red Book of Hergest, White Book of Rhydderch

---

127 RIB 1027.
128 Apologeticum 24:7, History of the Empire after Marcus 8.3.6.

Beli, meaning *"Shining"*, was the son of Mynogen, and the father figure of the House of Don, married to the goddess Don. One manuscript gives his wife as Ana, a variant of Anu/Danu, which reinforces the notion of a link between the goddesses Danu and Don.[129]

With Don he was the father of Amaethon, Arianrhod, Gilvaethwy, Govannon, Gwydion, Nudd and Penarddun, who were known as the *Children of Light*. He was also said to be the father of Caswallon. Beli was also known as Beli Mawr (meaning *"Great Shining"*) and as Beli Mawr he is given as the ancestor of the Gwynedd line of kings in one of the genealogies.[130]

Beli is mentioned in the *Book of Taliesin*, where he is described as *"victorious"* and as the *"son of Mynogen"* in the poem called *"A Bright Festivity"*.[131]

He has also been equated with the Irish god Bilé and the Gallic Belenus. The Romans equated him with the father god Dis Pater. The *Triads* refer to Rhun, the son of Beli, as one of the *"Three Blood-Stained Ones of the British Isles"*.[132] Another son, Jago, is mentioned as the recipient of one of the *"Three Infamous Blows with the Axe"*.[133]

Belisama

Name	Fire
Place of Origin	Lancashire
Place of Worship	Lancashire, Gaul

Belisama is a goddess whose name means *"Fire"*, and who was probably associated with the River Ribble (Lancashire).[134] Ptolemy's *Geography* has an estuary called Belisama where the Mersey should be, however his placement

---

129 MSS Harley 3859, Genealogy 10.
130 Harley MSS 3958.
131 Book of Taliesin ch. 69.
132 Triad 31.
133 Triad 48.
134 The Pagan Religions of the Ancient British Isles, Hutton, 1991, p218.

of towns indicates errors which make the River Ribble the most likely association.

A continental Latin inscription equates her to Minerva, and an inscription to her was also found at Nimes in Gaul. She may have been the consort of Belenus or of Beluctadros.

Bellona

Name	Battle
Known Period of Worship	2nd-5th century CE
Place of Origin	Rome
Place of Worship	Cumbria, Yorkshire

Bellona is a Roman war goddess, the sister of Mars, whose name means "Battle". She prepared her brother's chariot, and was depicted with dishevelled windswept hair, with a whip in one hand to incite the troops into battle-frenzy, and a torch in her other hand to light the enemy funeral pyres. A temple to her was set up outside York, and there was an altar inscription to her at Old Carlisle (Cumbria).[135]

Bé Néit

Name	The Wife of Néit
Place of Origin	Ireland
Place of Worship	Ireland
Other Names	See below
Literary References	Battle of Magh Rath, Cormac's Glossary, Tochmarc Émire.

"She is the Badb of battle and is called Bé Néit, 'the wife of Néit'."[136]

As can be seen from this quote and others, the name Bé Néit seems to function more as a title than be the name of a specific goddess, acting as a link equating

---

135 RIB 890.
136 Tochmarc Émire.

several of the war goddesses in Irish myth. In *Cormac's Glossary* we find her name being associated with Nemain:

> "*Néit, i.e. the God of Battle. Nemain is his wife*"; "*Bé Néit ... Nemon was his wife. This couple was venomous indeed.*"[137]

As Néit was described as a battle god, it emphasises the role of a war goddess or goddesses, as seen in the Battle of Magh Rath:

> "*Until they might learn upon which of the bands the fortune of the battle would descend and remain, and upon which of them battle-mourning Bé Néit would establish her mighty power.*"[138]

Bes

Name	Protector?
Place of Origin	Egypt
Place of Worship	Gloucestershire

Bes is a protective Egyptian lion-headed dwarf god. His name may come from the root Besa meaning *"To Protect"*. He was particularly associated with the protection of pregnant women. Two amulets have been found depicting him, one in the hoard at Gloucester.[139]

Bilé

Name	Tree
Place of Origin	Ireland
Place of Worship	Ireland
Literary References	Lebor Gabála Érenn

---

137 Cormac's Glossary.
138 The Banquet of Dun na n-Gedh and the Battle of Magh Rath, John O'Donovan (trans), 1842.
139 See The Religions of Civilian Roman Britain, Green, 1976, p58, p172, A Corpus of Roman Engraved Gemstones from British Sites (vol 2), Henig, 1974, p53.

Bilé is an Irish god whose name means *"Tree"*. The *Book of Invasions* says *"Bilé and Mílidh, it is from their progeny the Gaels come."*[140] As he is the father of Milidh, and grandfather of Donn, this suggests he may have been an ancestor god.

Black Annis

Black Annis is a figure found in English and Scottish folklore and may be a survival of the Cailleach Bheur, to whom she bears a distinct resemblance in appearance. Her name is thought to be derived from that of Anu.

In England Black Annis was also known as Black Agnes or Cat Anna, and was a blue-faced hag who lived in a cave in the Dane Hills, in Leicestershire, called *"Black Annis' Bower Close"*. She dug the cave out of the rock with her own long iron nails. The cave had a great oak in front of it, behind which she hid to leap out to catch and devour stray children and lambs. One version of the tale had Black Annis turning to stone if she came out in daylight, recalling the Cailleach Bheur turning into stone for the summer.

Black Annis was seen as a very real threat and affected the Leicestershire area greatly. The common people did not have window-glass in those days, so anti-witch-herbs were tied above the apertures to stop Black Annis reaching inside with her very long arms and grabbing their babies.

Every year on Easter Monday (known as Black Monday in this instance in honour of Black Annis), it was a local custom to hold a mock-hare hunt from her cave to the Mayor of Leicester's house. The bait was actually a dead cat rather than a hare, and it was drenched in aniseed. The cat was probably used to symbolise her under her name of Cat Anna. The use of aniseed, a protective herb, implies a protective propitiatory ritual.

Black Annis had the power of prophecy, and she prophesied that King Richard III would die when passed her on his way to the battle at Bosworth

---

140 Lebor Gabála Érenn.

and his spurs struck a stone pillar on the bridge. Annis said, *"It will be his head that will hit that stone when he comes back"*. After being killed in battle, his naked body was thrown across the saddle of a horse with his head hanging down as low as the stirrups, which hit that very same stone that his spurs had struck.[141]

Black Annis is also mentioned in Scottish tales as dwelling on the moors and hillsides of the Scottish Highlands. She is described as a witch-like hideous old hag with blue skin and a single piercing eye. If she captures human beings, she eats them, and is often referred to as sitting on a pile of bones outside her cave, with an oak tree (as with the English version).

She would carry humans off into her cave, suck them dry of blood and eat their flesh before draping their flayed skins out to dry on the oak's branches. She then made the skins into a skirt to wear. As she was also said to prey on animals, local shepherds would blame any lost sheep on her hunger.

Another form of Black Annis in Scotland was a weather spirit said to watch over the gales on the Firth of Cromarty. This area is known for its spasmodic squalls that can blow up in moments. As a result she had a reputation for treachery, turning up when least expected. She was often called Gentle Annie or Annis, probably in propitiation to try and calm her temper.

Blodeuwedd

Name	Flower Face
Place of Origin	Wales
Place of Worship	Wales
Literary References	Cad Goddeu, Red Book of Hergest, White Book of Rhydderch

The name Blodeuwedd means *"Flower Face"*. Blodeuwedd is created by Gwydion and Math from flowers in the tale of *Math the Son of Mathonwy* in the *White Book of Rhydderch* as a bride for Lleu to overcome Arianrhod's third curse. She is made from the blossoms of oak, broom and meadowsweet and

---

[141] Leicestershire and Rutland, Arthur Mee, 1937.

described as the fairest and most graceful maiden that man ever saw.[142] Whether she is a goddess is debatable, though many see her as such. Certainly her beauty and creation by two magickal gods could argue that point.

Blodeuwedd betrays Lleu when she falls in love with the huntsman Gronw Pebyr, and conspires with him to kill Lleu. This conflict clearly echoes the theme of the battle of summer and winter, the lords of light and dark. After Lleu is wounded he transforms to an eagle and flies away, to be restored and healed by Math. Math then transforms Blodeuwedd into an owl as punishment to be a creature of the night, hated by all the other bids. The nocturnal association fits with her choice of the *"dark"* Gronw over the *"light"* Lleu. Lleu subsequently kills Gronw, who agrees to take the same blow that he delivered to Lleu.

A section of *Cad Goddeu* in the *Book of Taliesin* almost certainly refers to Blodeuwedd. The references to the creation without parents, to Math and Gwydion and the flowers are a clear reference to Blodeuwedd's creation, even with the discrepancy in the types of flowers used in her creation. To further reinforce this, Gronw is mentioned a few lines later in the poem.

"Not of mother and father, when I was made,
did my Creator create me.
Of nine-formed faculties,
of the fruit of fruits,
of the fruit of the primordial God,
of primroses and blossoms of time hill,
of the flowers of trees and shrubs.
Of earth, of an earthly course, when I was formed.
Of the flower of nettles, of the water of the ninth wave.
I was enchanted by Math, before I became immortal,
I was enchanted by Gwydion the great purifier of the Brython."[143]

---

142 Math the Son of Mathonwy.
143 Cad Goddeu, Book of Taliesin, 8.

Boann

Name	White Cow
Place of Origin	Ireland
Place of Worship	Ireland
Other Names	Agda, Boand, Boind, Bovinda, Rigan
Literary References	Cath Maige Tuired, Dinshenchas, Táin Bó Fraích, Tochmarc Étaíne.

Boann is an Irish cattle and river goddess associated with the river Boyne. Her name Boann (or Boand or Boind) means *"White Cow"*. One of her titles is Agda which means *"Cow Goddess"*.[144] In one tale the Daghda desires Boann, and sends her husband Elcmar on an errand. He makes love with Boann, and also stops the sun, so that nine months pass for them and she is able to give birth to Angus Mac Og, whilst for Elcmar only one day passes and he is tricked into not knowing what has occurred.[145]

Due to the similarity in their names Boann is often equated to Boand, the Fomorian king Indech's daughter. In *Cath Maige Tuired* she first meets the Dagda when he is returning from the Fomorian camp with his distended belly after eating huge amounts of porridge, and satirises him and forces him to carry her. They then have sex at the ford where he had previously had sex with the Morrígan. Boand seems to be a powerful figure in her own right, for she says to the Daghda:

> *"She said that she would hinder the Fomorians, and she would sing spells against them … and she alone would take on a ninth part of the host."*[146]

There is a reference to Befind from the Sidhe, a sister of Boand, in *Táin Bó Fraích*. Befind has a son called Idath, whose son is Fraech.[147] The same text also refers to three sons of Boand who are harpers, called Gol-traiges

---

144 Dinshenchas 4:200.
145 Tochmarc Étaíne.
146 Cath Maige Tuired.
147 Táin Bó Fraích.

(*"Sorrow-strain"*), Gen-traiges (*"Joy-strain"*), and Suan-traiges (*"Sleep-strain"*), named after the music played by Uaithne, the Dagda's harp.

Boann is described using the title *rígan*, (the Gaelic word for "Queen"), the same term used to describe the Morrígan. In the *Dinshenchas* the gushing waters of her husband Nechtan's well injures her in a manner which exactly parallels the wounds the Morrígan receives from Cú Chulainn when she attacks him in animal forms at the ford. Hence:

"*As thrice she walked round about the well heedlessly,*
Three waves burst from it; whence came the death of Boann.
They came each wave of them against a limb; they disfigure the soft-blooming woman,
A wave against her foot, a wave against her perfect eye; the third wave shatters one hand."[148]

Boann and the Gallic cow goddess Bovinda may well be regional variations of the same goddess, as both names mean the same, i.e. *"white cow"*. This is reinforced by regional variations of the same title being used for them, Boann is called *Rígan*, (Gaelic for *"Queen"*), and Bovinda is called *Rigana*[149] (Gallic for *"Queen"*).

Bona Dea

Name	The Good Goddess
Known Period of Worship	2nd-5th century CE
Place of Origin	Rome
Place of Worship	Northumberland
Other Names	Fauna

Bona Dea is a Roman goddess worshipped only by women, also known as Fauna in her role as wife of Faunus. Her name means *"The Good Goddess"*, and only one altarstone has been found to her in Britain at Chesters.[150] The

---

148 Dinshenchas.
149 Textes gaulois et gallo-romains en cursive latine, II:Chamalière, Lejeune & Marichal, 1976.
150 RIB 1448.

inscription also refers to the goddess Caelestis and (possibly) equates them with Juno by use of the title Regina (*"Queen"*) which was frequently applied to her. Bona Dea was commonly associated with earth, nurturing and mother goddesses such as Cybele, Rhea, and Vesta.

Bonus Eventus

Name	Good Outcome
Known Period of Worship	1st-5th century CE
Place of Origin	Rome
Place of Worship	Monmouthshire, Yorkshire

Bonus Eventus is a Roman god whose name means *"Good Outcome"*. He is linked to specific outcomes of events, and is often associated with Fortuna, as shown by both the British dedications to him being shared with her.[131] Thirty-four engraved gems of him have been found dating to 1st-3rd century CE (not including a couple which are uncertain), mainly in southern England and the Welsh borders.[152]

He was associated with the bounty of crops and hunting as good outcomes, as seen when we examine the themes of the engraved gems. Of the gem intaglios, he holds a dish of fruit or patera in twenty-five of them, grapes in ten of them, and two ears of corn in twenty-three of them.

The game theme is indicated by the presence of a lagobolon (hooked hunting stick) twice bearing hares or twice bearing game on four of the gems. Two other gems show a bunch of grapes hanging from the lagobolon.

---

151 RIB 318, 642.
152 A Corpus of Roman Engraved Gemstones from British Sites (vol 2), Henig, 1974, p31-34, 100.

Braciaca

Name	God of Malt?
Known Period of Worship	2nd-5th Century CE
Place of Origin	Derbyshire
Place of Worship	Derbyshire

Braciaca is an unknown god mentioned in an inscription in Derby (Derbyshire),[153] whose name may derive from the Welsh root *"brag"* meaning *"malt"*, giving a possible meaning of *"God of Malt"*. The inscription equates him with Mars, though in what role is unclear.

Bran

Name	Raven
Place of Origin	Wales
Place of Worship	Wales
Other Names	Bendigeidfran, Pierced Thighs
Literary References	Cad Goddeu, Red Book of Hergest, White Book of Rhydderch

Bran is a Welsh god whose name means *"Raven"*, referring to his totemic bird. He was also known as Bendigeidfran, or Blessed Bran, and *"Pierced Thighs"*. He was described as one of the *"Three Blessed Kings of Britain"*.[154] In the *White Book of Rhydderch*[155] he led his troops across the sea to Ireland, but was so large that he waded across the sea, carrying the poets and musicians. During the fight, in which all the Irish men and all but seven of the Welsh were wiped out, Bran was mortally wounded by a poisonous spear. He instructed his companions to cut off is head and take it with them on their travels, foretelling how events will come to pass.

---

153 RIB 278.
154 Triad 35.
155 Branwen the Daughter of Llyr.

The companions do as Bran instructed them, and they spent seven years at Harddlech feasting with the head presiding and the birds of Rhiannon making sweet music for them. Then they spent eighty years at Gwales in Penfro with the head presiding, where they did not age. This idyll is ended when one of the companions opened a door he was told not to, and the companions took the head and buried it in London under the White Mount as they had been previously instructed by Bran, as an amulet to protect Britain. This they do, making the head of Bran one of the *"Three Happy Concealments"*.[156] Subsequently it was dug up and thrown into the Thames by King Arthur, who declared that he was the only defender the British Isles needed. This was one of the *"Three Unhappy Disclosures"*.[157]

The oracular severed head which continued to live and prophesy was a common theme in the ancient world, and parallels can be seen with the Norse giant Mimir and the Greek hero Orpheus. As the seat of the soul, the head of a magickal being was not dependant on the rest of the body in the same way as a human.

Bran is thus seen as a god of prophecy, and possibly of the arts, suggested by his carrying the poets and musicians rather than having them travel in the ships with the sailors and soldiers. The *Triads* also refer to him as one of the *"Three System Formers of Royalty"*,[158] and his family as the first of the *"Three Holy Families"*.[159]

Even after his *"death"*, Bran features in a later tale, fighting for Arawn against Amaethon, who has stolen a white roebuck and a whelp from Arawn. When Gwydion realises and sings Bran's name, Amaethon wins the contest.

> *"Sure-hoofed is my steed impelled by the spur;*
> *The high sprigs of alder are on thy shield;*
> *Bran art thou called, of the glittering branches.*

---

156 Triad 53.
157 Triad 53.
158 Triad 36.
159 Triad 18.

Sure-hoofed is my steed in the day of battle:
The high sprigs of alder are on thy hand:
Bran by the branch thou bearest
Has Amaethon the good prevailed."[160]

The references in this verse to alder as his emblem have resulted in it being considered the sacred tree of Bran, and we may also observe that his nephew was named Gwern, meaning *"alder"*.

Cwmbran in Wales may be named after Bran, with its meaning of the *"Valley of Bran"*, or *"Valley of the Raven"*. In this instance Bran is the name of the brook which runs through the valley. There is also Llyn Bran or *"Bran's Lake"* in Denbighshire and a nearby hill called Gorsedd Bran, meaning *"Bran's Throne"* which may also take their name from him.

Branwen

Name	White Raven or White Breast
Place of Origin	Wales
Place of Worship	Wales
Other Names	Bronwen
Literary References	Red Book of Hergest, White Book of Rhydderch

Branwen is the sister of Bran and Manawyddan, whose name means *"White Raven"*, or *"White Breast"*. Branwen's tale is told in the Second Branch of the *White Book of Rhydderch*, in the story called *Branwen the Daughter of Llyr*. Branwen was married to the Irish king Matholwch, but after a while he mistreated her.

During the initial flush of their relationship, Branwen was described as giving a *"brooch or a ring or a treasured jewel"* to every noble visitor to her court, hinting at a bountiful nature. She had a child by Matholwch, a boy called Gwern who was later killed at the Assembly held to bring peace after the war between the Irish and the Welsh. The slap she received from Matholwch was

---

160 Cad Goddeu, second later version.

known as one of the *"Three Fatal Blows"* because of the subsequent conflict between the Irish and the Welsh that arose from her mistreatment.[161]

Wisdom is indicated as one of Branwen's qualities, as the Irish have to call her to explain the vision of the mountain and woods that are seen in the sea. She explains that it is Bran with the Welsh fleet come to rescue her. She had previously taught a starling to speak and sent it across the Irish Channel to her brother Bran to tell him of her plight. This could hint at the starling as her totemic bird, and also demonstrates magickal ability, teaching the starling to speak.

Branwen died of a broken heart at Aber Alaw on Anglesey. There is a mountain in North Wales named after her, which is called Cadair Fronwen (Branwen's Seat).

Bregans

Name	High One?
Known Period of Worship	2nd-5th century CE
Place of Origin	Yorkshire
Place of Worship	Yorkshire
Other Names	Bregantis

Bregans (or Bregantis) is postulated as the tutelary god of the Brigantes tribe, and thus consort to Brigantia, whose name comes from the same root, indicating something like *"High One"*. However as the inscription is to the *"God of the Brigantes"* it could be simply a title rather than a name. The altar inscription was found at Slack (West Yorkshire).[162]

---

161 Triad 49.
162 RIB 623.

Bres

Name	The Glittering One?
Place of Origin	Ireland
Place of Worship	Ireland
Literary References	Cath Maige Tuired, Cath Muighe Tuireadh, Lebor Gabála Érenn, Oidheadh Chloinne Tuireann.

Bres is the half-Fomorian and half Túatha dé Danann god who initially acted as a hero but subsequently became a villain. His name may come from the root *"bregsos"* meaning *"The Glittering One"*. He first appears as the messenger of the Túatha dé Danann who parleys with the Fir Bolg hero Sreng after the Túatha dé Danann have landed in Ireland. He is described as the grandson of Néit.[163]

In *Cath Muighe Tuireadh*, there are two gods called Bres, one is the brother of Daghda and Ogma, and he is killed in the battle after slaying one hundred and fifty warriors. The better known Bres who marries Brigit is made high king after the battle because Nuada is no longer whole, having lost his hand to the Fir Bolg hero Sreng. Bres rules for seven years before his reign is challenged and he causes the Second Battle of Moytura.[164]

The conception of Bres is described in *Cath Maige Tuired*, as the son of the Túatha de Danann maid Eri and the Fomorian king Elatha. For the first seven years he grew twice as quickly as normal, so he appeared to be fourteen.[165]

After the Second Battle of Moytura, the offers made by Bres to spare his life imply he is a fertility god. He first offers that the cows will always produce milk, but is refused. He then offers a harvest every quarter, i.e. four a year. This is accepted and his life spared after he informs Lugh that the ploughing, sowing, reaping and harvesting must all be done on Tuesdays.[166]

---

163 Cath Muighe Tuireadh.
164 Lebor Gabála Érenn.
165 Cath Maige Tuired.
166 Cath Maige Tuired.

This is not the first time that Lugh spares his life, for he does so after the *Battle of Magh Mór an Aonaigh* when Bres led Fomorian raiders on a coastal raid and was defeated by Lugh.[167]

Brian

Name	Strong One
Place of Origin	Ireland
Place of Worship	Ireland
Literary References	Cath Maige Tuired, Leabhar Mór Leacain, Lebor Gabála Érenn, Oidheadh Chloinne Tuireann.

Brian, whose name means "*Strong One*", is one of the three sons of Danu[168] or the Morrígan[169] with his brothers Iuchar and Iucharba. The three brothers made weapons for the Túatha dé Danann to use in their battle with the Fomorians,[170] or gathered them in reparation according to *Oidheadh Chloinne Tuireann*.

In *Oidheadh Chloinne Tuireann*, Brian is the eldest and ringleader of the three brothers who kill Lugh's father Cian. In this tale he is the son of Tuirenn, and grandson of Ogma. He turns his brothers into dogs to locate Cian in pig form so they can kill him.[171] On the quest for the items that Lugh demands they fetch to make reparation he also turns himself and his brothers into hawks to steal three golden apples from the garden of the Hesperides.[172] To escape Brian transforms himself and his brothers into swans.

His ability to transform people into animal shapes with his druid rod indicates Brian was also a magician. This is also hinted at when his sister Ethne says:

---

167 Oidheadh Chloinne Tuireann.
168 Book of Lecan.
169 Book of Invasions.
170 Cath Maige Tuired.
171 Oidheadh Chloinne Tuireann.
172 Note the cross-over here into Greek myth.

> "O Salmon of the dumb Boinne, O Salmon of the Lifé River, since I cannot keep you here I am loath to part from you. O Rider of the Wave of Tuaidh, the man that stands best in the fight, if you come back again, I think it will not be pleasing to your enemy."[173]

Through the act of killing another member of the Túatha dé Danann the brothers were said to have caused Ireland to never again be free from strife.

Brigantia

Name	High One or Queen
Known Period of Worship	BCE-5th century CE
Place of Origin	North-East England
Place of Worship	Throughout Britain
Other Names	Bregantia

Brigantia is the tribal goddess of the Brigantes tribe of northern England, whose name comes from the root brig and means *"High One"* or *"Queen"*. She was associated with water and rivers (one inscription refers to her as the Nymph Brigantia), and the river Braint (in Anglesey) and river Brent (in Middlesex) were both probably named after her, and possibly the river Brechin in Scotland as well.

The Romans associated her with Victoria, goddess of victory, and Minerva, goddess of war and wisdom, as can be seen from inscriptions combining the names of these deities with Brigantia.

There are at least ten Roman inscriptions to Brigantia.[174] One image shows her bearing a spear and a globe, with a gorgon pendant around her neck and a shield behind her, which are all strongly reminiscent of Minerva. The Irish goddess Brigit and Gallic goddess Brigindo have also been identified with Brigantia.

---

173 Oidheadh Chloinne Tuireann.
174 RIB 88, 623, 627, 628, 630, 643, 1053, 1131, 2066, 2091, 2195.

Brigit

Name	High One or Exalted One
Place of Origin	Ireland
Place of Worship	Ireland
Other Names	Bride, Brighit
Literary References	Cath Maige Tuired, Cormac's Glossary

Brigit is an Irish Goddess whose name comes from the root *brig*, and means "High One" or "Exalted One". Brigit, Brigid or Brighit was the daughter of the Daghda, and was represented as both a single goddess and a triple goddess. She was the patron of a variety of crafts, including brewing, dyeing, smithing and weaving, medicine, poetry and seership. She was also particularly connected with childbirth and married to the Fomorian king Bres.

In *Cormac's Glossary* Brigit is described as:

"A female poet, daughter of the Dagda. This Brigit is a poetess, or a woman of poetry, i.e. a goddess whom poets worshipped, for very great and very noble was her superintendence. Therefore they call her goddess of poets by this name. Whose sisters were Brigit, woman of healing, Brigit, woman of smith-work, i.e. goddesses, from whose names with all Irishmen Brigit was called a goddess. Brigit then, i.e. breo-saigit, a fiery arrow."[175]

Brigit was married to the tyrannical king Bres, who was half Fomorian and half Túatha dé Danann. When her son Ruadán was killed by Goibniu she keened and shrieked and wept, which was the first time they were heard in Ireland. She also invented the whistle for signaling at night.[176]

Her feast day of Imbolc was on 1st February, one of the great Irish seasonal festivals. Indeed the month of February was named after her, being called *"Mí na Féile Bride"*, or *"The Month of the Festival of Brigit"*.

---

175 Cormac's Glossary.
176 Cath Maige Tuired.

Wells were commonly associated with Brigit, though they were to become St Bridget's wells. These include Tobar Bhride (Brideswell) in Co. Roscommon, Daigh Bhride (St Brigid's Well) at Liscannor in Co. Clare and St Brigid's Well in Ballinakill, Co. Galway. Many of the subsequent attributions to Brigit such as fire and virginity come from St Bride, so care needs to be exercised not to accrete the Christian associations onto the earlier goddess.

Britannia

Known Period of Worship	1st-5th century CE
Place of Origin	Northern England
Place of Worship	Northern England

Britannia is the tutelary goddess of Britain, after who the Romans named the British Isles following their invasion in 43 CE. Five Roman inscriptions to her have been found in northern England, and she was associated by the Romans with Minerva.[177] The image of Britannia combined with Minerva became the symbol of the British Empire. With the similarity of names and location of worship it is possible that Britannia was derived from Brigantia.

Búanann

Name	The Lasting One
Place of Origin	Ireland
Place of Worship	Ireland
Other Names	Búan
Literary References	Cormac's Glossary, Tochmarc Émire

Búanann is probably another war goddess. In some versions of the *Tochmarc Émire* she and the warrior woman Scáthach trained the hero Cú Chulainn.

The name Búanann means *"The Lasting One"*, and is also given in a shorter form as Búan. In this shorter form there is a well named after her in Iveragh,

---

177 RIB 88, 643, 2152, 2175, 2195.

Co. Kerry, called Búan's Well or St. Buonia's Well, reinforcing the idea that she was originally a goddess.

When the Morrígan offers herself to Cú Chulainn and is turned down by him, she introduces herself as *"Búan's daughter"*. In *Cormac's Glossary* she is equated to Anu: *"Búanann, the foster mother of the fiana, that is, the lady Anu."*[178]

In the nineteenth century the writer John O'Donovan made a connection between Búanann and the Roman goddess of war and wisdom, Minerva, though this has not been entirely substantiated.[179]

---

178 Cormac's Glossary.
179 Búanann; the Minerva of the pagan Irish – gloss from Supplement to O'Reilly's Irish-English Dictionary, John O'Donovan, 1864.

C

Caelestis

Name	Heavenly
Known Period of Worship	2nd-5th century CE
Place of Origin	Carthage
Place of Worship	Northumberland
Other Names	Tanith

Caelestis is a Romanized form of the Carthaginian and Phoenician moon goddess Tanith, whose name means *"Heavenly"*. Three inscriptions to her have been found, one with Jupiter Dolichenus, Brigantia and Salus; one with Bona Dea; and one with the constellation Virgo.[180]

Cailleach

Name	Veiled One, Old Woman or Nun
Place of Origin	Ireland?
Place of Worship	Ireland, Scotland, Isle of Man
Other Names	Caillagh ny Gromagh, Cailleach Beara, Cailleach Bheur
Literary References	Aithbe Dam Bés Mora, Compert Mongán, Leabhar Buidhe Lecain, Life of Saint Samson of Dol.

Cailleach or Caillighe can mean *"veiled one"*, *"old woman/crone"* or *"nun"*. The Cailleach Beara of Ireland, the Cailleach Bheur of Scotland and the Manx Caillagh ny Gromagh all seem to be representations of the same goddess. Tales of the Cailleach from all of these areas describe her forming the landscape by dropping stones out of her apron or slipping, and clearly

---

180 RIB 1131, 1448, 1791.

suggest that she was an earth goddess. Her protection of animals, control of the weather and association with the seasons all reinforce this attribution.

In the *Lament of the Old Woman of Beara* she is the Cailleach Bearra, a crone, recounting a monologue of nostalgia for her youthful beauty and royal lovers. This lament, written around 800 CE, contains elements of Christian and Pagan myths merged together, which may be where this name with its dual Pagan and Christian meanings comes from. Irish tales sometimes refer to her as Cailleach Mor, meaning *"great old woman"*, with *mor* being the same word that forms part of the name of the Morrígan.

The Cailleach Beara was described as having two sisters, Cailleach Bolus and Cailleach Corca Duibune, giving the triple form often seen in British deities. She was also described as being wed to the god Lugh. In Irish folklore she is described as possessing a white, red-eared cow, whose colours are symbolic of the otherworld.[181] This colouring is seen elsewhere in this context, such as when the Morrígan attacks Cú Chulainn as a hornless white red-eared cow, and the Welsh hounds of the otherworld (*Cwn Annwn*).

This cow makes an appearance in *The Conception of Mongán*, for Fiachna Finn needs the cow to heal King Eolgarg Mór, and the price the Cailleach demands is his aid to make war on the king of Lochlann. Fiachna does this, which sets up the circumstances for Manannán to make love with Fiachna's wife and sire Mongán in exchange for his aid in battle.

In the fourteenth century *Yellow Book of Lecan*, the Cailleach Beara is described as having seven youthful periods, marrying seven husbands, and having fifty foster-children who went on to found many tribes and nations. She was said to reside around the Beara peninsula, on the Cork-Kerry border.

The ninth century Christian hagiography, the Life of Saint Samson of Dol refers to the Cailleach in the manner of dismissive and belittling propaganda. Despite its Christian nature, there is a lot of pagan magickal symbolism in the story associated not only with the Cailleach but also Saint Samson himself.

---

181 Myth, Legend & Romance: An Encyclopaedia of Irish Folklore Tradition, D. Ó'hÓgain, 1990, p119.

Saint Samson was born to a previously barren woman, after her husband Amon had been told to present her with a silver rod equal in size to her height. Amon, gave his wife not one but three silver rods each equal to her height. The use of the faery metal silver and the triple motif are obviously not coincidental. The name of Saint Samson's mother was Anna, which may well be derived from Anu, as seen in the Welsh Genealogies. Anna was visited by God in a vision, who told her she would have a special child who *"Shall be holy and a high priest before Almighty God."*[182]

When St Samson was travelling one day he heard a dreadful shriek (which recalls the cries of the Morrígan), and saw a sorceress: *"in truth a very old woman with shaggy hair and that already grey, with her garments of red, holding in her hand a bloody trident."*[183] This woman, who by her age, hair and red garments was clearly representing the Cailleach, was chasing a man to death.

Saint Samson commanded her to stop in the name of Jesus and questioned her. After she had identified herself as a sorceress, the woman said *"I have eight sisters"*,[184] recalling the symbolism of the number nine associated with goddesses throughout the Celtic myths. The sorceress refused to change her ways and was killed by Saint Samson.

The Cailleach Bheur as Winter Queen is connected with another major deity, Bride, as the Queen of Summer who she holds captive in Ben Nevis to wash her mantle. She is rescued by the Summer King Angus, who is clearly reminiscent of Angus Mac Og. The Cailleach Bheur is described as having mackerel blue skin, one eye and red teeth.

A different version of the myth has her as the Queen of Winter who, at winter's end, drank from the Well of Youth. The waters transformed her into the Queen of Summer, a beautiful maiden. This seasonal change suggests an Earth Goddess whose form changes with the seasons.

---

182 Life of St. Samson of Dol.
183 Life of St. Samson of Dol.
184 Life of St. Samson of Dol.

Sir Walter Scott described the change back from maiden to crone at the end of the summer graphically:

"The appearance of the beautiful lady is changed into that of the most hideous hag in existence; one side is blighted and wasted, as if by palsy; one eye drops from her head; her colour, as clear as virgin silver, is now of a dun, leaden hue."[185]

The Cailleach Bheur is referred to as *"the daughter of Grianan"* or Grianaig, meaning *"little Sun"*. Little sun was a name for winter, as opposed to big sun being a name for summer.

The transformation of the Cailleach Bheur into the Maiden of Summer also demonstrates her shape-shifting ability. Shape-shifting occurs a number of times in the Cailleach myths. In Scottish myth she transforms into a number of birds, including cormorant, crow, eagle, gull, heron and raven. As Gyre Carling she assumes the form of a sow, the animal associated by the Celts with the Underworld Goddess.

This contrast of the Winter Queen and Summer Queen also occurs in the tale of *The Venomous Wild Boar of Glen Glass*, with the Cailleach being contrasted with the maiden Grainne, another Irish Goddess, but this time of the Sun.

A Scottish fragment of this tale has her as the Cailleach Bheur telling a Prior's daughter in Tiree how far back her memory stretches when asked how old she is, *"And I saw Leinster lake in Ireland when children could swim across."*[186]

In yet another different version of the myth she is reborn on every All Hallows Eve (Samhain) as the winter goddess returning to bring the winter and the snows. She carries a magickal staff, which freezes the ground with every tap.

She also guards the animals throughout the winter, and returns to the earth by turning to stone on Beltane Eve. The stone she turned into was said to remain *"always moist"*.[187]

---

185 Letters on Demonology and Witchcraft, Sir Walter Scott, 1831, letter 4:129.
186 Popular Tales of the West Highlands, J.F Campbell, 1860.

Before turning to stone she would throw her magick staff under a holly tree or gorse bush, which were her sacred plants. A local verse explains that this is why grass does not grow under holly trees: *"She threw it beneath the hard holly tree, where grass or hair has never grown."*[188]

One tale has the Cailleach ushering in winter by washing her huge plaid in the Corryvreckan whirlpool, one of her sacred sites.

"Before the washing the roar of a coming tempest is heard by people on the coast for a distance of twenty miles, and for a period of three days before the cauldron boils. When the washing is over the plaid of old Scotland is virgin white."[189]

Of all the animals the deer are most beloved of the Cailleach. She treats them as her cattle, herding and milking them and protecting them from hunters. However she also protects wild pigs and boars, wild goats, wild cattle and wolves.

The Manx version of the Cailleach is known as Caillagh ny Gromagh, which means *"Old Woman of Gloominess"*. If St Bride's Day was fine, she would go out to gather sticks to keep her warm for the rest of the summer. If it was wet she would stay hidden from the rain, and would have to improve the weather herself if she wanted to travel around the island. A fine 1st February was therefore seen as an augury of bad weather in the summer months. She was sometimes seen in the shape of a giant bird gathering sticks. The weather and avian connections are identical to those of the Scottish Cailleach Bheur.

Another Manx tale tells of how the Caillagh ny Gromagh fell into a crevice whilst trying to step from the top of Barrule to the top of Cronk yn Irree Lhaa, leaving the mark of her heel visible to this day.

In Scotland the Cailleach Bheur was said to have formed the hills of Ross-shire with earth and stones that fell off her back. Likewise she also dropped stones out of her pannier to form Ben Vaichaird.

---

187 Scottish Folk Lore and Folk Life, Donald MacKenzie, 1935, p138.
188 Witchcraft and Second Sight in the Scottish Highlands, J.G. Campbell, 1902, p254.
189 Myth, Tradition and Story from Western Argyll, K.W. Grant, 1925, p8,

"When standing on the site of the huge Ben Vaichaird, the bottom of the pannier is said to have given way, and the contents, falling through the opening, produced the hill, which owes its great height and vast extent of base to the accident."[190]

There is a hill called Beinn Chailleach Bheur in the parish of Strathlachlan and Strachur in Cowal (Argyllshire) named after her. A hill in Kidalton parish, Islay called Beinn na Caillich is named after her, and a furrow down its side called Sgrìoh na Caillich was said to be made by her as she slid down it in a sitting position.

At Sliab na Caillighe in Ireland there is a throne-shaped limestone boulder known as The Hag's Chair. Local tradition tells of how Cailleach Beara came down from the north to perform a magickal task, by which she could gain great power.

The Scottish Gyre Carling was described by Sir Walter Scott as the *"mother witch of the Scottish peasantry"*. In the correspondence Scott quoted the following lines from a poem in the *Bannatyne MSS* describing her unpleasant tastes:

> *"Thair dwelt ane grit Gyre Carling in awld Betokis bour,*
> *That levit [lived] upoun menis flesche [men's flesh]."*

She carries an iron club, which we can equate with the rod of winter carried by the Cailleach Bheur. When she is attacked by dogs she shape-shifts into a pig, showing an otherworld connection.

---

190 Scenes and Legends of the North of Scotland, Hugh Miller, 1835, p30

Callirius

Name	God of the Hazel Wood?
Known Period of Worship	BCE-5th century CE
Place of Origin	Essex
Place of Worship	Essex

A Roman temple near Colchester (Essex) has been excavated that was dedicated to a local god called Callirius, which may mean *"God of the Hazel Wood"*. We know nothing about this god except that the Romans equated him with their woodland god Silvanus.[191]

Camulos

Name	The Powerful One
Known Period of Worship	BCE-5th century BCE
Place of Origin	Belgium
Place of Worship	Dunbartonshire, Essex, London, Yorkshire

Camulos is a Belgian god whose name means the *"Powerful One"*, who was worshipped in England and Scotland. Evidence of his worship has been found in Colchester (Essex), Almondbury (Yorkshire) and Bar Hill (Dunbartonshire),[192] and in late 2002 a plaque dedicated to him was found in London. Associated place names for Camulos are Camulodunum (*"Fort of Camulos"*), which is now called Colchester, Camulosessa (*"Seat of Camulos"*) in southern Scotland, and possibly Cambodunum (Slack, Yorkshire).

British coins associated with Camulos from around Colchester (Essex) depict a ram-horned head, and two other coins dedicated to him show a boar, suggesting that he may have been seen as a horned god and hunter. Certainly

---

191 RIB 194.
192 RIB 2166.

the boar is a recurring motif in coins dedicated to him in Gaul, suggesting the boar was his sacred animal.[193] In Belgium and France he was associated with Mars by the Romans.

Carman

Name	She of the Weaving Beam
Place of Origin	Ireland
Place of Worship	Ireland
Literary References	Dinshenchas

Carman is a Fomorian goddess of magick in Ireland, whose name may mean *"She of the weaving beam"*. After the Túatha dé Danann had overcome the Fomorians, Carman and her sons blighted the corn of Ireland to try to destroy their conquerors. Carman used charms, spells and incantations, and her three sons Dian (*"Violent"*), Dothur (*"Evil"*) and Dub (*"Black"*) used dishonesty, plundering and violence.

The Túatha dé Danann overcame the family with magick, driving the sons across the sea, and holding Carman hostage. She died of grief, and an annual fair was instituted at her grave.[194]

Cautes

Name	Unknown
Known Period of Worship	2nd-4th century CE
Place of Origin	Persia
Place of Worship	Cumbria

Cautes is a divine companion of Mithras, representing light, the dawn and the Spring Equinox. Both he and his twin Cautopates bear torches, though his is

---

193 Pagan Celtic Britain, Ross, 1967, p309.
194 The Prose Tales in the Rennes Dinshenchas, W Stokes (Trans), 1894.

always lit and born upwards. He is depicted on an inscription on an altar found at Carlisle.[195]

Cautopates

Name	Unknown
Known Period of Worship	2nd-4th century CE
Place of Origin	Persia
Place of Worship	Co. Durham

Cautopates is a divine companion of Mithras, representing night, dusk and the Autumn Equinox. As with his twin Cautes he bears a torch, though his points downwards and is not always lit. He is referred to on an altar at Lanchester (Co. Durham), with Mithras.[196]

Ceres

Name	Creation
Known Period of Worship	2nd-5th century CE
Place of Origin	Rome
Place of Worship	Northumberland

Ceres is a Roman earth and corn goddess whose name means *"Creation"*. She was the daughter of Saturn and Vesta, particularly honoured at her festival of Cerealia (April 12th-19th). She was equated with the Greek Demeter, as seen by her being the mother by Jupiter of Prosperina (the Roman equivalent of Persephone), and also her role as an agriculture and earth goddess.

There is only one known inscription to her,[197] and she is much more commonly depicted on signet rings, worn by the villa owners who would have relied on her for good harvests of their crops. Eighteen such gemstones from rings have been found around Britain dating to 1st-3rd century CE, and

---

195 RIB 943.
196 RIB 1082.
197 RIB 1791.

in all of them she bears corn ears in her left hand and a bowl or basket of fruit in the right.[198]

Ceridwen

Name	Fair and Loved, or Crooked Woman
Place of Origin	Wales
Place of Worship	Wales
Other Names	Caridwen, Cyridwen
Literary References	Black Book of Carmarthen, Book of Taliesin, Red Book of Hergest, White Bok of Rhydderch

Ceridwen (or Caridwen) is a Welsh goddess associated with magick, poetry and transformation. Her name may mean *"Fair and Loved"* or *"Crooked Woman"*. She is referred to in the *White Book of Rhydderch* in the *Tale of Taliesin*. She was married to a man called Tegid Voel, and had a beautiful daughter called Creirwy (*"The Purest"*) and two sons, Morvran (*"Sea Raven"*) and Avagddu (*"Utter Darkness"*).

Avagddu was ugly so Ceridwen resolved to make a potion that would give him great knowledge so he would still be accepted despite his looks.

Morvran is mentioned in the tale of *Kilhwch and Olwen*, and in *Trioedd Ynys Prydein* where it is noted that he had hair on his face like a stag, and was not wounded in battle because the enemy thought he was a demon. He is also described as one of King Arthur's counselors in *The Dream of Rhonabwy*.

Ceridwen collected all the herbs and ingredients and put them in a Cauldron of Inspiration to boil for a year and a day, so that three drops would be distilled which would bestow inspiration onto the recipient of them. A blind man called Morda and a boy called Gwion Bach (*"little weaver"*) were in charge of keeping the cauldron boiling. Towards the end of the time three drops flew out onto the finger of Gwion Bach. Because of the heat he licked

---

198 A Corpus of Roman Engraved Gemstones from British Sites (vol 2), Henig, 1974, p39-41.

his finger and received the inspiration, which also caused the cauldron full of the remaining poisonous liquid to burst.

With his new knowledge Gwion Bach realised that Ceridwen would punish him, so he changed into a hare and fled, and she into a greyhound to chase him. Then he became a fish and she an otter, and then he a bird and she a hawk. Finally he became a grain in a barn and she a chicken, and she ate him. Nine months later she gave birth to him and could not kill him because of his great beauty, so she put him in a leather bag and cast him out to sea to the mercy of fate. He was rescued on May Eve and grew up to become the bard Taliesin (*"radiant brow"*).

Taliesin was not complimentary about Ceridwen in his descriptions of her when he recited his verses. He described her as *"a smiling black old hag"*, and when describing himself says *"Then I was for nine months in the womb of the hag Ceridwen"*.

Ceridwen is also referred to in the title of the piece *The Ode of Ceridwen*, linking her to minstrelsy and bardship, and two poems in this book refer to her connection with poetic inspiration (and it may be noted both use an identical line within them):

*"A successful song of fruitful praise,
relating to the bustling course of the host.
According to the sacred ode of Ceridwen,
the goddess of various seeds, the various seeds of poetic harmony,
the exalted speech of the graduated minstrel."*[199]

*"According to the sacred ode of Cyridwen, the Ogyrven of various seeds,
— The various seeds of poetic harmony,
the exalted speech of the graduated minstrel,
Cuhelyn the wise, of elegant Cymraec,
an exalted possession, Will skillfully sing"*[200]

---

[199] The Black Book of Carmarthen 3.
[200] The Black Book of Carmarthen, 4.

A chapter in *The Book of Taliesin* is called *The Chair of Ceridwen*, and contains reference to some of the qualities ascribed to her:

> *"My chair, my cauldron and my laws,*
> *And my parading eloquence, meet for the chair.*
> *I am called skilful in the court of Don."*[201]

Cernunnos

Name	Horned One
Place of Origin	Gaul
Other Names	Cernenus, Karnonos

Cernunnos is a horned god associated with nature and animals. His name is usually translated as *"Horned One"*, and he is also known as *"Lord of all Wild Things"*. There was dispute about his name, as it is derived from a piece of altar found in Notre Dame (Paris) dating to 17 CE which reads ERNUNNO, and depicts a bull-horned god, not the stag-horned god of the Gundestrup Cauldron.[202]

Inscriptions and finds from other parts of Europe have confirmed his name through the variants discovered, however. An inscription with the name Cernunnos was found at Polenza in Italy, and a variant, Cernenus at Verespatak in Rumania where he is equated with Jupiter. Other European inscriptions include one to *Deo Cernunico* at Seinsel-Rëlent in Germany and a Greek inscription at Montagnac in France to Karnonos.

Cernunnos is best known in modern times by association with the striking image on the Gundestrup Cauldron. However the worship of Cernunnos, and indeed his name, came from Gaul, where there were many representations of him. We are concerned with the British perception of the

---

201 Book of Taliesin, 16.
202 See e.g. The Gundestrup Cauldron, G.S. Olmsted, 1979; Cernunnos, F. LeRoux, 1953 in Ogam 25-6:324-29; and The Lost Beliefs of Northern Europe, H.R. Davidson, 1993, for arguments against the attribution of the name.

god and how he was recorded, and for these reasons the most likely representations of Cernunnos would be the unnamed bull-horned gods found around Britain.

The Romans encountered Cernunnos first in Gaul, and associated him with Mercury, although Julius Caesar likened him to Dis Pater as the major god.

Clídna

Place of Origin	Ireland
Place of Worship	Ireland
Other Names	Clíodna, Clíona
Literary References	Silva Gadelica

Clídna (alternatively spelt as Clíodna or Clíona) is an Irish otherworld goddess who possessed healing qualities, as one would expect from a goddess with watery associations. She also possessed three magickal singing birds, one blue with a red head, one red with a green head, and one speckled with a gold head, whose song lulled people to sleep and healed them, in a similar manner to the birds of Rhiannon. The birds are described in *Silva Gadelica*, in the voyage of the hero Tadhg mac Céin, who meets Clídna on an unknown island (implying the otherworld).[203]

The watery associations of the otherworld are also seen in the fact that Clídna has a wave named after her, Tonn Chlíona (*"Cliona's wave"*) on the Glandore strand.[204] Like Áine and Aoibheall, she became a fairy queen, hence her name of Clíona Ceaanfhionn (*"Fair-haired Clíona"*) and was claimed as an ancestor by the Ó Caoimh family of Munster. A contemporary lament has her foretelling the death of the bishop of Cork in 1726 CE.[205] She was also associated with Carriag Chlíona (*"Cliona's Rock"*) in Co. Cork.

---

203 Silva Gadelica, S. H. O'Grady, 1892, 1.342.
204 Silva Gadelica, 1.223; Banshenchus.
205 Amhráin Sheagháin Chláraigh Mhic Dhomhaill, An tAth P. Ua Duinnín, 1902, 49-50.

Cocidius

Name	The Red One?
Known Period of Worship	BCE-5th century CE
Place of Origin	Cumbria?
Place of Worship	Northern England and Scotland

Cocidius was a war god of the frontier of northern England and Scotland. He was associated by the Romans with Mars, and was invoked as the god of soldiers. The meaning of his name is unknown, though it has been linked to the Welsh root *"coch"*, hinting at a meaning of something like *"The Red One"*. This would certainly fit with his qualities as a war god.

A number of images show him hunting animals including stags, boars and hares, indicating a role as a god of the hunt, which would fit with the fact of his also being equated with Silvanus by the Romans.

There are at least twenty-three stone altars and two silver plaques bearing dedications to Cocidius, the majority of which are military altars.[206] One of the altars to Cocidius bears two dolphins at the base, though whether this indicates a connection to water is open to question. Another altar inscription equates Cocidius to both Mars and the native god Toutates (Teutates). As with Belatucadros, he is referred to six times as *sanctus* or *"holy"*.

The two silver plaques both bear similar images, of Cocidius bearing a spear and shield, and wearing a short cape-like garment. These images clearly reinforce his title as Cocidius, god of soldiers.

A major centre of his worship was at Bewcastle (Cumbria) which was known in Roman times as Fanum Cocidi, or The Temple of Cocidius.

---

206 RIB 602, 966, 985-9, 993, 997, 1017, 1102, 1207, 1577, 1578, 1583, 1633, 1683, 1872, 1885, 1955, 1956, 1961, 1963, 2015, 2020, 2024

Concordia

Name	Harmony
Known Period of Worship	2nd-5th century CE
Place of Origin	Rome
Place of Worship	Cumbria, Northumberland

Concordia is the Roman goddess of conciliation and harmony, which is the meaning of her name. The two known dedications to her at Carlisle (Cumbria) and Corbridge (Northumberland) are both at sites where more than one legion was based,[207] suggesting her influence was called on to limit the rivalry between the legions, which was known to cause incidents.

Condatis

Name	God of the Watersmeet
Known Period of Worship	2nd-5th century CE
Place of Origin	Tee basin
Place of Worship	Co. Durham, Lothian, Yorkshire
Other Names	Condatus

Condatis is an indigenous god worshipped in the Tee basin in northern England. His name means *"God of the Watersmeet"*, suggesting a healing attribution due to the watery association. The Roman settlement of Condate, now known as Northwich, in Cheshire, is named after him, indicating his worship was substantial.

As was often the case, the Romans equated him with Mars, and several Roman inscriptions bear his name.[208] The altars bearing these inscriptions were all found near rivers, two of them close to the junction of two rivers. In recent years an altar bearing an inscription to him has also been found at Cramond in Lothian.

---

207 RIB 964, 1125.
208 RIB 731, 1024, 1045.

Contrebis

Name	He Who Dwells Among Us
Known Period of Worship	2nd-4th century CE
Place of Origin	Lancashire
Place of Worship	Lancashire
Other Names	Gontrebi

Contrebis is an obscure god whose name may mean *"He who dwells among us"*, from the Welsh *tref* meaning *"town"* or the Latin words *treba* meaning *"dwelling"* and *con* meaning *"among, within"*. He is referred to in a dedication at Overborough (Lancashire)[209] where he is equated with another obscure god, Ialonus. A second inscription at the same site to *"Gontrebi deus san[cuts]"*, i.e. *"Gontrebis the holy god"* is probably a variant of his name.[210]

Corotiacus

Name	Lord of the Throwers?
Known Period of Worship	2nd-5th century CE
Place of Origin	Suffolk?
Place of Worship	Suffolk

Corotiacus is an obscure war god equated with Mars, the meaning of whose name is uncertain. The name may be derived from the words *koro* meaning *"throwing"* and *tiarn* meaning *"lord"*, giving a possible meaning of *"Lord of the throwers"*. Considering he is bearing an axe on the image of him this name does fit the depiction.

The only evidence for him is found at Martlesham (Suffolk) where he is shown on a bronze fragment as an axe-wielding mounted warrior riding over a prostrate foe, inscribed to Mars Corotiacus.[211]

---

209 RIB 600.
210 RIB 610.
211 RIB 213.

Coventina

Name	Unknown
Known Period of Worship	BCE-5th century CE
Place of Origin	Northumberland
Place of Worship	Northumberland, Somerset
Other Names	Conventina

Coventina (or Conventina) was a tutelary water goddess associated with the spring at Carrawburgh (Northumberland), where over sixteen thousand coins were found. This huge quantity of votive offerings suggests she was viewed as a healing goddess.

Fourteen inscriptions to her have been found, including two referring to her as nymphae (*"nymph"*) and, also as sancta (*"holy"*) and augusta (*"revered"*).[212] These latter two titles were more commonly used for Roman deities, showing the importance attached to Coventina. Despite numerous suggestions, the meaning of Coventina's name continues to defy translation.

A relief at her well shows Coventina in triple form, each image holding two water jars, one of which is held upright and the other has water pouring out of it. Another image shows her reclining on a large leaf, with her left arm resting on an urn and holding up a foliate branch in her right hand. This foliate imagery combined with her worship in conjunction with Nemetona does raise the question of whether she might also have had an earth goddess aspect as was sometimes the case.

She was worshipped in Bath with Sulis and Nemetona. It has been suggested that the city of Coventry takes its name from Coventina, but there is no evidence to substantiate this. Two sites in Spain (Os Curvenos and Santa Cruz de Loyo) and Narbonne in France also have dedicatory inscriptions to her, indicating her worship spread to the continent, probably through soldiers of the Roman army.

---

212 RIB 1522-35.

Creidhne

Place of Origin	Ireland
Place of Worship	Ireland
Literary References	Cath Maige Tuired.

Creidhne the Craftsman was one of a trio of Túatha dé Danann craft gods with Goibniu and Luchta. He made the rivets for the spears, hilts for swords and rimes and bosses for shields, taking only three actions to do so. He also helped Dian Cecht put the silver hand on Nuada after the First Battle of Moytura.[213]

Cuda

Name	Prosperity, Well-being
Place of Origin	Gloucestershire
Place of Worship	Gloucestershire

Cuda is the name on a sculpture of a mother goddess found in Cirencester (Gloucestershire), capital of the Dobunni tribe. She is shown bearing an object in her lap, possibly an egg or loaf, suggesting fertility, and has three Genii Cucullati with her. Another sculpture from Daglingworth nearby shows a similar group of figures and may also represent Cuda. Her name is thought to come from the word *cudd* meaning *"prosperity"* or *"well-being"*.

---

[213] Cath Maige Tuired.

Cunobelinus

Name	Hound of Belinus
Known Period of Worship	1st-5th century CE
Place of Origin	Essex?
Place of Worship	Essex
Literary References	Trioedd Ynys Prydein

Cunobelinus is a god represented on coins found at Harlow (Essex), shown wielding a club and bearing a severed head. He was a god of the Catuvellauni tribe and was often shown on coins having two faces, in a similar manner to the Roman god Janus. His name means Hound of Belinus, so he may be another form of the god Belenus.

He is described in the *Triads* as one of the *"Three Heroic Sovereigns of the Isle of Britain"*, though this may be referring to Cunobelin, ruler of the Catuvellauni tribe from 10-43 CE who is often confused with him.[214] The *Triads* also refer to his son, Gweirydd as one of the *"Three Primary Battle Princes"*.[215]

Cupid

Name	Desire
Known Period of Worship	1st-3rd century CE
Place of Origin	Rome
Place of Worship	Across Britain
Other Names	Eros

Cupid is a love god and son of Venus, depicted as a winged cherub, often with bow and arrow or torch. His name means *"Desire"*. Cupid is depicted on forty-two Roman engraved gems found across Britain dating from 1st-3rd

---

214 Triad 23.
215 Triad 24.

century CE.[216] He is depicted in a variety of poses and with a variety of animals.

Thus he is twice shown in duplicate, bearing grapes thrice, a butterfly and torch five times, a hoe, a bow, a spindle and a staff. He is shown thrice on a horse, once on a goat, thrice on a hippocamp, four times on a dolphin, and is also depicted accompanied by a goose, a hare, a fish, a goat, and a cock.

Cybele

Known Period of Worship	1st-5th century CE
Place of Origin	Phrygia
Place of Worship	Gloucestershire, London, Northumberland
Other Names	Kybele, Magna Mater

Cybele (or Kybele) is a Phrygian goddess whose worship influenced many other Mediterranean goddesses. She was a mother goddess and lady of the beasts who caught her shepherd god lover Attis being unfaithful and drove him mad. He castrated himself and bled to death. This is why priests of Cybele practiced castration in their devotion to their goddess.

Cybele was also known as the Magna Mater, or *"Great Mother"*. Her cult symbol was a black meteoric stone, which was moved from Asia Minor to Rome in 204 BCE.

In Britain the main areas of Cybele worship were in London, Gloucester, Corbridge (Northumberland) and Hadrian's Wall. Private shrines to her also seem likely based on the evidence from finds at Froxfield (Wiltshire) and Whatley (Somerset).[217]

---

216 A Corpus of Roman Engraved Gemstones from British Sites (vol 2), Henig, 1974, p21-6, 96, 98.
217 The Gods of Roman Britain, Green, 1983, p22-3.

D

Daghda

Name	The Good God
Place of Origin	Ireland
Place of Worship	Ireland
Other Names	Dagda, Eochaid Ollathair, Ruadh Rofhessa.
Literary References	Banshenchus, Cath Maige Tuired , Cath Muighe Tuireadh, Dinshenchas, Leabhar Buidhe Lecain, Lebor Gabála Érenn

The Daghda (or Dagda) is a fertility god and king of the Túatha dé Danann, whose name means the *"Good God"*. He was also known as Eochaid Ollathair, meaning *"Horse All-Father"*, and Ruadh Rofhessa meaning *"Red One Great in Knowledge"*.

The Daghda was said to control the weather and give good crops.[218] He is also described as a god of wizardry.[219] His skill at arms is indicated in *Cath Muighe Tuireadh*, where it says:

> *"The Dagda began the attack on the enemy by cutting his way through them to the west, clearing a path for a hundred and fifty."*[220]

He possessed a cauldron from which nobody ever went away hungry, which was one of the four treasures of the Túatha dé Danann.[221] His brothers were Ogma and Nuada, and his best known children were Angus Mac Og, and Sethor MacCuill (*"son of the hazel"*), Tethor MacCecht (*"son of the plough"*) and

---

218 The Yellow Book of Lecan, Cath Muighe Tuireadh.
219 Cath Muighe Tuireadh.
220 Cath Muighe Tuireadh.
221 Cath Maige Tuired.

Cethor MacGreine (*"son of the sun"*), the husbands of Banba, Ériu and Fotla. He also had sons called Aedh and Cermait.

In the Book of Invasions he is called the father of Brigid and Áine.[222] In the Dinshenchas, Dian Cecht is also called his son,[223] but the Book of Invasions calls Dian Cecht a cousin of the Dagda.[224] Elsewhere the Daghda is described as having an unnamed son, though it could refer to Angus Mac Og, and he also has a daughter called Echtgi:

> *"Pleasant Englec who did not spoil eloquence, was mother of the swift son of the Dagda. Echtgi the loathsome was daughter of the noble Dagda."*[225]

In Cath Maige Tuired, before visiting the Fomorians the Daghda made love with the Morrígan astride a ford, with feet on either bank, emphasising their giant size, as did the fact his club left a huge ditch behind as he dragged it along.

The Daghda was renowned for his love of porridge, and when he visited the Fomorian camp under a flag of truce before the Second Battle of Moytura they dug a huge hole in the ground and filled it with porridge, and forced him to eat it. He ate it all, and left with his belly distended. As he returned to his camp he was accosted by the Fomorian Boand, who satirised him and forced him into love-making, resulting in her defection to the Túatha dé Danann.

After the battle the Daghda accompanied by Lugh and Ogma went to reclaim his harp which had been stolen by the Fomorians. He had bound melodies into it so it did not play until he called it, suggesting a connection between him and harping. The Daghda ruled Ireland as king for eighty years, before handing the kingship to Lugh.

His son Aedh was killed by a jealous man called Corrgenn who thought he was too familiar with his wife. The Daghda laid a geas on Corrgenn to carry

---

222 Lebor Gabála Érenn.
223 Dinshenchas.
224 Lebor Gabála Érenn.
225 Banshenchus, pt 1.

Aedh's body until he found a stone the same size as Aedh to cover him, and then bury him in the nearest hill. Corrgen's heart burst as he carried the stone to the grave, and the hill where Aedh was buried was known afterwards as the Hill of Aileac (*"Hill of Sighs"*).

The Daghda desired Boann, and sent her husband Elcmar on a journey, working mighty magick that kept hunger and thirst from him, and nine months went past for him as one day. She gave birth to Angus Mac Og, without Elcmar knowing, and the Daghda took him away and fostered him elsewhere.

Following Lugh's reign, the Daghda ruled for eighty years.[226] After the Milesians defeated the Túatha dé Danann and they fled into the hollow hills, they still controlled the land and caused all the grass and grain to die until the Milesians agreed a treaty with them. The Daghda had four great underground palaces, of which he gave one to Lugh and one to Ogma, and kept two for himself. His other son Angus Mac Og was away at the time and given nothing. Angus tricked him into giving the finer of his two halls with the help of Manannán Mac Lir.[227]

Danu

Name	River
Place of Origin	Ireland
Place of Worship	Ireland
Other Names	Anu, Anand, Anann, Danand
Literary References	Leabhar Mór Leacain, Leabhar na h-Uidhri, Lebor Gabála Érenn

The two names of Anu and Danu are usually taken as referring to the same goddess. Danu means *"River"*, and may be the root of the name of the river Danube in Germany, where the Celts were known to live. Anu means *"wealth"* and implies a connection to the treasures of the earth.

---

226 Lebor Gabála Érenn.
227 The Taking of the Fairy Mound.

Danu is also recorded in some sources as Danand and Danann (and hence Túatha dé Danann), and Anu is recorded in places as Anand and Anann.

Danu was married to the Death God Bilé, with whom she gave birth to the Daghda. She is also described as the mother of the *"three Gods of Danu"*, Brian, Iuchar and Iucharba, who supplied the special weapons for Lugh to fight the Fomorians.[228] The *Book of Invasions* describes her as sister to Macha and Anu, and the sovereignty goddesses Ériu, Banba and Fotla.[229]

> *"The Morrígan ... and it is from her other name "Danu" the Paps of Ana in Luchair are named, as well as the Túatha dé Danann."*[230]

Danu and the Morrígan are sometimes equated, both directly and indirectly. In *The Book of Leinster*, the two are directly equated, and the earth connection referred to again:

> *"Badb and Macha and Anu, i.e. the Morrígan, from whom the Paps of Anu in Luachair are named, were the three daughters of Ernmas the witch."*[231]

Whereas the prophetic dream of Eochaid the Fir Bolg king in the First Battle of Moytura implies the same equation of the two goddesses by its symbolism (he dreams of the great flock of black birds invading representing the Túatha dé Danann).

In *The Book of Invasions* she is referred to as *"shapely Danand"*, emphasising her beauty.[232]

---

[228] Lebor Gabála Érenn, 4.64.
[229] Lebor Gabála Érenn 4.63-4.
[230] The Great Book of Lecan.
[231] The Book of Leinster.
[232] Lebor Gabála Érenn.

Deo Qui Vias et Semitas Commentus Est

Name	The God who Invented Roads and Pathways
Known Period of Worship	2nd century CE
Place of Worship	Yorkshire

The name of Deo Qui Vias et Semitas Commentus Est, meaning *"The God who Invented Roads and Pathways"*, is mentioned on a single Roman altarstone found at Catterick.[233]

Diana

Name	Heavenly or Divine
Known Period of Worship	1st-5th century CE
Place of Origin	Rome
Place of Worship	Across Britain

Diana is the Roman moon and hunting goddess, sister to the solar god Apollo. Her name may be derived from the root *"dyeus"* meaning *"heavenly"* or *"divine"*. Six inscriptions to her have been found across Britain,[234] as well as five engraved gems of her dating to 2nd-4th century CE (all in southern England and the Welsh borders), two of her head, and three as the huntress with bow and arrow.[235]

---

233 RIB 725.
234 RIB 138, 316, 1126, 1209, 2122, 2174.
235 A Corpus of Roman Engraved Gemstones from British Sites (vol 2), Henig, 1974, p38-9.

Dian Cecht

Name	Swift/Powerful Judge
Place of Origin	Ireland
Place of Worship	Ireland
Literary References	Bretha Déin Chécht, Cath Maige Tuired, Cath Muighe Tuireadh, Dinshenchas, Lebor Gabála Érenn

Dian Cecht was a god of healing, whose name may mean *"Swift/Powerful Judge"*. He is described as either the son of the Daghda,[236] or as the son of Esarg and grandson of Néit,[237] which would make him a cousin of Balor.

He had four sons, Miach, Cu, Cethen and Cian,[238] who was the father of Lugh with Ethne (daughter of Balor), and two daughters Airmed the healer and Etan the poet. He also had three brothers called Fir, Forus and Oll, who ambushed the Fir Bolg king Eochaid but were slain by an unnamed champion.[239]

During the war with the Fir Bolgs, Dian Cecht joined in the fighting, being one of the nobles who led the combat for the Túatha dé Danann.[240]

During the war with the Fomorians, Dian Cecht restored dead warriors to life in a healing well with the aid of his sons and daughter. He could restore any man, unless his head was cut off or his spine severed.[241]

Dian Cecht killed his son Miach for his attempt to heal Nuada's hand. He struck him three times with his sword, and each time Miach healed himself, then he struck him a fourth time in the head and killed him. From Miach's grave grew three hundred and sixty-five different healing herbs, one for each

---

236 Dinshenchas.
237 Lebor Gabála Érenn.
238 Or alternatively given as three sons, Miach, Cian and Octruil.
239 Cath Muighe Tuireadh.
240 Cath Muighe Tuireadh.
241 Cath Maige Tuired.

day of the year.²⁴² Dian Cecht mixed up the herbs so that there uses would not be clearly apparent and had to be learned through years of hard study. Dian Cecht also healed Midir (foster-father to Angus Mac Og), restoring his eye when it was put out with a piece of holly.

The eighth century text known as *Bretha Déin Chécht* ("*The Judgments of Dian Cecht*") was attributed to him, and deals with medical conditions and the treatment of wounds.

Disciplina

Name	Discipline
Known Period of Worship	2nd-5th century CE
Place of Origin	Rome
Place of Worship	Hadrian's Wall

Disciplina is the Roman goddess of discipline, which is also of course the meaning of her name. She was worshipped by the Roman legionnaires, and was the goddess who governed the strict discipline of the army. Seven inscriptions to her have been found, all at army bases in the area around Hadrian's Wall.²⁴³

Dolichenus

Name	After Doliche in Syria
Known Period of Worship	2nd-5th century CE
Place of Origin	Syria
Place of Worship	Northumberland
Other Names	Doliche

Dolichenus is a fusion of the Roman Jupiter with the Syrian iron and weather god Doliche, who was possibly named after the place of the same name as a local deity. He was worshipped particularly within the military, especially at

---

242 Cath Maige Tuired.
243 RIB 1127, 1128, 1497c, 1723, 1978, 2092, 2213c.

areas where iron was worked. A frieze from Corbridge (Northumberland) unites Dolichenus with Brigantia as consort, who herself is referred to as Caelestis, conflating her with that Syrian goddess. Two other inscriptions, from Bewcastle (Northumberland) and Old Penrith (Northumberland) give further evidence of worship of this god in the area of Hadrian's Wall.

Don

Name	River? / Gift?
Place of Origin	Wales
Place of Worship	Wales
Literary References	*The Chair of Ceridwen, Red Book of Hergest, White Book of Rhydderch*

The Welsh goddess Don, who was the mother of the Welsh pantheon of the *House of Don*, seems to be the Welsh form of the goddess Danu. If this is the case then her name may also be derived from the same root, meaning *"river"*. Alternatively it may come from the root *dfnu* meaning *"gift"*.

Don is married to the death god Beli, recalling Morrígan's marriage to Néit. She is referred to in reference to her children, without being present, in the *White Book of Rhydderch*. Taliesin mentions her in his description of himself, saying *"I was in the court of Don before the birth of Gwydion."*[244]

Don was the daughter of Mathonwy and sister of Math, the magick god, and had a number of children with Beli. These included her daughters Penarddun and the sky goddess Arianrhod, and her sons the agriculture god Amaethon, the smith god Govannon, the bard and magic god Gwydion (or Gwydyon), Gilvaethwy and Nudd.

The *Triads* mention two of these gods as her children, specifically Gwydion[245] and Arianrhod.[246] The early sixteenth century genealogy *Bonedd yr Arwyr*, which is a copy of an earlier lost manuscript, gives an extended list of children

---
[244] Taliesin in the White Book of Rhydderch.
[245] Triad 25.
[246] Triad 68.

for Don, adding Aidden (*"fiery?"*), Cynan (*"chief"*), Digant, Elawg, Elestron (*"iris"*), Eunydd (*"false mist"*), Hedd (*"peace"*), Hunawg and Idwal (*"lord of the wall"*) to the children listed above.[247] Eunydd and Elestron are also both mentioned in *Taliesin's First Address*,[248] after reference to Math and Govannon, as *"artful men"*, suggesting they may have been magicians.

Another mention of the court of Don is found in *The Chair of Ceridwen*, where Ceridwen declares she is called skilful in the court of Don, and Gwydion is also mentioned as the son of Don.[249]

Donn

Name	Lord or The Dark One
Place of Origin	Ireland
Place of Worship	Ireland
Literary References	Historia Britonum, Lebor Gabála Érenn, Togail Bruidne Da Derga

Donn is an Irish death god whose name means either *"Lord"* or *"The Dark One"*. Reference is made to three red horsemen riding red horses coming from his kingdom, emphasising his deathly association as red was the colour of death in the Celtic world.[250]

Donn was one of the Milesians who ousted the Túatha dé Danann, but offended Ériu and subsequently drowned and became a death god dwelling under the ground or on his island of Tech Duinn (i.e. either *"House of Darkness"* or *"House of the Lord"*).[251] On his death he said *"To me, to my house, come ye all after your deaths."*[252]

---

247 Bonedd yr Arwyr in Peniarth MS 127.
248 Red Book of Hergest.
249 Book of Taliesin, 16.
250 The Destruction of Da Derga's Hostel.
251 Lebor Gabála Érenn.
252 Historia Britonum, 249.

His association with death began on the voyage to Ireland with him cursing his brother Ir because he was rowing faster, causing the oar to break and kill him. For this Amergin cursed him as being unworthy of Ireland.[253]

Dylan

Name	Son of the Wave?
Place of Origin	Wales
Place of Worship	Wales
Literary References	Book of Taliesin, Red Book of Hergest, Stanzas of the Graves, White Book of Rhydderch

Dylan was the son of Arianrhod and brother of Lleu.[254] He was also known as the *"Son of the Wave"* because a wave never broke beneath him, a title which is also given as the meaning of his name.[255]

He had golden hair, could move better than a fish in the water and was described as taking the nature of the sea. Because of these qualities he has been suggested as a sea god. He was killed by his uncle Govannon out of jealousy, and this was known as *"The Third Fatal Blow"*.[256]

The death of Dylan is described in *The Death-song of Dylan, son of the Wave*, although it then raises the question of whom he and Govannon were competing for, as his uncle is obviously the opposing groom.

> *"An opposing groom, poison made, a wrathful deed,*
> *Piercing Dylan, a mischievous shore,*
> *violence freely flowing. Wave of Iwerdon, and wave of Manau,*
> *and wave of the North, And wave of Prydain,*
> *hosts comely in fours."*[257]

---

253 Lebor Gabála Érenn, Historia Britonum.
254 Math the Son of Mathonwy in the White Book of Rhydderch.
255 This title is also given in Cad Goddeu.
256 Triad 49.
257 The Death-song of Dylan, son of the Wave, from The Book of Taliesin, ch.63.

Following his death, Dylan's grave is mentioned in the *Stanzas of the Graves*, where it says:

> *"Where the wave makes a sullen sound,*
> *The grave of Dylan in Llan Beuno."*[258]

---

[258] Englynion y Beddau.

E

Edeyrn

Name	Eternal
Place of Origin	Wales
Place of Worship	Wales
Literary References	Red Book of Hergest, White Book of Rhydderch

Edeyrn is a god who name means "Eternal", and who is described as the son of Nudd and hence the brother of Gwyn ap Nudd. His main appearance is in the tale of Geraint the Son of Erbin in the *White Book of Rhydderch*, as the Sparrow-Hawk knight who fights Geraint. This title suggests that the sparrow-hawk was probably his totemic animal. He is described as being a knight of remarkable size on a similarly large horse.

When Geraint fights Edeyrn, every lance he uses breaks until he uses the one provided by the white-haired lord whose daughter Enid he fights for. Geraint overcomes Edeyrn and forces him to apologise for the previous insult he made to a maiden of Arthur's court.[259]

Edeyrn is also mentioned as the Prince of Denmark in the *Red Book of Hergest*, and as one of King Arthur's counsellors.[260] His men wear jet black with white-bordered scarves, ride black horses with white knees and white-topped shoulders, and bear jet-black banners with pure white tips. A variant of Edeyrn turns up in later French Arthurian tales as the character Sir Yder. Edeyrn in Gwynedd is named after him. Bodedern in Anglesey also takes its name from Edeyrn. Bod means *"dwelling place"*, so the name means *"Dwelling Place of Edeyrn."*

---

[259] Geraint the Son of Erbin, in the White Book of Rhydderch.
[260] The Dream of Rhonabwy, in the Red Book of Hergest.

Eostra

Name	East or Shining?
Known Period of Worship	Pre-7th century CE
Place of Origin	Germany?
Other Names	Eostre
Literary References	Works (Bede)

Eostra (or Eostre) is the Saxon goddess of the dawn whose name is thought to mean *"East"* or *"Shining"*. She may be derived from the German Saxon goddess Ostara, whose name comes from the same root. Bede recorded that the first month of Spring, called Eostre-monath (April in the modern calendar), was named after her.[261] Her name became Christianized into the feast of Easter. Modern writers have equated the custom of Easter Bunnies and eggs at Easter with Eostra, through a story involving an injured hare being transformed into a lapwing. There is however no evidence to support this idea.

Epona

Name	Divine Horse
Known Period of Worship	1st-5th century CE
Place of Origin	Gaul
Place of Worship	England and Scotland
Other Names	Atanta, Catona

The Gallic goddess Epona, whose name means *"Divine Horse"*, is linked to both Rhiannon and Macha as the horse goddess. She was popular amongst Roman cavalry soldiers, and was adopted by many of them, who brought her worship to Britain. In this context she was often shown paired with Mars. Her importance to the Romans is shown by the fact that she was the only *"Celtic"* deity included in the Roman calendar with her own feast day, 18th December (modern correlation).[262]

---

261 Works, Bede, 4:178-9.
262 Celtic Goddesses, Green, 1995, p184.

A number of inscriptions to her by Roman soldiers have been found in the North of Britain, at Carvoran (Northumberland) and Auchendavy (East Dunbartonshire).[263] A number of statues of her have also been discovered, including a bronze statue of her seated from Wiltshire, a statuette from Colchester (Essex), and part of a helmet with her portrayed in front of a horse.

Epona was also associated with birds. A fourth century tile from Roussas in Drôme, France, shows her riding on the back of a horned goose. More significantly a stela from Altrier, France shows her seated on a horse, with a raven and a hammer. Epona also had several titles in common with British goddesses. Inscriptions also refer to her as Regina (Latin for *"Queen"*) and Rigana (Gallic for *"Queen"*),[264] Catona (Gallic for *"Battle Goddess"*)[265], and Atanta (from the Gallic for *"Mother"*).[266]

Erce

Name	Unknown
Literary References	Æcerbot

It is not known if this is the name of a goddess, as the name only occurs in a tenth century Old English charm where the Christian God is also referred to.[267] If Erce was a goddess, then from the context she was clearly an earth and fertility goddess, possibly derived from Nerthus. The charm begins:

"Erce, Erce, Erce, Mother of Earth,
May the Almighty, the eternal Lord, grant you
Fields growing and thriving,
Increasing and strengthening, tall stems and fine crops,

---

263 RIB 1777, 2177.
264 CIL 3:7750 and CIL 3:12579 for Regina, and Textes gaulois et gallo-romains en cursive latine, II:Chamalière, Lejeune & Marichal, 1976, p151-6.
265 IEW: 534.
266 IEW: 71.
267 Cotton MS Caligula A.vii.

Both the broad barley
And the fair wheat,
And of all the crops of the earth ..."[268]

After this piece is spoken, the plough is driven forward and the first furrow opened, and the words continue:

"Hale may you be, earth, mother of mortals! Grow pregnant in the embrace of God, filled with food for mortals' use."

Ériu

Name	Earth or Soil?
Place of Origin	Ireland
Place of Worship	Ireland
Other Names	Eri
Literary References	Banshenchus, Battle of Tailtiu, Lebor Gabála Érenn

Together with her sisters Banba and Fotla, Ériu represented the sovereignty of Ireland, once again showing the triple motif. The kings of Ireland wed the three sisters to ensure their role as sovereigns.

Ériu was referred to as the daughter of Ernmas, though the *Banshenchus* calls her the daughter of Fiachra, and says *"Fierce Ériu was Cetar's consort"*.[269] Her name may translate as *"Earth"* or *"Soil"*, which would be extremely appropriate given her nature.

Ériu was also described as the mother of Bres, as Eri. After the Second Battle of Moytura, Ériu wed Lugh, but then later she was referred to as the wife of Cethor MacGreine (whose name means *"Son of the Sun"*).[270] Thus we can see references to three separate husbands to Ériu in different texts, emphasising her role as bestower of sovereignty.

---

268 Æcerbot (Field Remedy).
269 Banshenchus, pt 1.
270 Lebor Gabála Érenn.

A description of the goddess Ériu shows a crow connection, hinting at a link to (her sister) the Morrígan. She is described as alternating in appearance between being a beautiful woman one moment, and the next moment a grey-white crow.[271]

When the Milesians invade Ireland, they met Ériu at Usnech of Mide. She welcomed them and praised them, telling them that the land will be theirs forever. Ériu cleverly persuaded the Milesians to name Ireland after her, and to this day it still bears her name as Eire.

> "A gift to me, O sons of Mil and the children of Bregan,
> that my name may be upon this island!
> It will be its chief name for ever," said Amergin, "namely Ériu [Erin]."[272]

During the battle the Milesians kill Ériu, her sisters and their husbands, demonstrating that they will now have sovereignty over the land. However the land cannot die, and so neither can sovereignty. Hence the phrase, *"Ériu yonder, at the hands of Suirge ...Whatever the place wherein they sleep."*[273]

The key line is *"wherein they sleep"*, implying that the sovereignty embodied by Ériu is not destroyed, but recovering from the latest invasion. Also this is suggested by the drowning of Donn after the Milesians have conquered Ireland and the Túatha dé Danann have gone underground into the otherworld.

One version of *The Book of Invasions* has Ériu forming an army from sods of peat and a mountain to fight the Milesian invaders, showing her sovereignty over the land.

---

271 Battle of Tailtiu.
272 Lebor Gabála Érenn.
273 Lebor Gabála Érenn.

Ernmas

Name	Iron Death
Place of Origin	Ireland
Place of Worship	Ireland
Literary References	Leabhar na h-Uidhri, Lebor Gabála Érenn, Táin Bó Cúailnge

Ernmas, whose name means *"Iron death"*, is a mysterious goddess referred to in several Irish texts. The *Book of Leinster* calls her a witch, suggesting she was a magick goddess. The *Book of Invasions* refers to her as *"the she-farmer"*, suggesting she may have been an earth goddess. This would make sense considering her daughters include the earth goddess Anu and the triplicity of sovereignty goddesses.

She is described as being the mother of the three sovereignty goddesses Ériu, Banba and Fotla,[274] and of Badb, Macha and Anu[275] or the Morrígan. The *Book of Invasions* refers to her three sons Glon, Gaim and Coscar.[276]

> *"Badb and Macha and Anu, i.e. the Morrígan, from whom the Paps of Anu in Luachair are named, were the three daughters of Ernmas the witch."*[277]

The *Táin Bó Cúailnge* also describes her as the mother of the Morrígan. She was said to have been killed in the battle with the Fir Bolgs to conquer Ireland.

---

274 Lebor Gabála Érenn 4.63-4.
275 Lebor Gabála Érenn 4.62.
276 Lebor Gabála Érenn 4.64.
277 The Book of Leinster.

Étaín

Name	Unknown
Place of Origin	Ireland
Place of Worship	Ireland
Other Names	Étaín Echraide
Literary References	Cath Maige Tuired, Tochmarc Étaíne

Étaín is an Irish sovereignty goddess who features in the eighth century tale *Tochmarc Étaíne* ("The Wooing of Étaín"). The story of her abduction is given under the entry for Midir, so we shall consider the other relevant points within the story rather than repeating it.

When she is first seen Étaín is sitting by a spring holding in her hand a silver comb decorated with gold.[278] It is significant that she is by a spring, which is usually associated with healing and the otherworld, and by holding a comb she also shows a link to the otherworld, as the comb is commonly associated with the banshee.

The description of Étaín goes into great detail regarding her beauty, in a very similar manner to the sovereignty figure in *Echtra Mac Echach Muigmeddóin* ("The Adventure of the Sons of Eochaid Muigmedón"). The king, Eochaid, cannot rule without her, as his subjects ignore his summons when he is unwed. When he eventually gains her hand, Midir takes revenge on their descendants, causing the events of *The Destruction of Da Derga's Hostel*.

We may also note that Étaín has a horse title, being called Étaín Echraide, meaning *"of the horse tresses"* and is called swift Étaín.[279] This also suggests a divine connection. The *Banshenchus* describes her as one of *"the sorceresses of the Tuatha De"*.[280] In *Cath Maige Tuired*, she is described as having a son, Carpre the poet, who satirises the Fomorians.[281]

---

278 Tochmarc Étaíne
279 Banshenchus, pt 1.
280 Banshenchus, pt 1.
281 Cath Maige Tuired.

F

Fates

Name	Destiny
Known Period of Worship	1st-5th century CE
Place of Origin	Rome
Place of Worship	Cumbria, Lincolnshire
Other Names	Parcae

The Fates are the triple Roman goddesses of fate, known in Latin as the Parcae, meaning *"Birthing Ones"*. The word Fate comes from the Latin root *"fatum"* meaning *"destiny"*. Four inscriptions to them have been found,[282] two of which connect them to the Matres.

Faunus

Name	Befriend
Place of Origin	Rome
Place of Worship	Norfolk
Other Names	Ausecus, Blotugus, Narius, Saternius, Medigenus

Faunus is a Roman earth god, associated with the woods and fields, and protecting the fertility of the animals. He was also the guardian of treasure and could send oracular dreams. His name means *"to befriend"*. Significantly he was sometimes referred to in the plural as Fauni, which fits in with the common British triple deity motif. His feast, the Faunalia, took place on December 5th.

---

282 RIB 247, 881, 951, 953.

Votive offerings to Faunus include bezelled rings showing woodpeckers, suggesting that it may have been a sacred animal to him.[283] Seven silver spoons all engraved to Faunus were found at Thetford (Norfolk).[284]

Amongst the titles he was given in these inscriptions are Ausecus (*"Long Ear"*), Blotugus (*"Bringer of Spring Blossom"*), Narius (*"Lord"*), Saternius (*"Giver of Plenty"*) and Medigenus (*"Mead Begotten"*). Some of these titles may refer to British gods with whom he was conflated.

Fea

Name	Death, That Which Causes Death, or To Attack
Place of Origin	Ireland
Place of Worship	Ireland
Literary References	Historia Britonum, Lebor Gabála Érenn

Fea is probably an Irish war goddess, if we consider her name which can be translated as *"death"*, *"that which causes death"*, or *"to attack"*. Fea is described as being one of the two wives of the battle god Néit with Nemain,[285] and also as the daughter of the Fomorian god Balor. There is also a reference to *"the plundering host of Fea, who were aided by poison."*[286]

Fedelm

Name	Unknown
Place of Origin	Ireland
Place of Worship	Ireland
Literary References	Leabhar na h-Uidhri, Longes mac nUsnig, Táin Bó Cúailnge, Tochmarc Émire

---

283 Faunus at Thetford, C.Johns, 1986 in Pagan Gods and Shrines of the Roman Empire, p93-105.
284 RIB 2420.11-22.
285 Lebor Gabála Érenn.
286 Historia Britonum, 135.

Fedelm is a prophetic goddess who is found in *Táin Bó Cúailnge*. The meaning of her name is unknown. As Queen Medb is about to leave Cruachain with her army she sees a beautiful maiden in a chariot drawn by two black horses approaching. She has yellow hair in three plaits, two up and one hanging down to her calves (recalling the faery associations of the banshee, and also the triple motif), and her eyes have triple irises. A woman alone in a chariot in the myths usually indicates a goddess in the Irish myths, and the eyes and triple motifs reinforce this supposition.

In her hands she has a weaver's beam of white bronze, or in other versions such as in the *Book of Leinster* she is weaving a fringe. The weaving motif is highly significant as it is classically associated with the weaving of fate e.g. the Norns in Norse myth and the Fates in Greek myth.

When asked who she is, she replies, *"I am Fedelm the poetess of Connaught"*.[287] Medb asks if she has the power of prophecy called *"imbass forosna"* (*"divination which illuminates"*),[288] and Fedelm answers yes. Imbass forosna in this context is the chewing of the flesh of the thumb to gain insight and wisdom.

Other examples of this are seen when Demne sticks his thumb in his mouth after being burned by the salmon of wisdom, and when Gwion Bach sticks his thumb in his mouth after being burned by the three drops of Awen from the cauldron of Ceridwen. In both cases the individual is transformed, Demne becomes Fionn MacCumhill, and Gwion Bach becomes Taliesin.

Fedelm then tells Queen Medb that Cú Chulainn will perform heroic deeds and decimate her army. When Medb asks why she has come bearing bad news, Fedelm replies that she is promoting Medb's interests by gathering together the warriors of the great provinces to go with her to fight (for although Cú Chulainn will be heroic he does get killed).

---

287 In The Book of Leinster version Fedelm says "I am Fedelm the prophetess from Síd Chrúachna" making her faery connection evident.
288 Imbas Forosnai, N.K. Chadwick, in Scottish Gaelic Studies IV 2:97-135, 1935.

Fedelm is mentioned in the conversation between Cú Chulainn and the maiden Emer, when they are talking in riddles using magical place and people names to confuse Emer's maidens, who are listening in. Her name occurs between other goddess names, implying that she is one as well:

> "The foam of the two steeds of Emain Macha; over the Morrigu's Garden ... over the Marrow of the Woman Fedelm ... over the Washing-place of the horses of Dea."[289]

Fedelm is described as having a son, Fiachna, who is slain in *The Exile of the Sons of Usnech*.[290] Emer also refers to her when setting the tasks Cú Chulainn must perform to win her hand in marriage, saying, *"Where the quick froth of Fedelm makes Brea leap."*[291]

Fergus

Name	Strong or Vigorous Man
Place of Origin	Ireland
Place of Worship	Ireland
Other Names	Ro-ech
Literary References	Longes mac nUsnig, Scéla Conchobair maic Nessa, Táin Bó Cúailnge

Fergus may have been a horse god, as suggested by his name as son of Ro-ech, or *"Great Horse"*. His name means *"Strong/Vigorous Man"*. He is described in the texts as having very large genitals, which fits with him being a horse god, and also his virility as a fecundity god. If he did not sleep with his divine wife Flidais, it took seven women to satisfy him sexually.[292]

A detailed description in *The Tidings of Conchobar son of Ness*, indicates the giant size of Fergus, and also the number seven, which may have been his sacred number.

---

289 Tochmarc Émire.
290 Longes mac nUsnig.
291 Tochmarc Émire.
292 Táin Bó Cúailnge.

> "Seven feet between his ear and his lips, and seven fists (42 inches[293]) between his eyes, and seven fists in his nose, and seven fists in his lips. The full of a bushel-cup was the moisture of his head when being washed. Seven fists in his penis. A bushel-bag in his scrotum. Seven women to curb him unless Flidais should come. Seven pigs and seven vats of ale and seven deer to be consumed by him, and the strength of seven hundred in him."[294]

The same text also describes him shaping the earth in a manner only seen by giant beings (e.g. the Daghda and the Morrígan):

> "... cut off the three Formaela of Meath--that is, the three blows he gave the earth when his anger with Conchobar came to him, so that those three hills are still there, and will remain there for ever."[295]

In *The Exile of the Sons of Usnech*, there is reference to Fiacha, a son of Fergus, who is treacherously slain trying to save Naisi from spear thrusts. In revenge Fergus burned Emain to the ground, and was exiled.[296]

Flidais

Place of Origin	Ireland
Place of Worship	Ireland
Literary References	Cath Muighe Tuireadh, Cóir Anman, Oidheadh Chloinne Tuireann, Táin Bó Flidais

Flidais is an Irish goddess associated particularly with deer and cattle. She is described in one source as riding a chariot pulled by deer.[297] These associations suggest she may have been a lady of the beasts or earth goddess. In *Táin Bó Flidais* she brings a magickal cow called Maol Flidais ("hornless

---

293 A fist is 6 inches (15cm).
294 Scéla Conchobair maic Nessa, 13.
295 Scéla Conchobair maic Nessa, 18.
296 Longes mac nUsnig.
297 Die irische Helden und Königsage, R Thurneysen, 1921, p318.

Flidais") with its herd from the otherworld to be a partner for the White-horned Bull.[298]

Her first husband was Ailill Finn (*"the fair-haired"*) but she loved the god Fergus. After a conflict which was settled with her agreeing to supply food from her herd to the men of Ireland, she left Ailill for Fergus who became her second husband. If she did not sleep with him it required seven women to satisfy him, suggesting her virility and fertility, as does the herd of cows that supplies all the food for the Irishmen.[299] Elsewhere she is described as the wife of Adammair.[300]

Flidais had four daughters, Argoen, Dinand, Be Theite and Bé Chuille. The last of these, Bé Chuille is described as one of the two foster mothers of the Morrígna.[301]

There is a tantalizing reference to the *"cloak of the daughters of Flidais"* worn by Lugh in the tale of *Oidheadh Chloinne Tuireann*. This might hint at the daughters being weaver goddesses.

Fortuna

Name	Fortune
Known Period of Worship	1st-5th century CE
Place of Origin	Rome
Place of Worship	All across Britain

Fortuna is the Roman goddess whose name embodies her quality, that of Fortune. As such she was also associated with gambling, and presided over bath houses, where fortunes were often made and lost through the social interaction that occurred there.

---

298 Táin Bó Flidais.
299 Táin Bó Flidais.
300 Cóir Anman, 295.
301 Cath Muighe Tuireadh.

More inscriptions have been found to Fortuna than to any other goddess, Roman or otherwise. A total of thirty-four inscriptions to her have been found all across Britain.[302] These include three dedications to Fortuna as Conservatrix (*"the Preserver"*), four as Redux (*"the Home-Bringer"*), one as Servatrix (*"the Deliverer"*), and one as Populi Romani (*"of the Roman People"*). Seven sculptures of Fortuna have also been found in villas and town houses in Britain.

Fortuna is often depicted with a wheel or cornucopia. Images show her with a wheel (Rudston, Yorkshire), or wheel and globe (Chilgrove, Sussex), or even wheel and globe and rudder (Llantwit Major, Glamorgan). Two figures show her with cornucopia and patera (Kingscote, Gloucestershire and Stonesfield, Oxfordshire).

The wheel can be seen as the prototype for the later symbol of the *"wheel of fortune"*. The cornucopia, patera and globe all indicate her bountiful nature, and the rudder indicates her ability to steer men through troubled times.

Of the twenty-five engraved gems of her all dating from 1st-4th century CE, fifteen show her with rudder in left hand and cornucopia in right, and the other ten with patera and cornucopia.[303]

Fotla

Name	Unknown
Place of Origin	Ireland
Place of Worship	Ireland
Other Names	Fodla
Literary References	Banshenchus, Leabhar Méig Shamhradháin, Lebor Gabála Érenn

Fotla or Fodla was a sovereignty goddess of Ireland with her sisters Banba and Ériu, and was also sister to Badb, Macha and Anu.[304] The original

---

302 RIB 317, 318, 445, 575, 624, 644-5, 730, 760, 764, 812, 840, 968, 1029, 1073, 1210-12, 1423, 1449, 1536-7, 1684, 1724, 1778-9, 1873, 2093-5, 2146, 2189, 2217, 2335.
303 A Corpus of Roman Engraved Gemstones from British Sites (vol 2), Henig, 1974, p46-8.

meaning of her name is unknown. She was wed to Sethor MacCuill, one of the Daghda's sons.[305]

She was usually described as a daughter of Ernmas, though the *Banshenchus* calls her a daughter of Fiachra. That text also mentions a husband, saying *"Fotla's Husband, Detar, was no slacker."*[306] As with her sister Ériu she is thus depicted in different texts with different husbands.

In *Leabhar Méig Shamhradháin* there is an interesting reference which distinguishes between Fotla and Banba, where it says:

> *"Their rivalry in desire of Banbha's Land has deprived them of thick-grassed Fodla."*[307]

This comment could suggest that whereas Banba was being seen as the land itself, Ériu was being perceived as the plant life on the earth.

Frigg/Freya

Name	Beloved or Noble (Frigg); Lady or Woman (Freya)
Place of Origin	Scandinavia
Other Names	Frea
Literary References	Brut, Rune Poem

Frigg was a Saxon fertility goddess, and wife of Woden. In the Norse pantheon, Freya and Frigg were originally the same goddess, but became divided into two separate goddesses, still sharing many of the same characteristics.[308] The meaning of the names also indicates this, Frigg meaning *"beloved"* or *"noble"*, and Freya meaning *"lady"* or *"woman"*.

---

304 Lebor Gabála Érenn, 4.63-4.
305 Lebor Gabála Érenn.
306 Banshenchus, pt 1.
307 Leabhar Méig Shamhradháin, XXIII.2.
308 For evidence of this, see Freya and Frigg by Stephan Grundy, in The Concept of the Goddess, 1996, p56-67.

There may have been a re-assimilation of the two goddesses, though this is speculative based on the reference to Friday, in a thirteenth century poem by the poet Laymon:

> *High she is and holy; nobles love her for this;*
> *She is called Frea, well does she direct them ...*
> *Frea, our Lady; we give to her Friday."*[309]

The qualities assigned to the goddess here under the name of Frea (Freya) are in keeping with those of Frigg as the noble and devoted wife of Woden, rather than the sexual warrior goddess Freya. This may be where the idea that Friday comes from *"Freya's-day"* originates, when in fact it is derived from the old English, Frigedæg.

Frigg is also referred to in the *Rune Poem*. The rune Ger has its stanza dedicated to her:

> *"Fruitful year, is the hope of men, when Frigg. Heaven's queen, makes the earth give forth bright crops for rich and poor."*[310]

A number of place names were derived from Frigg and these include Frobury, Froyle, Freefolk (Hampshire); Fretherne (Gloucestershire), Friden (Derbyshire), Fryup and Fridaythorpe (Yorkshire).

---

309 Brut, R. Allen (trans), 1992, 11.6943-6952.
310 Rune Poem, stanza 12, trans. Tony Linsell in Anglo-Saxon Mythology, Migration and Magic.

G

Garmangabi

Name	She who takes hold of the Weaver's Beam?
Known Period of Worship	2nd-5th century CE
Place of Origin	Germany?
Place of Worship	Co. Durham

Garmangabi is an obscure (possibly Germanic) goddess referred to in a single inscription at Lanchester (Co. Durham),[311] about whom nothing is known. The inscription was made by a member of the Suevi tribe, who were Germanic Celts living on the Rhine, suggesting Garmangabi was a Germanic goddess.

It has been suggested her name may be derived from the proto-Celtic words *karb-agno* meaning *"weaver's beam"* and *gab-yo* meaning *"take hold"*. This would give a suggested meaning of something like *"She who takes hold of the weaver's beam"*. Were this to be the case it might suggest a goddess of fate, as this is the most common weaving association.

Geat

Name	Unknown
Literary References	Life of King Arthur (Asser)

Geat is an unknown Saxon god who is mentioned once by Asser, the biographer of Alfred the Great, as being a divine ancestor of Alfred's, tracing

---

311 RIB 1074.

him all the way back to Adam as was done in the ancient genealogies.[312] Asser quotes the fifth century CE Christian poet Sedulius' reference to Geat:

> *"When gentile poets with their fictions vain,*
> *In tragic language and bombastic strain,*
> *To their god Geat, comic deity,*
> *Loud praises sing, &c."*[313]

The poem *Beowulf* also refers to the tribe of the Geats in southern Sweden, to which Beowulf belonged, who were a historical tribe originally from northern Germany. As with the Ingaevones they may have taken their name from a god they worshipped, i.e. Geat.

Gilvaethwy

Name	Unknown
Place of Origin	Wales
Place of Worship	Wales
Literary References	Red Book of Hergest, White Book of Rhydderch

Gilvaethwy is a god in the *White Book of Rhydderch* who was one of the children of the divine couple of Don and Bilé. Gilvaethwy raped the maiden Goewin whose lap was the resting place for Math's feet.

He was transformed by Math into different animals as punishment for his behaviour. He was a stag for a year, then a wild boar for a year, then a wolf for a year. Each time he fathered a baby on Gwydion who was also cursed in the same manner. His sons from the three periods were called Hydwn (*"deer"*), Hychdwn (*"swine"*) the tall and Bleiddwn (*"wolf"*).[314]

---

312 The Life of King Alfred by Bishop Asser.
313 The Life of King Alfred.
314 Math the Son of Mathonwy.

Gobannos

Name	Smith
Place of Origin	Gaul
Place of Worship	Kent
Other Names	Gobannus

Gobannos (or Gobannus) is a Gallic smith god who was also worshipped in Britain. His name means *"Smith"*, clearly demonstrating his role, and also indicating his role as the proto-figure on whom Goibniu and Govannon were later based.

An inscription to him was found at Canterbury (now in the British Museum), and there were several important continental items found, including an inscription and a cauldron dedicated to him (France), and the Berne zinc tablet (Switzerland).

Goibniu

Name	Smith
Place of Origin	Ireland
Place of Worship	Ireland
Other Names	Goibhniu
Literary References	Cath Maige Tuired, Lebor Gabála Érenn, St Gall Codex

Goibniu or Goibhniu was an Irish smith god,[315] whose spears never missed and always took life when they struck.[316] His name is indicative of his role, meaning *"Smith"*. He was one of a triad of craft gods, with Luchta, who made the spear shafts, and Creidhne who made the rivets, Goibniu made the spear heads. Goibniu only required three actions to make a spear head, javelin or sword.

---

315 Lebor Gabála Érenn 4.62.
316 Cath Maige Tuired.

When he was attacked by Ruadán, Goibniu pulled the spear out with which he had been wounded and hurled it back, killing him. Dian Cecht then healed Goibniu in the healing well he had set up.[317] Goibniu also hosted the otherworld feast, providing magickal ale which gave immortality to all who drank it.[318]

As a blacksmith and maker of sharp objects, it is interesting that he should also be called upon to remove sharp objects, as in this charm to remove a thorn from the *Codex of St Gall*:

"Very sharp is Goibniu's science, let Goibniu's goad go out before Goibniu's goad!"[319]

Govannon

Name	Smith
Place of Origin	Wales
Place of Worship	Wales
Literary References	Red Book of Hergest, White Book of Rhydderch

Govannon was a Welsh smith god (the meaning of his name) who was the son of Don and Beli, and brother to Penarddun, Arianrhod, Amaethon, Gwydion, Gilvaethwy and Nudd. He is mentioned in the tale of *Kilhwch and Olwen*[320] in regard to being the only person capable of removing the iron from a piece of land, as appropriate for a smith. He was also responsible for the death of Dylan. He is often equated to the Irish smith god Goibniu.

Govannon is also mentioned in *Taliesin's First Address*, with a hint that he is also a magician, where it says:

"I have been with artful men,
with Math or with Govannon
With Eunydd, with Elestron,

---

317 Cath Maige Tuired.
318 The Craftsman in early Celic literature, Gillies, 1981, p70-85.
319 St Gall Codex.
320 White Book of Rhydderch

my journey with the furrow-maker,
A year in Govannon's fortress."[321]

Abergavenny in Monmouthshire takes its name from Govannon. Aber means *"mouth of a river/stream"* and Gavenny is derived from Govannon, being the name of the river.

Grannos

Name	Sun
Known Period of Worship	2nd-5th century CE
Place of Origin	Gaul
Place of Worship	Midlothian
Other Names	Grannus

Grannos (or Grannus) is a Gallic god associated with healing who was imported to Britain and is referred to at Musselborough (Midlothian).[322] The Romans equated him with Apollo as Apollo Grannus, which is not surprising for a healing deity. He may also have been a solar deity, as his name derives from the word Grián, meaning *"Sun"*. In Gaul he was paired with the healing water goddess Sirona.

Grián

Name	Sun
Place of Origin	Ireland
Place of Worship	Ireland
Other Names	Griánne
Literary References	Aithed Gráinne re Diarmait ua nDuibne, Dunaire Finn, The Venomous Wild Boar of Glen Glass

Grián (or Griánne) is described as being the sister of Áine, the Fairy Queen, whose name means *"Sun"*. In many instances sisterhood or a mother-

---

321 Red Book of Hergest.
322 RIB 2132.

daughter relationship is used to indicate different representations of the same goddess.

We may note that Griánne means *"ugliness"*, which has interesting connotations in light of the ugly hag/beautiful maiden transformation found in a number of stories. She elopes with the young beautiful Diarmuid because she does not want to be with the ageing hero Finn.[323]

Not only does she lay a geis (taboo restriction) on him to help her escape, but she lays another one on him to sleep with her. After being chased by Finn for a year and a day, hiding in megalithic tombs (known locally in Ireland as Diarmuid and Grainne's Bed), they made peace with him and lived peacefully for a while, until sixteen years later. Then Diarmuid was gored by a boar and died as Finn refused to heal him.[324]

Much of this story is echoed in the Scottish tale of *The Venomous Wild Boar of Glen Glass*, where Griánne is Diarmaid's wife that he has eloped with, and the poisonous boar kills him as he kills it.

Gwenwynwyn

Name	Thrice Blessed or Blessed White and Fair
Place of Origin	Wales
Place of Worship	Wales
Literary References	Red Book of Hergest, White Book of Rhydderch

Gwenwynwyn is a shadowy figure who has been largely overlooked, despite being one of the sons of Arianrhod. His name comes from a threefold repetition of the word *"gwyn"* meaning *"white"*, *"blessed"* or *"fair"*, so it can literally mean either *"thrice blessed"* or *"blessed, white and fair"*.

---

323 Aithed Gráinne re Diarmait ua nDuibne.
324 Dunaire Finn.

He is mentioned twice in the *Triads*, as one of the *"Three Fleet Owners"*,[325] and as a member of one of the *"Three Hosts that departed from this Island, and never returned."*[326] In the first of these he is described as the son of Naf, but in the second he is described with his brother Gwanar as a son of Arianrhod and Lliaws mab Nwyfre.

Gwydion

Name	One Born of Wood or Wood Knowledge
Place of Origin	Wales
Place of Worship	Wales
Other Names	Gwydyon
Literary References	Cad Goddeu, The Chair of Ceridwen, Red Book of Hergest, White Book of Rhydderch

Gwydion is a Welsh god displaying characteristics of eloquence and magick, whose name may mean *"One Born of Wood"*, or *"Wood Knowledge"*. He was one of the sons of Don and Beli. Gwydion is described as one of the *"Three Shepherd Retinues"* in *Trioedd Ynys Prydein*.[327] He is also described as one of the *"Three Renowned Astronomers"*, with the power of prediction from the stars.[328]

He is described as the best teller of tales in the world, suggesting he was a bard.[329] Gwydion created a charm of twelve horses and twelve dogs in exchange for Pryderi's pigs. After a day the horses and dogs disappeared, and in the subsequent fighting with Pryderi, Gwydion killed him with the aid of his magic and charms. Gwydion also assisted Gilvaethwy in raping the maiden Goewin.

As a punishment Math transformed both Gwydion and Gilvaethwy into deer for a year, then wild pigs for a year, then wolves for a year. Each time

---

325 Triad 13.
326 Triad 32.
327 Triad 87.
328 Triad 89.
329 Gwydion's tale is told in Math the Son of Mathonwy.

Gwydion was the female animal, and the two brothers produced a baby animal, which Math transformed into a boy.

Gwydion raised Lleu and tricked his sister Arianrhod into giving him a name and weapons, first causing himself and Lleu to appear as shoemakers, and subsequently using his magic to raise up the semblance of an army outside her castle when they were there disguised as bards.

With Math he produced the flower maiden Blodeuwedd as a bride for Lleu. After Lleu was mortally wounded by Blodeuwedd's lover Gronw, Gwydion found him in his eagle form and charmed him back into human form and healed him. In punishment for her betrayal, Gwydion transformed Blodeuwedd into an owl.

References are also made to Gwydion in *The Chair of Ceridwen*, where he is described as *"Gwydion the son of Don, of toil severe"*,[330] and reference is made to his role in creating Blodeuwedd and bringing pigs from the south (i.e. after killing Pryderi).

An intriguing description in this piece indicates a battle between Gwydion and another magickal person or being, for it says:

"I saw a fierce conflict in Nant Frangeon On a Sunday, at the time of dawn, between the bird of wrath and Gwydion Thursday, certainly they went to Mona to obtain whirlings and sorcerers."[331]

Gwydion is referred to twice in *Cad Goddeu* (*"The Battle of the Trees"*). He is described as exalting the Brython, being the purifier of the Brython, and enchanting Blodeuwedd.[332]

Gwydion plays a part in the short tale also called *Cad Goddeu*, where he realises the identity of the unnamed warrior fighting as a champion for

---

330 Book of Taliesin, 16.
331 Book of Taliesin, 16.
332 Cad Goddeu, Book of Taliesin.

Arawn against his brother Amaethon, and sings two verses which name him as Bran, giving the victory to Amaethon.[333]

Bryn Gwydion, or Gwydion's Hill, is located in Gwynedd near the coastal village of Clynnog Fawr.

Gwyn ap Nudd

Name	White son of Nudd
Place of Origin	Wales
Place of Worship	Wales
Literary References	Cad Goddeu, St Collen and Gwyn ap Nudd, Black Book of Carmarthen, The Dialogue of Gwyddno Garanhir and Gwyn ap Nudd, Red Book of Hergest, White Book of Rhydderch

The Welsh god Gwyn ap Nudd has a variety of roles. The first part of his name, Gwyn means *"white"* but with connotations of *"fair"*, and *"blessed"* or *"holy"*, and Ap Nudd means *"son of Nudd"*, the war god. He was variously the faery king, Lord of the Otherworld and leader of the Wild Hunt.

Gwyn has a brother Edeyrn, who is the Sparrow-Hawk knight in *Geraint the Son of Erbin*.[334] Gwyn was one of the *"Three Renowned Astronomers"*, able to read the future accurately from the stars, and knowing their natures and qualities.[335]

Several of his qualities are described in *The Dialogue of Gwyddno Garanhir and Gwyn ap Nudd*,[336] where he is described with qualities which indicate a war god, as:

> *"Bull of battle was he, active in dispersing an arrayed army, The ruler of hosts, Indisposed to anger, Blameless and pure his conduct in protecting life."*[337]

---

333 Cad Goddeu, second later version.
334 In the White Book of Rhydderch.
335 Triad 89.
336 The Black Book of Carmarthen, 33.
337 The Black Book of Carmarthen, 33.

A reference in *Cad Goddeu* may be to Gwyn ap Nudd, as it mentions the *"bull of battle"*,[338] a term used elsewhere for him, as seen in the previous reference.

His horse is described as hound-hoofed and the torment of battle,[339] reminiscent of the cwn annwn (*"hounds of the underworld"*), the magickal white hounds with red ears that he leads on the Wild Hunt.

In the story of *Kilhwch and Olwen*[340] Gwyn ap Nudd is one of the characters who goes with Kilhwch and King Arthur to fulfill the quests that have been set for Kilhwch to win Olwen's hand in marriage. In this tale it is mentioned that Gwyn fought with Gwythyr ap Greidal (*"victor son of fierce"*) every Beltane for the hand of the maiden Creiddylad, who he had previously abducted by force. When Gwythyr and his forces battled Gwyn ap Nudd and his army they were defeated and Gwythyr's men imprisoned.

The annual battle until the end of time was Arthur's solution to the conflict., enabling him to release all the imprisoned warriors to fight for his causes The battle between the two protagonists seems to be another battle of light and dark, fought on May Eve for the hand of the eternal maiden who represents the land. It has been suggested that Creiddylad daughter of Llys was anglicized by Shakespeare into Cordelia daughter of Lear in his play *King Lear*.

The giant Yspaddaden describes him as *"whom God has placed over the brood of devils in Annwn."*

Gwyn appears in the tale of *St Collen and Gwyn ap Nudd* as King of the Faeries and the otherworld. St Collen was the abbot of Glastonbury and he was invited by Gwyn to visit his faery realm under Glastonbury Tor. He saw the most beautiful faery realm and responded by throwing holy water everywhere, at which it all disappeared.

---

338 The Book of Taliesin, 8.
339 The Black Book of Carmarthen, 33.
340 In the White Book of Rhydderch.

A fourteenth century Latin manuscript refers to him, saying that Welsh soothsayers would repeat the following before divination:

> "To the King of Spirits, and to his Queen, Gwyn ap Nudd, you who are yonder in the forest, for love of your mate, permit us to enter your dwelling."[341]

---

[341] Medieval folklore: an encyclopedia of myths, legends, tales, beliefs, and customs, ed. Carl Lindahl, John McNamara, John Lindow, 2002, p190.

H

Harimella

Name	Unknown
Known Period of Worship	2nd-5th century CE
Place of Origin	Dumfries & Galloway
Place of Worship	Dumfries & Galloway

Harimella is an unknown, possibly indigenous, goddess mentioned in an inscription at Birrens, Scotland.[342]

Harpocrates

Name	Horus the Child
Known Period of Worship	1st-5th century CE
Place of Origin	Greece
Place of Worship	London
Other Names	Harpokrates

Harpocrates is a Greek form of the Egyptian god Horus as the child of the mother goddess Isis, his name meaning *"Horus the Child"*. Two statues of Harpocrates, one bronze and one silver have been found in London. Both show him with his right hand raised to his lips in the gesture of silence. An engraved carnelian intaglio found in Bath dating to the first century CE shows Harpocrates sitting on a lotus.[343] Another undated gem from Colchester (Essex) shows the youthful god with Greek lettering on the reverse.[344]

---

342 RIB 2096.
343 A Corpus of Roman Engraved Gemstones from British Sites (vol 2), Henig, 1974, p52.
344 A Corpus of Roman Engraved Gemstones from British Sites (vol 2), Henig, 1974, p53.

Helioserapis

Name	Fusion of Helios and Serapis
Place of Origin	Rome

Helioserapis is an amalgam of the Greek sun gods Helios and Serapis. Two rings with red jasper settings have been found depicting his head, at Warlingham (Surrey) and Chesterholm (Northumberland).[345]

Helith

Name	Unknown
Place of Origin	Cerne Abbas
Place of Worship	Cerne Abbas
Other Names	Helis

Helith, or Helis is a name used for the Cerne Abbas hill figure, showing a priapic naked giant with club. It has been suggested that this figure was a depiction of the sky god, and that the name may be derived from Hercules.[346]

Hercules

Name	Glory of Hera
Known Period of Worship	1st-5th century CE
Place of Origin	Greece
Place of Worship	Across Britain
Other Names	Herakles

Hercules is the divine son of Jupiter, derived from the Greek Herakles. His name means *"Glory of Hera"*, a somewhat ironic name considering the troubles she put him through! He was a popular god with the Roman army, as a warrior hero, which is reflected in the eighteen inscriptions found to him

---

345 A Corpus of Roman Engraved Gemstones from British Sites (vol 2), Henig, 1974, p53.
346 Religious Cults at Roman Godmanchester, Green, 1986, p44.

across Britain.[347] A relief from Corbridge (Northumberland) shows him with Minerva, under whose protection he fought.

Twelve engraved gems from around Britain dating to 1st-3rd century CE show Hercules in a variety of poses. There are two busts, one with club and bow, two with club and lion skin, three wrestling the Nemean lion, one wrestling a giant, one subduing Cerberus, one wrestling Antaeus watched by Minerva, and one of him holding his club and urinating.[348]

Ptolemy's third century CE work *Geography* refers to a place called Hercules Promontory, which equates to the modern location of Hartland Point in Devon.

Herne

Name	Uncertain
Place of Origin	Windsor?
Literary References	The Merry Wives of Windsor

Herne is compared by many to Cernunnos, and his name could be a Saxon form of the Celtic name, though it has also been seen as a shortening of Herian, a title of Odin. Herne the Hunter is first mentioned in writing by Shakespeare in *The Merry Wives of Windsor*. However the myth seemed widespread by then. Herne is a horned god of the hunt, who leads the Wild Hunt.

> "There is an old tale goes that Herne the hunter,
> Sometime a keeper here in Windsor Forest,
> Doth all the winter-time, at still midnight,
> Walk round about an oak, with great ragg'd horns;
> And there he blasts the tree, and takes the cattle,
> And makes milch-kine yield blood, and shakes a chain

---

347 RIB 67, 214b, 648, 796, 892, 946, 1129, 1199, 1200, 1213-5, 1264, 1580, 1781, 2040, 2140, 2177.
348 A Corpus of Roman Engraved Gemstones from British Sites (vol 2), Henig, 1974, p61-2, 95.

In a most hideous and dreadful manner:
You have heard of such a spirit, and well you know
The superstitious idle-headed eld
Received, and did deliver to our age,
This tale of Herne the hunter for a truth."[349]

Originally he was seen as a ghostly figure with antlers on his head who haunted Windsor Forest. The story goes that Herne was a gamekeeper to King Richard II, who rescued the king when he was about to be gored by a stag. Herne was gored as he slit the stag's throat, but healed by a magician called Philip Urswick. Urswick had made a pact with the other keepers, who were envious of Herne's skill and prestige, to cause him to lose his skills. Urswick cut off the stag's antlers and tied them to Herne's head.

Herne recovered but the antlers grew to his head and he lost his skills. Heartbroken, he rode to the forest and hanged himself from the oak that bears his name. A peddler saw the body, but when he returned with others, it was gone, and that night the oak was struck by lightning.

The frightened gamekeepers consulted Urswick, who told them to go to the oak that night, which they did, and Herne appeared to them. He ran into the forest and the gamekeepers chased him. Urswick then appeared and demanded his payment for cursing Herne, telling them they must ride with the Wild Hunt forever.

For a while Herne and his hunt poached deer, killed men, and vandalised parks. Finally the king in frustration confronted Herne. Herne told the king he rode for revenge, and he would not stop raiding the king's lands until the gamekeepers (who were still alive and riding with him) were hanged. So Richard had the men hanged, and they became the Wild Hunt, collecting souls of the dead.

The tale is most likely mediaeval in origin as it names historical individuals, though it may well have been based on an earlier myth. There other versions

---

[349] The Merry Wives of Windsor, Shakespeare.

of the tale, where he committed suicide after the King disgraced his daughter, or in shame for having poached the king's deer, or because he was accused of witchcraft. The Wild Hunt appears in all the versions of the tale though. The imagery of the Wild Hunt is both Saxon and Celtic in origin, and also occurs in Norse myth.

That the myth was earlier is indicated by the Hunt being described in *The Anglo Saxon Chronicles* in 1127:

> "...it was seen and heard by many men: many hunters riding. The hunters were black, and great and loathy, and their hounds all black, and wide-eyed and loathy, and they rode on black horses and black he-goats. This was seen in the very deer park in the town of Peterborough, and in all the woods from the same town to Stamford; and the monks heard the horn blowing that they blew that night. Truthful men who kept watch at night said that it seemed to them that there might be about twenty or thirty horn blowers. This was seen and heard...all through Lenten tide until Easter."

Hiccafrith

Name	The Trust of the Hiccas
Place of Origin	Cambridgeshire
Place of Worship	Cambridgeshire

Hiccafrith, whose name means *"The Trust of the Hiccas"*, seems to be a Fenland version of the Wheel God. He survived in the tales of the giant Tom Hickathrift, who carried a wheel and club. As with Black Annis, the tales have degenerated, and give him a cannibalistic bent.

> *"He ate a cow and a calf, an ox and a half*
> *The church and the steeple, and then all the people*
> *And still had not enough."*[350]

Earlier tales have him portrayed as a defender of the people and provider. He carried on his back as much straw as would fill a wagon. He also killed a

---

[350] Cambridgeshire Customs and Folklore, E. Porter, 1969, p188.

giant using a club made from a tree trunk, using his wheel as a shield, and conquered ten thousand rebels who were ravaging the fenland. Another tale has him fighting the Devil, and throwing a javelin over four miles in their contest.[351]

Horus

Name	The Distant One or High or Above
Place of Origin	Egypt
Place of Worship	Surrey

Horus is an Egyptian hawk-headed god of the sky and warrior god. Although he was worshipped more in the Greek form of Harpocrates, a statue of falcon Horus was found at Farley Heath (Surrey).[352]

Hreda

Name	Glory?
Literary References	Works

Hreda is an obscure Saxon goddess who we only know of due to Bede referring to her as the goddess after whom March was named in the Anglo-Saxon calendar, being called Hredmonath.[353] Her name may derive from the Old High German word *"hruod"* or the Old Norse word *"hróðr"*, both of which mean *"glory"*.

---

351 Cambridgeshire Customs and Folklore, E. Porter, 1969.
352 The Gods of Roman Britain, Green, 1983, p26.
353 Works, Bede, 4:178-9.

Hu Gadarn

Name	Hu the Mighty
Place of Origin	Wales
Place of Worship	Wales
Literary References	Book of Taliesin, Red Book of Hergest, White Book of Rhydderch

Hu Gadarn, or Hu the Mighty was said to be the leader of the settlers who first settled in Britain in ancient times, becoming the first ever king of the British Isles. It was he who called Britain the White Island (*"Ynys Wen"*) and the Island of the Mighty Ones.

The material on Hu Gadarn comes largely from Iolo Morgannwg, who was known to *"add"* to his copies of manuscripts. The result of this is that most of the material on Hu is questionable as all the Triad references come from his copy, which is longer and has a number of references not found in any of the other sources.

Thus all the following material including footnotes quoted from the *"extended Triads"* should be treated as questionable. In the *Triads* he has several titles, perhaps not surprising as he was said to have written them! He was one of the *"Three Benefactors of the Race of Cymry"*,[354] one of the *"Three Over-Ruling Counter Energies of the Isle of Britain"*,[355] one of the *"Three Primary Inventors of the Cymry"*,[356] and one of the *"Three Pillars of the Race of the Island of Britain"*.[357]

Amongst his deeds, Hu Gadarn was said to have invented the Ogham, being one of the *"Three Inventors of Song and Record of the Cymry nation"*,[358] who first applied vocal song to strengthening memory and record. He invented glass

---

[354] Triad 56.
[355] Triad 54.
[356] Triad 57.
[357] Triad 4.
[358] Triad 92.

making, and to have promoted agriculture. He was also renowned as a peacemaker.

The *Triads* refer to Hu Gadarn with reference to the *"Three Primary and Extraordinary Works of the Isle of Britain"*.[359] During Hu's reign, there were many floods, and he discovered these were caused by the afanc, a monster which lived in the lake of Llyn Llion.

With his large horned oxen he dragged the afanc from its lake to the land, which stopped the lake from bursting forth. Hu used his oxen to drag the afanc to Llyn y Ffynnon Las, where he magickally imprisoned it (for it to later turn up in the Arthurian stories).[360]

There is one other reference to Hu Gadarn in the *Triads*, where it says:

"There were three social tribes on the Isle of Prydein. The first was the tribe of Cymry, who came to the Isle of Prydein with Hu the Mighty, because he would not possess a country and lands by fighting and pursuit, but by justice and tranquility."[361]

For verifiable information, we can say that Hu is referred to in the *Red Book of Hergest* and the *White Book of Rhydderch*, in the story called *The Expedition of Charlemagne to Jerusalem and Constantinople, and his adventures with Hu Gadarn*. Another reference is found in the *Book of Taliesin*:

"Disturbed is the isle of the praise of Hu, the isle of the severe recompenser."[362]

---

359 Triad 97.
360 Hu the Mighty, in The Welsh Fairy Book, Thomas, 1907.
361 Triad 5.
362 The Elegy of Aeddon, in The Book of Taliesin.

Hygiaea

Name	Health
Known Period of Worship	2nd-5th century CE
Place of Origin	Rome
Place of Worship	Cheshire, Lancashire

Hygiaea is the Roman healing goddess whose name means *"Health"*. She was the daughter of Aesculapius, with whom she is associated in both the inscriptions found dedicated to her, at Chester and Overborough (Lancashire).[363]

---

[363] RIB 235, 609.

I

Ialonus

Name	God of the Glade
Known Period of Worship	1st-5th century CE
Place of Origin	Lancashire
Place of Worship	Lancashire
Other Names	Ialanus

Ialonus is a god referred to at Lancaster,[364] whose name means *"God of the Glade (or Lea)"*. It has been suggested that he was a river god, giving his name to the local river Lune. He is also equated with the god Contrebis on one inscription. We may also note that a goddess called Ialona was worshipped at Nîmes in Provence, France.

Ing

Name	Foremost One?
Known Period of Worship	4th-8th century CE?
Place of Origin	Germany?
Other Names	Ingeld, Ingui
Literary References	Beowulf, Exodus, Rune Poem

Ing is a Germanic fertility god of peace and plenty, whose symbol was the boar. His name may mean *"Foremost One"* and he was also known as a god of brightness. Linsell describes him as the son of Nerthus and brother of Eostra.[365] The rune Ing is named after him, and the *Rune Poem* gives further indications of his nature.

---

364 RIB 600.
365 Anglo-Saxon Mythology, Migration and Magic, Linsell, 1994, p102.

> *"Ing was first among the East Danes seen by men.*
> *Then he went back over the waves his wagon behind him.*
> *Thus the warriors named the hero."*[366]

It has been suggested that Ing and Frey were the same god, and there are certainly parallels, such as the boar and wagon symbolism. Significantly Frey was also known as Yngvi, which comes from the same root as Ing.

The Ingaevones were a proto-Germanic tribe known as North Sea Germans, who probably took their name from their god Ing, and settled on the North Sea coast. They went on to become the Angles, Saxons, Jutes and Frisians, who brought Ing to Britain.

Anglo-Saxon poetry contained a number of references to Ing, such as in the poem *Exodus to the Ingefolc* (*"people of Ing"*),[367] and in *Beowulf* the Danish king is called Frea Ingwina (*"Lord of the friends of Ing"*).[368]

Isis

Name	Throne
Known Period of Worship	1st-5th century CE
Place of Origin	Egypt
Place of Worship	London

Isis is the Egyptian mother goddess of magick, whose worship prevailed in the Greco-Roman world. Her name means *"Throne"*, reflected in her headdress which is shaped like a throne. Her spouse was originally Osiris, but became Serapis in the Greco-Roman myths, and her son became transformed from Horus to Harpocrates.

Evidence of her worship in Britain has been found in an inscription on a jug found in Southwark (London).[369] The inscription on the jug indicates an

---

366 Rune Poem, stanza 22, trans. Tony Linsell in Anglo-Saxon Mythology, Migration and Magic.
367 Exodus.
368 Beowulf.

Iseum (Isis temple) in London, but the location of this temple has yet to be determined. An altar found in Blackfriars records the restoration of a temple to Isis in the third century CE, further reinforcing evidence of her worship.[370]

It has been suggested by some modern writers that the river Isis in Oxfordshire was named after this goddess, though this may in fact be a coincidence. The name of the river Isis is most probably a contraction of the name Thamesis. It is likely that *"Thamesis"* is a Latinisation of the Celtic river names *"Taom"*(Thames) and*"Uis"*(is), giving *"Taom-Uis"*meaning *"The pouring out of water"*.

An engraved onyx intaglio found at Wroxeter (Shropshire) dating to the third century CE shows Isis bearing a sistrum in her right hand.[371] Another gem from Lockleys (Hertfordshire) dating to the fourth century CE shows Isis standing between Bes and a lioness, all surrounded by a serpent ouroboros.[372]

Iuchar

Name	July?
Place of Origin	Ireland
Place of Worship	Ireland
Other Names	Iuchair
Literary References	Cath Maige Tuired, Leabhar Mór Leacain, Lebor Gabála Érenn, Oidheadh Chloinne Tuireann

Iuchar (or Iuchair) is one of the three sons of Danu[373] or the Morrígan[374] with his brothers Brian and Iucharba. Alternatively he is described as the son of Turenn.[375] The three brothers made (or acquired) weapons for the Túatha dé

---

369 RIB 2503.127.
370 RIB 39b.
371 A Corpus of Roman Engraved Gemstones from British Sites (vol 2), Henig, 1974, p52.
372 A Corpus of Roman Engraved Gemstones from British Sites (vol 2), Henig, 1974, p53.
373 Leabhar Mór Leacain.
374 Lebor Gabála Érenn.
375 Oidheadh Chloinne Tuireann.

Danann to use in their battle with the Fomorians.[376] The name Iuchar is Gaelic for the month of July.

Iucharba

Place of Origin	Ireland
Place of Worship	Ireland
Other Names	Iuchairba
Literary References	Cath Maige Tuired, Leabhar Mór Leacain, Lebor Gabála Érenn, Oidheadh Chloinne Tuireann

Iucharba (or Iuchairba) is one of the three sons of Danu[377] or the Morrígan[378] or Turenn[379] with his brothers Brian and Iuchar. He made (or acquired) weapons with his two brothers, as described above. The meaning of his name is unknown, but it can be seen to be very similar to that of his brother Iuchar.

---

376 Cath Maige Tuired, Oidheadh Chloinne Tuireann.
377 Leabhar Mór Leacain.
378 Lebor Gabála Érenn.
379 Oidheadh Chloinne Tuireann.

J

Juno

Name	Vital force?
Known Period of Worship	2nd-5th century CE
Place of Origin	Rome
Place of Worship	Cumbria
Other Names	Regina

Juno is the queen of the gods of the Roman pantheon, the wife of Jupiter. The meaning of her name is uncertain; it may derive from the Etruscan goddess Uni, or from the root *"yeu"* meaning *"vital force"*. She is the second deity of the Capitoline triad, in which role she was known as Regina (*"Queen"*).[380] Juno was the mother of Mars, Vulcan and Hebe. An inscription at Carlisle (Cumbria) includes Juno in its list of deities.[381]

There are five known engraved gems found of her in Britain, dating to 2nd-3rd century CE.[382] In all of them she wears a chiton and carries a sceptre in her right hand. In two she wears a diadem, and in the other three she does not but bears a patera.

Jupiter

Name	Father God
Known Period of Worship	1st-13th century CE?
Place of Origin	Rome
Place of Worship	Throughout Britain

---

380 RIB 213, 331.
381 RIB 964b.
382 A Corpus of Roman Engraved Gemstones from British Sites (vol 2), Henig, 1974, p34-5.

Jupiter is the king of the gods of the Roman pantheon. He is the first deity of the Capitoline triad, and his name means *"Father God"*. Jupiter has more inscriptions than any other deity, with over one hundred and thirty having been found so far in Britain.[383] As such an important and popular deity it is not surprising that the Romans equated other deities with him, including the Egyptian Ammon and the Syrian Dolichenus

Seventeen engraved gem intaglios of Jupiter have been found in Britain dating from 1st-3rd century CE.[384] Six of these have him accompanied by the eagle, his cult bird. He is also commonly shown bearing a sceptre (four times) or lance (three times) and a patera (six times). In two images he has corn ears; in one he is feeding a goat, which would be the one that suckled him. There have also been six gems found showing Ganymede offering a cup to an eagle (Jupiter) dating from 1st-3rd century CE.

An Anglo-Saxon amulet of Jupiter was kept in St Albans Abbey (Hertfordshire) and used to help women in childbirth. The amulet is now lost, but it is recorded in a manuscript and referred to in later writings.[385] It was a large onyx cameo, too large to hold in one hand, depicting Jupiter with a sceptre in one hand and a Victory in the other, and accompanied by an eagle. The sceptre has a serpent wound around it, suggesting there may have been some identification with Aesculapius. Æthelred the Unready was said to have presented the amulet to the abbey and it was kept on the shrine for anyone to use. With an invocation to St Alban it was placed between the breasts of the pregnant woman and then moved down her body to encourage the baby to come out.

---

383 RIB 89, 103, 215, 235, 319, 320, 452-53, 636, 649, 708, 761-62, 778, 792, 797, 814-835, 893-5, 897-99, 913, 915-17, 964b, 969, 991-92, 1021-23, 1030, 1130-1, 1216-20, 1299-1301, 1316-17, 1330, 1366, 1450-2, 1581-89, 1686-90, 1725-27, 1782-83, 1874-7, 1879-83, 1885-92, 1894-5, 1979-83, 1984-6, 2041-2, 2057, 2062, 2097-9, 2117, 2123, 2134, 2158, 2176, 2332, 2334-36.
384 A Corpus of Roman Engraved Gemstones from British Sites (vol 2), Henig, 1974, p8-10.
385 British Library MS Cotton Nero D.1, fig VI.oo, and see also the writings of Matthew Paris.

K

Kymideu Kymeinvoll

Name	Pregnant in Battle
Place of Origin	Ireland
Literary References	Red Book of Hergest, White Book of Rhydderch

Kymideu Kymeinvoll is referred to in the tale of *Branwen the Daughter of Llyr* in the *White Book of Rhydderch*. From the description given of her, it is likely that she is one of the primal Fir Bolgs. Her attributes as an unkillable hideous giant woman bearing a cauldron of rebirth fit with her being a war goddess from earlier times. The meaning of her name is *"pregnant in battle"*, which describes her ability to produce full-grown warriors from conception in six weeks.

She is described as rising from the waters of a lake, after her cauldron-bearing husband Llassar Llaesgyvnewid, who is a giant, though she is twice his size. She could produce a child every month, who would grow in two weeks to be a full-grown skilled warrior.

The Irish trapped her and her husband and children in an iron house, and heated it to white heat, killing all her sons but not her or her husband. They escaped to Wales and gave the cauldron to Bran, who subsequently (and unfortunately) returned it to the Irish. Her subsequent sons were scattered around Wales as soldiers.[386] That even the iron house could not contain her shows that Kymideu Kymeinvoll was divine rather than a fairy being.

The magickal property of her cauldron was that any man who was slain could be thrown in the cauldron and he would be restored to life the next day,

---

386 Branwen the Daughter of Llyr in the White Book of Rhydderch.

except unable to speak. The cauldron was destroyed by Bran's step-brother Evnyssien, who pretended to be dead and was thrown inside, and burst the cauldron from the inside, killing himself in the process.

L

Latis

Name	Goddess of the Pool or Goddess of Beer
Known Period of Worship	2nd-5th century CE
Place of Origin	Northumberland?
Place of Worship	Northumberland

Latis is a water goddess associated with bogs and pools (and possibly beer), whose name means either *"Goddess of the Pool"* or *"Goddess of Beer"*. She is mentioned in dedications at Birdoswald and Fallsteads.[387]

Lenus

Name	Unknown
Known Period of Worship	2nd-5th century CE
Place of Origin	Gaul
Place of Worship	Wales
Other Names	Lenumius?

Lenus is a Gallic healing god, two inscriptions to whom have been found on the pedestal of a large broken statue in Wales at Caerwent.[388] The inscriptions equate Lenus to three other gods, the Roman Mars, and the British god Ocelos and Vellaunes (a Gallic god equated by the Romans to Mercury).

The broken statue shows only the feet of the god and the webbed feet of a bird, probably a goose as this was associated with war by the Celts (and the Romans as an effective guard animal).

---

387 RIB 1897, 2043.
388 RIB 126, 309.

The meaning of his name is unknown, and a dedication from Benwell to the god Lenumius may refer to the same god or another unknown god.

Lir

Name	The Sea
Place of Origin	Ireland
Place of Worship	Ireland
Literary References	Lebor Gabála Érenn, Oidhe Chloinne Lir

Lir is an Irish sea god, whose name means *"The Sea"*. He does not feature heavily in the Irish myths as he went to live under a hill in County Armagh after not being selected as king of the Túatha dé Danann.[389] He was the father of the sea god Mannanan.

Lir also had four children by his first wife Aobh. These children were his daughter Fionnula, his son Aodh and the twin sons Fiachra and Conn. After her death he married her sister Aoife, who in jealousy transformed his children into swans for nine hundred years.[390]

Lleu Llaw Gyffes

Name	Bright One of the Skilful Hand
Place of Origin	Wales
Place of Worship	Wales
Literary References	The Deceiving of Huan, Red Book of Hergest, Stanzas of the Graves, White Book of Rhydderch

Lleu Llaw Gyffes is a Welsh god whose name means *"Bright One of the Skillful Hand"*, a name his mother Arianrhod was tricked into giving him. Lleu Llaw Gyffes and his elder brother Dylan were born when Arianrhod stepped over

---

389 Lebor Gabála Érenn.
390 Oidhe Chloinne Lir.

Math's magick wand.[391] Gwydion snatched him up and hid him, and raised him, and he grew up twice as fast as a normal boy.

When Gwydion took Lleu disguised as shoemakers to trick Arianrhod, she saw him shoot and hit a wren, and made the comment which gave him his name. From this he also was known as the "Third Gold Shoemaker".[392] The hitting of the wren recalls the old custom of the hunting of the wren on Boxing Day, hinting at solar associations for Lleu, who was also linked with the Irish god of light, Lugh, and the Gallic god Lugus.

The second time Gwydion and Lleu visited Arianrhod disguised as bards, and Gwydion caused the semblance of an army to appear outside the castle, whereupon Arianrhod gave them both arms, and breaking her second stricture on Lleu. On discovering this she laid her third curse that he should never marry a woman of human race.

Lleu married Blodeuwedd, the flower maiden created by Math and Gwydion. She betrayed Lleu with Gronw, the Lord of Penllyn, and managed to inveigle out of him the unusual manner in which he could be killed. The only way to kill Lleu was with a spear which took a year to make, and was only worked on during the time of Sunday church services, and he had to be standing with one foot on a horse's back and the other on the edge of a cauldron.

At her request Lleu demonstrated the position, and was wounded by Gronw with his poison spear. He transformed into an eagle and flew away. This transformation may suggest a totemic connection with the eagle, which is a solar bird.

Gwydion managed to find Lleu and transformed him back into human form and healed him. After this Lleu demanded reparation of Gronw, and caused him to stand in his place by the river, with Lleu taking Gronw's ambush position. Despite Gronw holding a stone in front of his chest, Lleu's spear went through it and killed Gronw. This death is similar to the killing of Fer Diad by the hero Cú Chulainn, with the gae bolga spear piercing the stone in

---

[391] Math the Son of Mathonwy in the White Book of Rhydderch.
[392] Triad 124.

front of Fer Diad's chest, and of course Cú Chulainn was the son of Lugh in those myths.

The solar connection for Lleu would also fit with his horse, described in the *Triads* as one of the *"Three Bestowed Horses"*: *"Pale yellow of the Stud, horse of Lleu Skilful-hand"*. Not only was the horse seen as solar to the Celts, but the colour of the horse is also appropriate.[393]

An old Welsh genealogy gives Lleu as the son of Gwydion, (*"Lou hen map Guidgen"*, i.e. Lleu son of Gwydion)[394] which would explain why Gwydion snatched him up and raised him. This of course raises the issue of incest between Gwydion and Arianrhod.

Another source gives an alternative retelling of the end of the tale, called *The Deceiving of Huan*.[395] In this short piece Lleu is renamed Huan ap Don, making him the son of Don and therefore brother of Arianrhod rather than her son. The name Huan means *"Sun"*, maintaining the light associations of the name Lleu.

The text known as the Stanzas of the Graves presents us with a very different impression of Lleu to the other tales. The verse referring to him implies he is dishonest, and his connection with the sea may well refer to his brother Dylan:

"The grave of Llew Llawgyffes under the protection of the sea,
With which he was familiar
He was a man that never gave the truth to any one."[396]

There is a brook in Gwynedd called Nantlle, which used to be called Nant y Llew or *"Lleu's Brook"*. This may well be associated with the place where Lleu is wounded and subsequently takes his revenge.

---

393 Triad 38.
394 The Brycheiniog list in Harleian MS 3859.
395 Peniarth MS 112, 880-1.
396 Englynion y Beddau.

Llyr

Name	Sea
Place of Origin	Wales
Place of Worship	Wales
Other Names	Llyr Llediath
Literary References	Red Book of Hergest, White Book of Rhydderch

Llyr is a Welsh sea god, also connected with healing and magic. His full name is Llyr Llediath, meaning *"Sea Half-Speech"*. He was married to Penarddun, and fathered Manawyddan, Bran and Branwen.

Collectively his children were called Children of Darkness as opposed to Don's Children of Light.[397] He was often equated with the Irish sea god Lir. Llyr is referred to in the *Triads* as Llyr the Bellipotent, one of the *"Three Battle-Knights of the Sovereign of the Isle of Britain"*.[398]

He is also mentioned as one of the *"Three Exalted Prisoners of the British Isles"*.[399] In this Triad he is described as the captive of Eurosswydd, which would explain how Eurosswydd came to be the second husband of Penarddun.

Loki

Name	Breaker?
Place of Origin	Scandinavia

Loki is the Norse trickster god who plays a major role in many of the Norse Sagas and their derivative Saxon variants. His name may come from the root *"leug"* meaning *"to break"*. Loki is referred to in the old Fenland charm which survived into recent times, *"For God, for Wod and for Lok"*, which also includes

---

[397] White Book of Rhydderch.
[398] Triad 29.
[399] Triad 52.

Woden. There does not seem to have been any exclusive worship of Loki, and he was demonized by the Christian Church into a form of Satan.

London Hunter God

Name	N/A
Known Period of Worship	2nd-5th century CE
Place of Worship	London

The so-called *"London Hunter God"* is a figure depicted in a Phrygian soft cap, found in three unnamed statues from London, at Bevis Marks, Goldsmiths and Southwark. It is likely that these are in fact depictions of Attis.

Loucetius

Name	Lightning or Bright One
Known Period of Worship	1st-5th century CE
Place of Origin	Gaul
Place of Worship	Somerset
Other Names	Leucetius

Loucetius (or Leucetius) is a European import, equated with Mars as warrior and healer, and partnered with the goddess Nemetona.[400] His name can mean *"Lightning"* or *"Bright One"*, and he was worshipped at Bath and around the Severn Estuary.

Luchta

Name	Unknown
Place of Origin	Ireland
Place of Worship	Ireland
Other Names	Luchtaine, Lucraidh
Literary References	Cath Maige Tuired

---

400 RIB 140.

Luchta (or Luchtaine or Lucraidh) the Joiner or Wright was the maker of spear shafts and shields. He required only three chippings to make a complete spear shaft. He is one of a trio of craft gods of the Túatha dé Danann with Creidhne and Goibniu.[401] The meaning of his name is unknown.

Ludd

Name	Unknown
Place of Origin	Wales
Place of Worship	Wales
Other Names	Lludd Llaw Ereint, Lud
Literary References	Black Book of Carmarthen, Red Book of Hergest, Stanzas of the Graves, White Book of Rhydderch

Ludd (or Lludd or Lud) was the eldest of the four sons of Beli, along with Caswallon,[402] Nynyaw and Llevelys. The meaning of his name is not known. He is featured in the tale *Ludd and Llevelys* in the *White Book of Rhydderch*. He rebuilt London, which he loved most of all places, and it took its name from him. He was also called Lludd Llaw Ereint, or *"Ludd Silver Hand"*, which is one of the reasons why he is equated with the Irish god Nuada.

In the tale of *Ludd and Llevelys*, three plagues befall Britain and need to be overcome. The first was a race called the Coranians who heard everything said about them no matter where it was spoken. The second was a fierce shriek every May-eve which left women, plants and animals barren, made men lose their strength, and young men and women lose their senses (caused by two dragons fighting).[403] The third was that no matter how great the store of provisions gathered in the king's court, everything not consumed on the first night disappeared (caused by a giant magician). With the aid of his brother he overcame all three plagues and ruled prosperously for the rest of his days.

---

401 Cath Maige Tuired.
402 Though the Triads give him as Ludd's son, Triad 17.
403 Ludd had these dragons buried in the fortress of Pharaon among the rocks of Snowdon, this being one of the Three Concealments, Triad 53.

Ludd's son Mandubratius was one of the *"Three Men Who Exposed Themselves and Their Progeny to Disgrace"*, as the person who invited the Romans under Caesar to come to Britain, and who gave them the Isle of Thanet.[404] Another son is mentioned in retrospect in the *Black Book of Carmarthen*, where it says *"The grave of Tavlogan, the son of Ludd, is far away in Trewrudd."*[405]

Ludd is also mentioned as having a daughter, Creiddylad, who is described as being the most splendid maiden in the British Isles, for whose hand Gwyn ap Nudd and Gwythyr ap Greidal fight every year at Beltane.[406]. Ludd may well be derived from Nudd, as many writers have suggested. It has also been suggested that Ludd and Creiddylad were the inspiration for Shakespeare's *King Lear* and his daughter Cordelia.

Lugh

Name	Shining One
Known Period of Worship	1st-10th century CE?
Place of Origin	Ireland
Place of Worship	Ireland
Other Names	Lugh Lamfada
Literary References	Baile in Scáile, Cath Maige Tuired, Lebor Gabála Érenn, Oidheadh Chloinne Tuireann

Lugh is the son of Ethne (daughter of Balor) and Cian (son of Dian Cecht). His name may mean *"Shining One"*. He was fostered with the smith god Goibniu who taught him all crafts, and he gained the name Lugh Lamfada, or *"Lugh of the Long Arm"*.

Lugh was the god of all crafts, and when challenged at the gate of Tara, replied that he was a builder, a smith, a champion, a harper, a warrior, a poet and historian, a sorcerer, a physician, a cupbearer and a brazier, i.e. the master

---

404 Triad 100.
405 The Stanzas of the Graves.
406 Kilhwch and Olwen.

of all crafts. He also defeated all opponents in the game of fidchell.[407] Thus it is easy to see why Caesar would equate Lugh with Mercury, the skilled god.

The Spear of Lugh, one of the four treasures of the Túatha dé Danann, ensured that no battle was ever won against whoever held it in their hand.[408]

Lugh avenged his father Cian, who was killed shamefully by the three sons of Turenn.[409] In this story he is described as being like the sun, emphasising his solar nature. In this tale he forces the three brothers to go on a quest for various magickal items.

These are three golden apples of the Hesperides; the magickal pig skin of the Greek king Tuis; the Luin spear of the King of Persia; the chariot and horses of Dobar the King of Siogair; the seven regenerating pigs of Easal, King of the Golden Pillars; Fail-Inis, the whelp belonging to the King of Ioruaidh, the Cold Country; the cooking-spit of the women of Inis Cenn-thinne, the Island of Caer of the Fair Hair; and then give three shouts on the Hill of Miochaoin in the north of Lochlann.

> "Bres, son of Elathan, rose up and said: 'It is a wonder to me the sun to be rising in the west to-day, and it rising in the east every other day.' 'It would be better for us it to be the sun,' said the Druids. 'What else is it?' said he. 'It is the shining of the face of Lugh, son of Ethlinn,' said they."[410]

In the Second Battle of Moytura he fulfilled the prophecy made for him, killing his grandfather Balor of the Evil Eye, by slinging a missile which sent the eye through Balor's head. It is interesting to note that before his encounter with Balor, Lugh assumed the corrguinecht cursing posture and recited a chant to encourage his troops.[411]

---

407 Cath Maige Tuired.
408 Cath Maige Tuired.
409 Oidheadh Chloinne Tuireann.
410 Oidheadh Chloinne Tuireann.
411 Cath Maige Tuired.

Lugh ruled Ireland for forty years after the battle:

> "till Lugh the spear-slaughterous was made king--
> the many-crafted who cooled not.
> Forty to Lugh--it was balanced--
> in the kingship over the Palace of Banba;
> he reached no celestial bed of innocence;"[412]

Elsewhere Lugh is also identified as a solar god and otherworld god in association with the Gallic goddess Rosmerta.[413] He was the father of the hero Cú Chulainn, and helps him by healing him and fighting in his place when he is badly wounded.

Lugh can be equated to the Welsh Lleu Law Gyffes and the Gallic Lugus, after whom Luguvalium (*"Strong in the god Lugus"*), which later became called Carlisle, was named.

The Christians assimilated and canonized Lugh, as Saint Lughaidh. Lugh also appeared in *Baile in Scáile*,[414] where he appears in a vision to the Christian King Conn of the Hundred Battles, and gives his agreement to the sovereignty goddess giving Conn a drink from her cup, signifying his right to rule.

---

412 Lebor Gabála Érenn.
413 Baile in Scáile (The Frenzy of the Phantom).
414 Baile in Scáile.

M

Mabon

Name	Son
Place of Origin	Wales
Place of Worship	Wales
Literary References	Black Book of Carmarthen, Red Book of Hergest, Stanzas of the Graves, White Book of Rhydderch

Mabon is a Welsh god mentioned in the *White Book of Rhydderch*. His name means *"Son"*, and he is described as the son of the goddess Modron. He was stolen from his mother when he was three days old, and curiously is known as the oldest of men or beasts living on earth. He is rescued after his location is revealed by the Salmon of Llyn Llyw.

His aid is required by Kilhwch in the tale of *Kilhwch and Olwen* as he is the only huntsman who can handle the dog Drudwyn, and he retrieves the razor and comb needed by Kilhwch from between the ears of the magic boar Twrch Trwyth. He is also described as one of King Arthur's counselors in *The Dream of Rhonabwy*.

A passing reference is also made to Mabon in the poem *"What man is the Gatekeeper?"* in the *Black Book of Carmarthen*,[415] where he is described as a wizard.

A reference to Mabon in the *Stanzas of the Graves* makes clear one of the obvious points about him, that little is actually known:

---

415 Ch. 31 of The Black Book of Carmarthen.

> *"The grave in the upland of Nanllau;*
> *His story no one knows.*
> *Mabon the son of Modron the sincere."*[416]

There is also a place name associated with Mabon, that of Ruabon in Denbighshire. Ruabon is a corruption of Rhiw Fabon, meaning "Hillside of Mabon".

Macha

Name	Pasture, Field or Plain
Place of Origin	Ireland
Place of Worship	Ireland
Other Names	Macha Mongruad
Literary References	Cath Maige Tuired, Cath Muighe Tuireadh, Cormac's Glossary, Dinshenchas, Lebor Gabála Érenn, Noínden Ulad 7 Emuin Macha, MSS Trinity H.3.18

The name Macha means *"Pasture"*, *"Field"* or *"Plain"*, and suggests her role as an earth goddess, also possibly also alluding to her function as a horse goddess (giving links to Rhiannon and Epona). She is a war goddess and champion of the power of women, demonstrating her superiority to boastful men when challenged. Macha appears as three distinct characters in the Irish myths.

In the *Book of Invasions* she is described as being sister to Badb and Anu, and the three sovereignty goddesses Ériu, Banba and Fotla.[417] With the Morrígan and Badb she is one of the trio of sorceresses in the battle with the Fir Bolgs.[418] In this aspect she is very martial, and the severed heads collected by warriors after battles were known as *"Macha's Acorn Crop"* in her honour.

This is how she is described in an old manuscript:[419]

---

416 Englynion y Beddau.
417 Lebor Gabála Érenn 4.63-4.
418 Cath Muighe Tuireadh.
419 MSS Trinity H.3.18.

> "*Macha, that is a crow; or it is one of the three Morrígna, that is Macha and Badb and Morrígan. Whence Mesrad Machae, Macha's mast, that is the heads of men after their slaughter. As Dub Ruise said: There are rough places yonder, where men cut off Macha's mast; where they drive young calves into the fold; where the raven-women instigate battle.*"[420]

Macha was a triple Goddess in that she is described as having three different depictions in semi-divine or mortal form. The first is as the wife of Nemedh (*"Sacred One"*), when she was a prophetess who foretold the destruction of the country that would be wrought in the future Táin conflict. Her husband named a plain after her, and she died of a broken heart when she saw what devastation would be wrought there by the Táin.

The second depiction is as the divine (though mortal) bride of Crunnchu, when she cursed the Ulstermen. Crunnchu (or Cruinn) was a wealthy farmer, and one day the beautiful Macha appeared and married him. She brought him great prosperity and his crops all did extremely well (showing her qualities as bountiful earth goddess), but she warned him that he must never boast about her.

Crunnchu of course did not listen to Macha, and boasted that his wife could run so swiftly that she could even outrun the king's horses (implying her role as a horse goddess). The king heard about the boast and imprisoned Crunnchu. He then told Macha that the only way to save her husband was to run in the horse race at the great Ulster Assembly and prove his boast true.

Macha appealed to the king and the crowd to let her deliver her babies before she ran, appealing to them saying *"A mother bore each one of you"*. Even though she was nine months pregnant, Macha was forced to run, and she warned that she would curse the whole of Ulster for what they were doing to her. She won, but died giving birth to twins.[421]

---

420 The version in Cormac's Glossary is shorter and variously dated between the 9th-12th century: "Macha, that is a crow; or it is one of the three Morrígna., Mesrad Machae, Macha's mast, that is the heads of men after their slaughter."
421 This tale is recounted in Noínden Ulad 7 Emuin Macha. This text may date back to the mid ninth century, and certainly no later than the tenth century.

With her dying breath she cursed the Ulstermen with the *ces noinden*, the weakness curse which caused them to become as helpless as a woman in childbirth for five days and four nights whenever their strength was needed most. This curse would last for nine generations, and laid the foundations for future events, i.e. the circumstances which cause the death of Cú Chulainn as he had to fight alone without the Ulstermen.

Her third depiction was as the divine legendary warrior-ruler of Ireland, Macha Mongruad (*"Macha of the Red Tresses"*). The tale of the founding of the site of Emain Macha (*"the Twins of Macha"*) describes how she was challenged by the five sons of Dithorba, and visited them feasting after a hunt, disguised as a leper. Even though she was in the form of a leper and repellant, all the brothers desired her. Macha Mongruad slept with each man in turn, overpowered them and enslaved them, and forced them to build the stronghold which was named after her.[422]

In *Cormac's Glossary* a description is given which implies her divine nature. He writes, *"Thus was the outline of the fort described by the woman (Queen Macha), when she was sitting she took her pin from her garment to measure around her with her pin."* This description implies gigantic stature to Macha Mongruad, indicating her divine nature, as giant size did in Irish stories.

Macha was described as being married to the ex-king of the Túatha dé Danann, Nuada, who lost his hand in the First Battle of Moytura.[423] In the Second Battle of Moytura, Macha and Nuada were killed by Balor when he opened his all-destroying eye. However she re-appeared in subsequent tales, so her death did not seem to be a permanent event.

In the *Metrical Dinshenchas* Macha is linked with the solar goddess Grián on two occasions. *"And men say that she was Grián Banchure, 'the Sun of Womanfolk'."*[424] The two are also linked in the same sentence, indicating

---

[422] MSS RIA 23 N10.
[423] Cath Maige Tuired.
[424] Rennes Dinshenchas, no. 94.

connection, when the phrase *"bright Grián and pure Macha"* is used in a similar manuscript.[425]

Armagh (Ard Macha) is named after the Macha, as is recorded in the *Dinshenchas*:

> *"And after this she died, and her tomb was raised on Ard Macha, and her lamentation was made, and her gravestone was planted. Whence Ard Machae, Macha's Height."*[426]

Manannán MacLir

Name	Him from the Isle of Man the Son of the Sea
Place of Origin	Ireland
Place of Worship	Ireland
Literary References	Cath Maige Tuired, Compert Mongán, Duanaire Finn, Lebor Gabála Érenn, Oidheadh Chloinne Tuireann, Serglige Con Culainn, Tochmarc Étaíne

Manannán is an Irish sea and magick god who was the son of Lir. His name Manannán means *"Him from the Isle of Man"*, and MacLir simply means *"Son of Lir"*. Manannán is married to Fand, who falls in love with the hero Cú Chulainn, but after a brief period with him as lovers, Manannán returns and waves his cloak between the two, causing them to forget.[427] He has two daughters, Niamh of the Golden Hair and Clíodna, and later a son Mongán by the wife of Fiachna Finn.

In some versions of *The Wooing of Étaín*, it is Manannán who kills the woman Fuamnach for her treatment of Étaín. He was linked to the otherworld journey on the sea, and wore a great cloak which could assume any colour.

He had other prized possessions; these were his flying ship Scuabtuinne (*"The Sweeper of the Waves"*), his sword Fragarach (*"The Answerer"*) and his horse

---

425 Metrical Dinshenchas, Part 4:127
426 Rennes Dinshenchas, no. 94.
427 Serglige Con Culainn.

Aonbharr ("*One Mane*").[428] Another name for waves was Manannán's horses.[429]

Manannán also carried his magickal crane-bag, made from the skin of a crane, in which he kept his most treasured possessions. This crane had been the woman Aoife, who was transformed into a crane.[430] The bag contained his shirt, knife and house, a fish-skin belt, the bones of the pig of Asal, the shears of the King of Scotland, the helmet of the king of Lochlann, and the smith's hook and belt of Goibniu.

In *The Conception of Mongán*, Manannán sleeps with the wife of Fiachna Finn, fathering the child Mongán, in exchange for his aid in battle. He then returned when Mongán was three days old and took him to the otherworld until he was twelve.

The Isle of Man was under his protection, and may have been seen as an otherworld isle. His pigs were the main food of the Túatha dé Danann, which magickally regenerated and were alive again the next day after being killed. He also had martial qualities, bearing an invincible sword, invulnerable armour and a helmet which glinted like the sun on the water. He gave all these items to Lugh to aid in the fight with the Fomorians.[431]

Manannán is a significant god, as he rules over the Blessed Isles of the Otherworld--Tír na mBean (the land of women), Tír fo Thonn (the land beneath the wave), Tír Tairnigir (the land of promise), Tír na nOg (the land of youth), Emhain Abhlach (the Plain of Apples), and Magh Mell (an afterlife paradise).

Manannán figures in the medieval tale *The Voyage of Bran, Son of Febal*, appearing in his chariot which he rides over the sea. He recites verses glorifying the son he will have when he returns to Ireland, and then leaves again.

---

428 Oidheadh Chloinne Tuireann.
429 Cath Maige Tuired.
430 Duanaire Finn, MacNeil, 1904.
431 Cath Maige Tuired.

Manannán seems to have had a previous incarnation, for in the *Book of Invasions* it refers to a previous name and his death. Even here his nature as a sea god is indicated by the lake bursting forth when he is buried:

> "Orbsen was the name of Manannán at first, and from him is named Loch Orbsen in Connachta. When Manannán was being buried, it is then the lake burst over the land."[432]

Manawyddan

Name	He Who Came from the Isle of Man
Place of Origin	Wales
Place of Worship	Wales
Literary References	Black Book of Carmurthen, Red Book of Hergest, White Book of Rhydderch

Manawyddan was a Welsh god often identified with the Irish sea god Manannán. He was the brother of Bran and Branwen, and was one of the seven Welsh survivors of the war between Ireland and Wales.

Manawyddan was one of the *"Three Humble Princes"*[433] and also one of the *"Three Ungrasping Chieftains"*, i.e. a lord without land. He first appears in the *Second Branch* of the *White Book of Rhydderch*, in the tale *Branwen the daughter of Llyr*, as one of the companions of Bran who travels to Ireland.

After the eighty years in the presence of Bran's head and its burial under the White Mount in London, Pryderi bestowed the hand of his mother Rhiannon on Manawyddan.[434] With Rhiannon, Pryderi and his wife Kicva, they traveled the land after their court disappeared. Manawyddan made first saddles, then shields, then shoes, and excelled in each to such an extent that they were forced to flee each place or be slain by jealous artisans. For making such fine

---

432 Lebor Gabála Érenn 4.64.
433 Triad 38.
434 Manawyddan the Son of Llyr.

shoes with golden clasps he was called *"One of the Three Makers of Golden Shoes."*[435]

Rhiannon and Pryderi were magickally captured, and once again he made shoes. Then he returned home and grew the finest wheat ever. However the wheat was stolen by enchanted mice, and he caught one of them. He resolved to kill the mouse, until he was offered reparation by the source of his problems by the magician Llwyd, whose pregnant wife was the mouse. He had caused all the problems for revenge on Pwyll for his treatment of Grawl the suitor of Rhiannon.

He is also mentioned as Manawyddan the son of Llyr in the tale of *Kilhwch and Olwen*, as one of the heroes who helps finally catch and kill the giant boar Twrch Trwyth.[436]

The poem *"What man is the Gate-keeper?"* refers to the wisdom of Manawyddan, saying:

> *"Manawyddan son of Llyr whose council was profound*
> *Manawyd brought shattered shields from Tryfrwyd."*[437]

Maponus

Name	Divine Youth
Known Period of Worship	BCe-5th century CE
Place of Origin	Northern England?
Place of Worship	Northern England and Southern Scotland
Other Names	Maponos

Maponus (or Maponos) is a northern English and Scottish god often identified with Mabon, whose name means *"Divine Youth"*. Four of the five Roman inscriptions found to him equate Maponos to Apollo,[438] including as

---

435 Triad 124.
436 Kilhwch and Olwen in the White Book of Rhydderch.
437 Black Book of Carmarthen.
438 I.e. RIB 583, 1120-2; the one which does not is RIB 2063.

Cithareodus (*"the Harper"*) which may explain his association with poetry and music. A silver pendant inscribed to him was found at Vindolanda (Northumberland).[439] Maponus was also frequently connected with a dog companion, which may have been his sacred animal.[440]

The centre of his worship may have been on the Scottish borders, as the dedications occur in Cumbria, Lancashire and Northumberland, and associated place names include Lochmaben in Dumfriesshire and a stone called the Clochmabenstane near Annan.

Mars

Name	Unknown
Known Period of Worship	1st-5th century CE
Place of Origin	Rome
Place of Worship	Across Britain

Mars is the tutelary god of the Romans. He was worshipped as a war god, but also as an agriculture god, his earlier attribute which never really went away. His name may be derived from the Etruscan agriculture god Maris.

The month of March is named after him, and 1st March was celebrated by all Roman soldiers as the birthday of Mars Pater Victor (*"Mars the Victorious Father"*). March was also the beginning of the growing season, appropriate to an agricultural deity.

With these considerations in mind, it is not surprising that of all the Roman gods, Mars is the one most often equated with the indigenous British gods. At least eighty-seven inscriptions to Mars have been found all across Britain, making him the second most common god after Jupiter.[441]

---

439 RIB 2431.
440 Roman Inscriptions from Scotland: some additions and corrections to RIB I, Keppie, 1983.
441 RIB 71, 120, 126, 131, 140, 187, 191, 213, 216-19, 248, 274, 278, 282, 305, 307, 309, 310, 454, 584-85, 601-2, 616-17, 622, 650-51, 711, 731, 742-43, 779-80, 837-38, 900, 918, 948-50, 970, 1055, 1077-81, 1100, 1132, 1221-3, 1332-33, 1590-97, 1691, 1784, 1898-1901, 1986-87, 2024, 2044, 2100, 2159, 2166, 2177, 2190.

Mars is referred to by a large number of titles in the inscriptions. He is twice called Augustus (*"Imperial"*), once called Conservator (*"the Preserver"*), twice called Militarus (*"Military"*), once called Pacifer (*"the Peacemaker"*), once called Pater (*"Father"*), once called Ultor (*"the Avenger"*), and Victor (*"the Victorious"*) six times.

Twenty-one engraved gems of Mars dating between 2nd-3rd century CE have been found, and in all of these he bears a spear in his right hand and shield in his left.[442] The naturalisation of Mars is emphasised in a figure found in the Southbroom (Wiltshire) hoard, where he is shown holding two ram-headed serpents, a classic Celtic emblem.

This is alao illustrated through his connection to indigenous gods, including Alator, Barrecis, Braciaca, Belatucadros, Camulos, Cocidius, Condatis, Corotiacus, Lenus, Loucetius, Medocius, Nemetius, Nodens, Ocelus, Olloudius, Rider God, Rigisamus, Rigonemetos, Segomo, Teutates and Tiw.

Math Mathonwy

Name	Bear?
Place of Origin	Wales
Place of Worship	Wales
Literary References	Red Book of Hergest, White Book of Rhydderch

Math seems to be a magick god. In the White Book of Rhydderch[443] it is mentioned that if anyone spoke of him no matter how quietly and the wind heard them, it carried their words back to Math. Unless he was at war Math's feet had to rest in a virgin's lap at all times. The maiden who served him in this way was a fair maiden called Goewin. After her rape by Gilvaethwy, Math took Goewin for his wife.

Following the death of Pryderi and shaming of Goewin he used his magick wand to turn Gwydion and Gilvaethwy into deer for a year, then wild pigs

---

442 A Corpus of Roman Engraved Gemstones from British Sites (vol 2), Henig, 1974, p16-19.
443 Math the Son of Mathonwy.

for a year, and then wolves for a year. Math transformed the baby animals they produced into human boys. Math also helped Gwydion create the flower maiden Blodeuwedd

That Math was a magick god can be seen from him being one of the *"Three Illusive and Half-Apparent Men"*, able to generate illusions as he desired.[444] He was also the third of the *"Three Major Enchanters"*,[445] and he produced one of the *"Three Great Enchantments"*.[446] His name may be derived from the root *matu* meaning *"bear"*.

Matunus

Name	Divine Bear
Known Period of Worship	3rd-5th century CE
Place of Origin	Gaul?
Place of Worship	Cambridgeshire

An inscription at Risingham (Cambridgeshire) refers to Matunus, meaning *"Divine Bear"* (from the Gallic *"matus"* meaning *"bear"*), suggesting there may have been a bear god worshipped in the area.[447] That some burials in this area have contained small jet bear carvings also strengthens this supposition.[448]

Medb

Name	Drunk Woman or Intoxicating One
Place of Origin	Ireland
Place of Worship	Ireland
Other Names	Maeve
Literary References	Fled Bicrenn, Leabhar na h-Uidhri, Táin Bó Cúailnge, Táin Bó Flidais

---

[444] Triad 90.
[445] Triad 136.
[446] Triad 25.
[447] RIB 1265.
[448] Celtic Goddesses, Green, 1995, p 166.

Medb, whose name means *"Drunk Woman"* or *"The Intoxicating One"*[449] is a warrior queen who shows the skills and appetites associated with the Morrígan. Her name is pronounced Maeve, to which it is often anglicized, and it is likely that the faery queen Mab was derived from her.

Medb could run faster than the swiftest horse, and sight of her deprived men of two thirds of their strength. It was Medb who was the great rival of Cú Chulainn. Medb led the forces with the Children of Cailitín (who she had trained) that finally killed the hero Cú Chulainn.

Medb is described as *"a woman, tall, beautiful, pale and long faced. She had flowing, golden-yellow hair. She wore a crimson, hooded cloak with a golden brooch over her breast. A straight, ridged spear blazing in her hand."*[450]

Medb is clearly a sovereignty figure, as all her husbands become kings. Thus she is married to Conchobar (King of Ulster), who she forsakes due to *"pride of mind"*, then Tinne (King of Connacht). After Eochaid is killed by Conchobar, who subsequently rapes her,[451] she takes Eochaid Dala as her husband (who becomes King of Connacht with Medb's consent). By the time of the Táin she has married her fourth husband, Ailill mac Mata. The duration of her reign also indicates her divinity, as she is taking husbands when she has adult grandchildren

Medb is a great warrior and also has an insatiable sexual appetite, sleeping with thirty men a day. In one story she sleeps with Cú Chulainn,[452] and offers her thighs in exchange for the loan of the Brown Bull of Cúailnge, she also sleeps with the hero Fergus to gain his assistance, being the only other woman apart from Flidais who can satisfy him, and entices Fer Diad to fight Cú Chulainn for her.

---

449 In this context it is interesting to note that the word mead comes from the same root.
450 Táin Bó Cúailnge.
451 This is suggested as being the initial cause of the Táin, and indicates an attempt to take the sovereignty by force, a fact that causes war as the other kings are not happy about this.
452 Fled Bicrenn.

The last consideration is one that demonstrates Medb's divine power in an unusual manner. When her army is retreating, Medb's bleeding begins and she needs to urinate. Menstrual blood and urine both have long histories as symbols of sexual potency, and also as protective substances. Medb uses this to cover her retreat:

> "Then her issue of blood came upon Medb (and she said: "O Fergus, cover) the retreat of the men of Ireland that I may pass my water" ... Medb passed her water and it made three great trenches in each of which a household can fit."[453]

In another tale[454] Medb again urinates when retreating, but in this instance the urine has a destructive quality on the land, for *"neither root nor underbrush nor stick of wood was left .... And neither root nor growth nor grass, in its pure, lovely ripeness, was left in that place forever after."*

The Gallic river Goddess Meduana, (*"the Intoxicatress"*) referred to at hot springs near Trier,[455] may be another form of Medb, emphasising the water aspect of the goddess.

Medigenus

Name	Mead begotten
Known Period of Worship	2nd-5th century CE?
Place of Origin	Norfolk
Place of Worship	Norfolk

Medigenus means *"Mead begotten"* and seems to be the name of a Celticised form of the Roman god Faunus. Finds at Thetford (Norfolk) where there are numerous inscriptions on spoons, including twelve to Faunus with other names, and seven inscriptions of just the British names.

---

453 Leabhar na h-Uidhri.
454 Táin Bó Flidais II.
455 CIL 13:7667.

Medocius

Name	Unknown
Known Period of Worship	2nd-5th century CE?
Place of Origin	Essex
Place of Worship	Essex

Medocius is a name of an unknown god on a bronze panel from Colchester (Essex), associated with Mars.[456]

Mercury

Name	Merchant?
Known Period of Worship	1st-5th century CE
Place of Origin	Rome
Place of Worship	Across Britain

Mercury is the Roman god of communication, magick and merchants. His name may come from the root *"merx"* meaning *"merchandise"*. He is the son of Jupiter and the nymph Maia. He was a precocious child, inventing the lyre when he was a few days old. He was a great joker and mischief and theft are also qualities associated with him.

So far eighteen inscriptions to him have been founding Britain.[457] A fine bronze figure from St Albans (Hertfordshire) shows a very Romano-Celtic Mercury, he has a caduceus and moneybag in his hands, and is accompanied by a cock and a ram, with a large torc around his neck. Another figure, from the Southbroom (Wiltshire) cache shows Mercury with his winged helmet, bearing a patera and a rattle.

As a thief god, Mercury was appealed to for the return of stolen property. Documents found at Uley (Gloucestershire) and Kelvedon (Essex) both

---

456 British Museum Catalogue 37, figure 29.
457 RIB 190c, 193,214, 244, 270, 321, 655, 952, 1133, 1303-4, 1693, 2102-3, 2148, 2339, 2432.6-7.

petition Mercury for the return of stolen property.[458] The Uley site also revealed several hundred lead defixiones (curse tablets) to Mercury, further emphasising this role.[459]

Thirty-three engraved gem intaglios of Mercury have been found dating from 1st-3rd century CE.[460] In these he is commonly shown with his caduceus and money bag (twenty-three times), and occasionally with just one of the items (three times with only the caduceus and twice with just the money bag).

Mercury was sometimes combined with native gods, including a reference to the obscure name which occurs nowhere else and whose meaning is unknown, Mercury Andescociuoucus.[461]

Methe

Name	Drunkenness
Place of Origin	Rome

Methe is a Roman nymph or goddess whose name means *"Drunkenness"*, which she personified. From this perspective of her name meaning it is interesting to note the similarity of her name to that of the Irish goddess Medb.

Three engraved gems of her have been found all dating to the first century CE, in Caerwent, Bath and Sea Mills (Bristol).[462] All three show her naked with diadem and mantle, about to drink from a cup.

---

458 Religion in Roman Britain, Henig, 1986, p144.
459 The Gods of Roman Britain, Green, 2003, p35.
460 A Corpus of Roman Engraved Gemstones from British Sites (vol 2), Henig, 1974, p13-6.
461 RIB 193.
462 A Corpus of Roman Engraved Gemstones in the British Isles, Henig, p227.

Midir

Name	Unknown
Place of Origin	Ireland
Place of Worship	Ireland
Literary References	Banshenchus, Cath Muighe Tuireadh, Leabhar Méig Shamhradháin, Tochmarc Étaíne

Midir is an Irish otherworld god who is described as being very beautiful, and whose beauty is used as a poetic device to illustrate the beauty of others.[463] Midir is referred to as the foster-father of Angus Mac Og. In Cath *Muighe Tuireadh*, Midir is one of the chiefs of the Túatha dé Danann who leads the battle against the Fir Bolgs.[464]

In the story *Tochmarc Étaíne* (*The Wooing of Étaín* in *The Yellow Book of Lecan*) he plays chess with the Irish king Eochaid Airem for his wife Étaín, who had been his love in a previous life. He asks permission to embrace Étaín as his prize, which Eochaid agrees to but not until the end of the month.

At the end of the month Eochaid fortifies himself in his court, making it impossible to gain entry, but Midir appears in the middle of the court. He puts his weapons in his left hand and his right arm around Étaín, and they rise through the skylight. All that is seen is two swans which circle around Tara before leaving, Midir having transformed himself and Étaín into swans in a similar manner to Angus and Caer.

Eochaid spent a year digging up mounds to find his wife, and when he discovered Midir's mound, was given a choice. After two white ravens have flown out as Eochaid digs up the mound, Midir brought out Étaín with fifty other identical women and Eochaid had to choose one. He chooses, but picks his daughter rather than his former wife.

---

463 See e.g. Leabhar Méig Shamhradháin IX.38.
464 Cath Muighe Tuireadh.

When Eochaid realises his mistake he returns and sacks Midir's mound and takes Étaín with him. As Eochaid is also called Airem, meaning *"the ploughman"*, this tale may be indicative of the classic battle of the lords of light and dark for the earth goddess.

Midir also had three magick cranes which warned off visitors from entering his dwelling, and drained warriors of their strength. The crane is commonly associated with the powers of life and death in Irish myth,[465] so this symbolism fits his nature.

The *Banshenchus* refers to Midir as having two daughters:

> "Ogniad was daughter of good Midir. Bri Bruachbrec was his other daughter who did not prepare open treachery."[466]

Minerva

Name	Mind?
Known Period of Worship	1st-5th century CE
Place of Origin	Rome
Place of Worship	Across Britain

Minerva is the Roman goddess of wisdom and martial strategy. Her name may come from the root *"men"*, for *"mind"*, or alternatively it may be derived from the Etruscan wisdom goddess Menrva, the meaning of whose name is unknown. She is the third deity in the Capitoline triad with Jupiter and Juno. Nineteen inscriptions to her have been found across Britain,[467] three of which are from Bath, where she is conjoined with Sulis.

A relief from Corbridge (Northumberland) shows Minerva with Hercules, who towers over her with his club. Twenty-one gem images have been found

---

465 See e.g. the tales of the hero Finn, and of course Manannan's crane bag.
466 Banshenchus, pt 1.
467 RIB 91, 110, 141, 146, 150, 429, 457,964b, 1101, 1134, 1200, 1266-68, 1542-3, 1788, 2104, 2177.

of Minerva dating to 1st-3rd century CE.[468] Three of these show her head in helmet, the rest show her with spear and shield, and occasionally another item like a patera (twice) or the goddess Victoria (five times).

Mithras

Name	Friend
Known Period of Worship	1st-5th century CE
Place of Origin	Persia
Place of Worship	Anglesey, London, Northumberland

Mithras is a Persian light and warrior god adopted by the Roman army as their tutelary deity. His name means *"Friend"*. Mithras was the emissary of Ahura Mazda, the supreme power of good, who battled Ahriman, the supreme evil. Mithras slew the divine bull to release its life-giving blood into the earth, and creatures that served Ahriman like scorpions and serpents tried to stop this happening.

Mithras was often depicted with a pointed cap, and a number of reliefs show him in the act of slaying the bull. As a solar god he was directly equated to Sol Invictus by the Romans, as can be seen from inscriptions.[469] Twelve inscriptions to him have been found to date.[470]

There were seven grades in the Mithraic mysteries, which were only open to free men. The Mithraic cult was highly tolerant of other deities, as is evidences by depictions of other gods in the shrines. Also as the soldier god, priesthoods were known to bring their statues to the Mithraea (temples) for protection when danger threatened.

The Mithraea were usually small, and have preserved their mysteries to an extent as little writing remains from them. A relief from Housesteads (Northumberland) shows Mithras bearing a sword and spear rising from an

---

468 A Corpus of Roman Engraved Gemstones from British Sites (vol 2), Henig, 1974, p35-8, 95.
469 See e.g. RIB 4, 1993.
470 RIB 4, 322, 1082, 1395, 1397, 1544-46, 1599, 1600, 1993-94.

egg, surrounded by a hoop depicting the signs of the zodiac. A silver amulet found at St Albans similarly depicts Mithras rising from a pile of stones.

More commonly images on altars showed him sacrificing a bull, such as at Rudchester (Northumberland), Carrawburgh (Northumberland) and the London Mithraeum. There are now five known Mithraea in Britain, those at Caernarvon, Carrawburgh, Housesteads, London and Rudchester. Of these all were purely military apart from the London Mithraea.

Modron

Name	Mother
Place of Origin	Wales
Place of Worship	Wales
Literary References	Cad Goddeu, The Ford of Barking, Red Book of Hergest, Stanzas of the Graves, White Book of Rhydderch

Modron is a sovereignty goddess whose name is derived from Matrona, meaning *"Mother"*.[471] A later reference calls her *"Modron the sincere"*.[472] She is also mentioned in *Cad Goddeu*, though without any context.

The children of Modron and her husband Urien were Owein and Morfydd. Owein is best known for his game of chess with King Arthur in *The Dream of Rhonabwy*.[473] During this chess game Arthur's men start slaying Owein's ravens, but as the game proceeds the tables are turned and the ravens slay many of Arthur's men. The supernatural raven motif is a common one in British myths.

Another Welsh tale, *The Ford of Barking*[474] also brings several of these figures together.[475] In this tale the hero Urien Rheged goes to the ford to discover why the dogs have stopped barking. He finds a woman washing there (i.e.

---

471 Morgan le Fee and Celtic Goddesses, R.S. Loomis, 1940, p194
472 Englynion y Beddau.
473 From the Red Book of Hergest.
474 Rhyd y Gyfartha.
475 MSS Peniarth 147, c. 1556 CE.

the Washer at the ford). They have sex (reminiscent of the union of the Morrígan and the Daghda), and she tells him that she is the daughter of the King of Annwn[476] and if he returns in a year she will present him with a child. When he returns she presented him with twins – Owein and Morfydd.

Mogons

Name	The Great One
Known Period of Worship	2nd-5th century CE
Place of Origin	Germany
Place of Worship	Cumbria, Northumberland
Other Names	Mogti, Mouno, Mounti

Mogons, whose name means *"The Great One"*, was worshipped in northern England and Scotland.[477] An inscription from High Rochester (Northumberland) refers to him in plural form (Dis Mountibus), which would probably have been a triple form.[478] Inscriptions show he was also worshipped in Gaul and Germany, indicating he was thus not a localized tribal deity. Variants of his name include Mogti, Mounti and Mouno.

Morrígan

Name	Great Queen, Terrible Queen, Phantom Queen
Place of Origin	Ireland
Place of Worship	Ireland
Other Names	See below
Literary References	Cath Maige Tuired, Cath Muighe Tuireadh, Dinshenchas, Leabhar Mór Leacain, Lebor Gabála Érenn, Táin Bó Cúailnge

Morrígan can be translated in a number of ways, as *"Great Queen"*, *"Terrible Queen"*, *"Phantom Queen"*, *"Fairy Queen"*, *"Queen of Death"*, *"Sea Queen"* or *"Witch Queen"*. Great or Terrible Queen are the most commonly used

---

476 The underworld in Welsh myth.
477 RIB 921, 922, 971, 1225, 1226, 1722.
478 RIB 1269.

meanings of her name, but as fairy queen, water goddess and earth goddess all the other possibilities are also relevant. As the queen of battle, the Morrígan never fought on the losing side.

The name Morrígan first occurs in Irish literature around 876/7 CE. Her name also found in a glossary to the Books of the Old Testament, referring to *Isaiah* 34:14. The word lamia is described as *"monstrum in femine figura i.e. morigain"* (*"monster in female form, that is a Morrígan"*).[479]

The connection with the Lamia is interesting, as this recalls the carving of three Lamiae at the Roman fort of Benwell in Northern Britain.[480] The Lamiae were beautiful phantom women who seduced men, and killed them for their flesh and blood. That the Lamiae are in triple form and at a military fort suggests a connection to the Morrígan.

The Morrígan is best known for her role in the conflicts in Ireland, and as the tutelary goddess of Cú Chulainn. She is also a magick goddess, described as *"Morrígan – source of enchantments."*[481] With Macha and Badb she performed magick to keep the Fir Bolgs in their fortress:

> *"bringing down enchanted showers of sorcery and mighty showers of fire, and a downpour of red blood upon the warrior's heads, preventing them from moving for three days and nights."*[482]

She also made love with the Daghda and ensured the Túatha dé Danann win the battle with the Fomorians. This liminal event occurs at Samhain, and the Morrígan has sex with the Daghda astride the ford (i.e. across the magickal waters), with a foot on each bank, before the Second Battle of Moytura.[483]

"He [the Daghda] beheld the woman at Unius in Corann, washing herself, with one of her two feet at Allod Echae, to the south of the water, and the other at Loscuinn, to the

---

[479] MSS Regina 215.
[480] CIL (Corpus Inscriptionum Latinarum),7:507, Berlin, 1862.
[481] Lebor Gabála Érenn.
[482] Cath Muighe Tuireadh.
[483] Cath Maige Tuired, and also Dinshenchas.

north of the water. Nine loosened tresses were on her head. The Daghda conversed with her, and they made a union. 'The Bed of the Couple' is the name of the place thenceforward. The woman that is here mentioned is the Morrigu."[484]

She was equated with a number of other goddesses, including Danu, the Cailleach, Nemain, Badb, and Macha.[485] She also had many roles, including as warrior, oracle, washer at the ford, magician, earth goddess, faery queen, bestower of sovereignty and lady of the beasts. Her powers include prophecy, shape-shifting, her death screech and many others.

"The Morrígan daughter of Ernmas came from the síd and sat on the pillar-stone in Temair Cúlainge, warning the Donn Cúlainge about the men of Ireland." [486]

Her shape-shifting ability is particularly emphasised in the *Táin Bó Cúailnge*, where the Morrígan appeared in a wide range of forms, as a maiden and a crone, as a crow, and in the eel, wolf and cow forms which she used to attack Cú Chulainn. This ability is specifically referred to in the *Dinshenchas*, where it says *"The Daghda's wife found her; the shape-shifting Goddess."*[487]

Her power of prophecy is indicated when she warns the Brown Bull of Cúailnge of forthcoming events, and also particularly in her victory prophecy delivered after the victory of the Túatha dé Danann over the Fomorians.[488]

From the eleventh century CE we see the Morrígan being equated with classical figures whose names are incorporated into the Irish tales. So we see her equated with the Greek Fury Alecto: *"Alecto came for a while, that is, the Morrígan, in the form of a bird which perched on the pillar-stone."*[489]

"The Morrígan was the mother of Brian, Iucharba, and Iuchar."[490]

---

484 Dinshenchas.
485 See The Guises of the Morrígan, Rankine & D'Este for more on this.
486 Táin Bó Cúailnge.
487 Dinshenchas.
488 Cath Maige Tuired.
489 Táin Bó Cúailnge Rescension I.
490 Leabhar Mór Leacain.

Although the references are fleeting, they do indicate she had sons, though these three sons are more often called the sons of Danu. The tales in *The Great Book of Lecan* also mention her son Mechi, who was killed by Mac Cecht at Magh Fertaige, which was subsequently called Magh Mechi. Mechi had three serpents in his three hearts, which would have desolated all of Ireland if they had been allowed to grow.

Gort na Morrígna (the Morrígan's Field) in Co. Louth is named after her. The Corryvreckan whirlpool, which lies between the northern end of Jura and the isle of Scarba in the Inner Hebrides, as well as being known as Coire-Bhrecain (the cauldron of Brecan) was also known as *"The Morrígan's Cauldron"*.

N

Nantosuelta

Name	Winding River
Known Period of Worship	2nd-5th century CE
Place of Origin	Gaul
Place of Worship	Nottinghamshire

Nantosuelta is a Gallic goddess whose name means *"Winding River"*. Her consort is the hammer god Sucellos. The raven is the main symbol of Nantosuelta, along with the dovecote, indicating a more domestic aspect. She is also sometimes depicted with a cornucopia (horn of plenty), implying a bountiful earth goddess aspect.

A small carved stone found in East Stoke (Nottinghamshire) is thought to represent Nantosuelta, as is a relief of a god and goddess, here being Nantosuelta with Sucellos.

Nechtan

Name	The Pure One
Place of Origin	Ireland
Place of Worship	Ireland
Other Names	Nechtain
Literary References	Banshenchus, Lebor Gabála Érenn

Nechtan (or Nechtain) is an Irish water god associated with the sacred well of knowledge at Sidh Nechtan, who is also the husband of Boann. His name, appropriately, may be translated as *"The Pure One"*. His well was situated under nine hazel trees (associated with wisdom), and the nuts fell into the well where they were eaten by the salmon of wisdom.

The *Book of Invasions* mentions a brother of Nechtan called Caicher, and describes them both as being the sons of Nama.[491] The same verse describes Nechtan slaying the Milesian hero Cairpre, and being killed with a poisoned weapon by the hero Sigmall.

The *Banshenchus* however describes his parentage differently, saying:

> "*Nechtan was son of busy Labrad Lesbric, a strong man, quick in battle heroic and fierce.*"[492]

Néit

Place of Origin	Ireland
Place of Worship	Ireland
Other Names	Net
Literary References	Banshenchus, Cath Maige Tuired, Cath Muighe Tuireadh

Néit (or Net) is an Irish Fomorian battle god. He is described as the father of Donn and grandson of Balor,[493] although elsewhere he is the grandfather of Balor.[494] He is also described as the husband of several of the Irish war goddesses like Nemain and Badb.

The *Banshenchus* describes him as: "*mighty Net a greater man than pleasant Hector. (From him is famed the cairn at Ath Feindead where he fought a duel).*"[495]

---

491 Lebor Gabála Érenn 4.63.
492 Banshenchus, pt.1.
493 Versions of Cath Maige Tuired and Cath Muighe Tuireadh.
494 Banshenchus, pt 1.
495 Banshenchus, pt 1.

Neith

Name	The Terrifying One
Place of Origin	Egypt

The Egyptian goddess Neith is a war and creator goddess whose name may mean *"The Terrifying One"*. She was one of the earliest of the Egyptian deities, and was said to have come from the primal waters of Nun. An amulet depicting her was found at Gloucester.[496]

Nemain

Name	Frenzy, Panic or Venomous
Place of Origin	Ireland
Place of Worship	Ireland
Other Names	Nemon
Literary References	Banshenchus, Cogadh Gaedhel re Gallaibh, Cormac's Glossary, Lebor Gabála Érenn, Táin Bó Cúailnge

Nemain means *"Frenzy"*, *"Panic"* or *"Venomous"*, and indicates the battle fury of this Irish warrior goddess, intimidating the side that was going to lose with her shrieks, and exhorting the side she had decided would win to victory.

Nemain is described in *Cormac's Glossary*, as the wife of Néit, further emphasizing the interchangeability and connection of these different guises of the Morrígan:

> "Néit, i.e. the God of battle. Nemain is his wife"; "Bé Néit ... Nemon was his wife. This couple was venomous indeed."[497]

---

496 See The Religions of Civilian Roman Britain, Green, 1976, p58, p172.
497 Cormac's Glossary.

Nemain is directly identified with Badb in later texts: *"Nemain, i.e. the Badb of battle, or a hooded crow."*[498] She is also mentioned in a stanza with Fea, further indicating the connection to this little-known guise:

"Banba, Fotla, and Fea, Nemain of prophetic stanzas, Danu, mother of the Gods."[499]

When Nemain shrieked at the Connacht army facing Cú Chulainn one hundred soldiers dropped dead with fright in the night.[500] Before this she had promised both sides they would win, even though she had decided the Ulstermen would, she was also known for her (at times) fickle nature.

If we consider the deathly shriek combined with the prophecy of imminent death, we can see a clear parallel to the Banshee, indeed in Munster the Badb was referred to as the Bean Sídhe or Banshee.

Accounts record the appearance of Nemain at the Battle of Clontarf in 1014 CE,[501] as a raven flying overhead, also instilling terror into the opposing Vikings and thus protecting her land from invasion.

It has been suggested that Nemain is linked to the British goddess of the Sacred Grove, Nemetona. However apart from a similarity of name there is little to connect these two goddesses.

Nemesis

Name	Dispenser of Dues
Place of Origin	Greece
Place of Worship	Northumberland

Nemesis was originally a Greek goddess of vengeance and justice, whose worship was taken up by the Romans. Her name means *"Dispenser of Dues"*.

---

498 Glossary, Michael O'Clery, 1643 CE.
499 Lebor Gabála Érenn .
500 Táin Bó Cúailnge.
501 Cogadh Gaedhel re Gallaibh , 12th century CE, and Annals of Lough Cé, 13th century CE
.

Three inscriptions to her have been found, a lead defixione table at Caerleon (Monmouthshire), and inscriptions at Chester and Hadrian's Wall.[502] One engraved gem as found at Braughing (Hertfordshire) showing her winged and bearing a patera.[503]

Nemetius

Name	Sacred
Known Period of Worship	2nd-5th century CE
Place of Origin	Germany
Place of Worship	Yorkshire

Nemetius is another obscure god equated with Mars by the Romans. His name means *"Sacred"*, and he is referred to in an inscription at Rokeby (Yorkshire). He was worshipped on the west bank of the Rhine, and may have been brought to Britain with the Roman army.

Nemetona

Name	Goddess of the Sacred Grove
Known Period of Worship	2nd-5th century CE
Place of Origin	Unknown
Place of Worship	Somerset

Nemetona is a goddess whose name means *"Goddess of the Sacred Grove"*, who was particularly popular in Bath. She was paired with Mars by the Romans.[504] One image shows her seated with a sceptre, surrounded by a ram and three hooded figures.

Nemetona may have been worshipped throughout the Celtic world, with place names to her being found across Gaul, though these could refer to sacred groves (the nemetons) that were not specifically for her worship. In

---

502 RIB 323, 573b, 2065.
503 A Corpus of Roman Engraved Gemstones from British Sites (vol 2), Henig, 1974, p43.
504 RIB 140.

Britain there were several Roman sites that had nemeton names, including Medionemeton on the Antonine Wall in Strathclyde, Nemetostatio in North Devon (now North Tawton), and Vernemetum in Nottinghamshire (now Willoughby).

There were two tribes in Europe with names derived from the same word who may have worshipped her. These were the Nemetate of northern Spain, who are mentioned by Ptolemy, and the Nemetes who were a Germanic tribe living by the Rhine, and referred to by Caesar[505] and Tacitus.[506]

Neptune

Name	God of Moisture?
Known Period of Worship	2nd-5th century CE
Place of Origin	Rome
Place of Worship	Across England

Neptune is the Roman sea god, celebrated in his festival of Neptunalia on 23rd July. His name may come from the root *"nebh"* meaning *"moisture"*, giving a meaning of *"God of Moisture"*. He was originally associated with springs and streams before his identification with the Greek sea god Poseidon. He has been equated with Nodens, though he was also worshipped in his own right, as shown by the ten inscriptions found in northern England.[507]

A fine silver plaque found at Chesterford (Essex) depicts his head as a mask. A mosaic from Frampton (Gloucestershire) shows Neptune flanked by dolphins. Two bronze rings dating to the third century CE bear images of Neptune, one accompanied by dolphin was found at Woodeaton (Oxfordshire), the other at South Shields (Co. Durham).[508]

---

505 The Gallic Wars 6.25.1.
506 The Annals 12.27.
507 RIB 66, 91, 706e, 839, 1319, 1694, 1929d, 1990, 2105, 2149.
508 A Corpus of Roman Engraved Gemstones from British Sites (vol 2), Henig, 1974, p10.

Nerthus

Name	North?
Place of Origin	Germany
Place of Worship	England
Literary References	Germania (Tacitus)

Nerthus is a Germanic earth goddess whose worship was imported to Britain, and whose name may mean *"North"*. The Roman historian Tacitus mentions her in his writings, giving her a whole (short) chapter, and as this is the main source it is worth quoting for the relevant information.

> *"They worship in common Nerthus, that is Terra Mater and believe she intervenes in human affairs and goes on progress through the tribes. There is a sacred grove on an island of the ocean, and in the grove is a consecrated wagon covered with a cloth. Only one priest is allowed to touch it; he understands when the goddess is present in her shrine and follows with profound reverence when she is drawn away by cows. Then there are days of rejoicing: the place she considers worthy to entertain her keep holiday. They do not go to war, do not use weapons, all iron is shut away, peace and quiet are so much esteemed and loved at that time, until the same priest returns the goddess to her sanctuary. Directly, the wagon, the covering cloth, and, if you like to believe this, the goddess herself, are washed in a secluded lake. Slaves are the ministers; immediately, the same lake swallows them."*[509]

From this we may note a number of points. The sacred grove was common to many deities, and is especially appropriate to an earth goddess. Tacitus calls her earth mother (*"Terra Mater"*), clearly indicating her role. The places she stopped were wherever the cows decided to stop, as the wagon had no drover except the goddess herself.

Tacitus also describes the boar as the emblem of Nerthus, worn for peace of mind and even as a replacement protection for weapons. Thus we see her sacred animal is the boar.[510]

---

509 Germania, 40.
510 Germania, 45.

The peaceful nature of Nerthus is highly emphasised, and the reference to all iron being shut away is interesting, as it may hint at a retinue of other spiritual beings, who disliked iron, like the faery folk. The washing of the statue, wagon and covering cloth all suggest a need for return to the purity of the grove, unsullied by the unconsecrated people and places she had visited. And finally, Tacitus indicates the slaves are killed after having touched the goddess and her wagon (*"the same lake swallows them"*), though this may be propaganda of the kind seen in descriptions of the druids and their practices.

An interesting echo of this practice in local custom was recorded some fifteen hundred years later by a German couple visiting Eton on 14th September 1598 CE, who described the statue of an earth goddess being carried in a wagon.

"By lucky chance we fell in with the county-folk celebrating their harvest home. The last sheaf had been crowned with flowers and they had attached it to a magnificently robed image, which perhaps they meant to represent Ceres. They carried her hither and thither with much noise; men and women were sitting together on the wagon ..."[511]

This type of practice was still going on two centuries later at the end of the eighteenth century, being described as occurring in Northumberland by the antiquarian William Hutchinson. This demonstrates the persistence of the earth goddess in the country practices as the harvest queen.

Nodens

Name	He Who bestows Wealth or The Cloud-maker
Known Period of Worship	BCE-5th century CE
Place of Origin	Gloucestershire
Place of Worship	Across England
Other Names	Nodons

Nodens (or Nodons) is a god of healing and water, whose name may have meant *"He who bestows wealth"* or alternatively *"The Cloud-maker"*.[512] His main

---

511 England as seen by Foreigners in the Days of Elizabeth and James I, W. B. Rye (ed), 1865.

temple was at Lydney Park (Gloucestershire) on the banks of the river Severn, and was a major religious centre. His worship was spread over a considerable area, as demonstrated by inscriptions at Cockersand Moss (Lancashire) and Chesterholm (Northumberland).

The Romans equated Nodens with Mars and Silvanus, and a fragment from Chesterholm (Northumberland) equates him to Neptune. That there were also inscriptions just to him without any other gods shows his significance as a god in his own right.

Pavements (now destroyed) and friezes from the temple show scenes of sea monsters and fish, fishermen and tritons bearing conch shells and anchors; and a fragmentary bronze relief shows a sea deity bearing a shell and an anchor. The amount of sea imagery found at the temple clearly suggests he was a sea god as well as a healing water god, as does his equation to Neptune.

Cult objects retrieved at the temple also represented the sun, such as a bronze showing a sun god with whip driving a four-horse chariot followed by tritons with anchors, indicating that Nodens may also have had a solar aspect.

There are nine instances of dogs being represented with Nodens inscriptions. As there have been no anthropomorphic figures of this god found, it could indicate either that he has a dog form, or that the dog is his sacred animal. Nodens is often equated with the Irish Nuada and the Welsh Nudd. See also the entries for Mars, Neptune and Silvanus.

---

512 RIB 305-7, 616, 617.

Nuada

Name	Unknown, possibly from Nudd
Place of Origin	Ireland
Place of Worship	Ireland
Other Names	Nuadu
Literary References	Cath Maige Tuired, Cath Muighe Tuireadh, Lebor Gabála Érenn

Nuada was the king of the gods of the Túatha dé Danann. Nuada possessed an invincible sword that none could resist, which was one of the four treasures of the Túatha dé Danann.[513] He ruled the Túatha dé Danann for seven years before they went to Ireland,[514] and is described as being *"large breasted"* and *"flaxen-maned"*.[515]

Nuada had his hand cut off in the First Battle of Moytura with the Fir Bolgs,[516] an event predicted by the prophetic dream of the Fir Bolg king Eochaid.

"I saw a great flock of black birds coming from the depths of the ocean. They settled over all of us, and fought with the people of Ireland. They brought confusion on us and destroyed us. It seemed to me that one of us struck the noblest of the birds and cut off one of its wings."[517]

Dian Cecht replaced it his missing hand with a silver hand, leading to his title of Nuada of the Silver Hand. As he was no longer whole of body he could no longer be king, and Bres replaced him. However following the retreat of Bres he again became king, until he was killed by Balor at the Second Battle of

---

513 Cath Maige Tuired.
514 Lebor Gabála Érenn.
515 Lebor Gabála Érenn.
516 Cath Muighe Tuireadh.
517 Cath Muighe Tuireadh.

Moytura.[518] This is a confusing point, because Nuada is also described as ruling for twenty years after the battle, indicating he was not killed.[519]

Nudd

Name	Catcher or Mistmaker
Place of Origin	Wales
Place of Worship	Wales
Literary References	Red Book of Hergest, White Book of Rhydderch

Nudd is a war god whose name means either *"Catcher"* or *"Mistmaker"*. He was the father of Gwyn ap Nudd and his brother Edeyrn.[520] In the *Triads* there is mention of a third son Dryan, who has one of the *"Three Noble Retinues"*;[521] whose name may be derived from the word *draen* meaning *"thorn"* or *"bramble"*. Alternatively if the name is Dreon as shown in one text it could mean *"host"*. Nudd is also described as one of the *"Three Generous Princes"*.[522] Nudd is often equated with Ludd, and also with Nuada.

Nyx

Name	Night
Known Period of Worship	2nd-5th century CE
Place of Origin	Greece
Place of Worship	Essex
Other Names	Nox

Nyx (or Nox) is the primal Greek goddess of Night (the meaning of her name), also worshipped by the Romans. An inscription to her has been found at Westwood (Essex).[523]

---

518 Cath Maige Tuired.
519 Lebor Gabála Érenn.
520 Kilhwch and Olwen in the White Book of Rhydderch.
521 Triad 28.
522 Triad 2.
523 RIB 2157.

O

Oceanus

Name	Ocean
Known Period of Worship	2nd-5th century CE
Place of Origin	Greece
Place of Worship	London, Tyne & Wear, Yorkshire

Oceanus is a Roman sea god, who gives his name to the *"Ocean"*. Oceanus was the eldest of the Titans, and married his sister Tethys. He was akin to Neptune, and worshipped in a propitiatory manner for protection from the forces of the sea. A dedicatory plaque in Greek from York,[524] an inscription at Newcastle-upon-Tyne (Tyne & Wear)[525] and a statue of Oceanus from the London Mithraea all indicate his worship in Britain.

Ocelus

Name	Unknown
Known Period of Worship	BCE-5th century CE?
Place of Origin	Cumbria
Place of Worship	Cumbria, Monmouthshire
Other Names	Ocelos

Ocelus (or Ocelos) is thought to have been a tribal god of the Silures tribe. The meaning of his name is unknown, but as was often the case, the Romans equated him with Mars.[526] An inscription at Caerwent also equates Ocelus with Lenus and the Gallic god Vellaunus.

---

524 RIB 663.
525 RIB 1320.
526 RIB 309, 310, 949.

There is a reference to an Ocelius Promontory in Ptolemy's *Geography* which may be Spurn Head in Humberside, and could refer to Ocelus, which would indicate he was a fairly well known deity.

Ogma

Name	*Unknown*
Place of Origin	*Ireland*
Place of Worship	*Ireland*
Other Names	*Oghma, Ogmia*
Literary References	*Cath Maige Tuired, Cath Muighe Tuireadh*

Ogma or Oghma is the Irish god of poetry and eloquence, son of Danu and the Daghda. He was often identified with the Gallic Ogmios. He was the creator of the Ogham script, and was also a mighty fighter, being able to hold his own against the Fomorian king and twenty-seven of his men.[527] When he fought, *"his track was marked with crimson blood."*[528]

A native relief found at Richborough shows a figure with the name Ogmia, so we can assume it is Ogma, possibly in a localized form. He has long curling hair with solar rays coming from his head and bears a whip (associated with Sol Invictus).[529] This image combined with his other names clearly suggests Ogma has qualities as a solar god, as do his other names.

Ogma was also called Ogma Grianainech (*"Sun-face"*), Ogma Trenfher (*"Strongman"*), and Ogma Cermait (*"Honeymouth"*).

---

527 Cath Maige Tuired.
528 Cath Muighe Tuireadh.
529 Third Report on the Excavations of the Roman Fort at Richborough, Bushe-Fox, 1932, p185, plate 63.

Olloudius

Name	Great Tree? / He who holds all?
Known Period of Worship	2nd-5th century CE
Place of Origin	Belgium
Place of Worship	Gloucestershire

Olloudius is a war god whose name may mean *"Great Tree"*.[530] An alternative suggestion for the meaning of his name is *"He who holds all"*, from the roots *oljo* meaning *"all"* and *dalge* meaning *"hold"*, which is interesting when considering the double cornucopia imagery.

A depiction of him in Custom Scrubs (Gloucestershire) equates him to Mars, but unusually has him bearing a double cornucopia, indicating a strong fertility aspect and recalling the agricultural aspect of Mars. He was worshipped widely in Belgium, and may well have been imported from there.

Olwen

Name	White Track
Place of Origin	Wales
Place of Worship	Wales
Literary References	Red Book of Hergest, White Book of Rhydderch

Olwen is the heroine of the tale *Kilhwch and Olwen* in the *White Book of Rhydderch*. Her name means *"White Track"*, referring to the white clovers which appear wherever she treads. She is the daughter of the giant Yspaddaden Penkawr.

The mere mention of her name makes Kilhwch fall in love with her. To gain her hand he has to undertake an almost impossible quest, for when she is wed her father will die. Kilhwch enlists the aid of his cousin King Arthur and many of his men and fulfills the quest and gains her hand.

---

[530] RIB 131.

The description of Olwen emphasises both her beauty and her connection to the land (as does her name), as she may well have been a sovereignty goddess. She is described as:

> "More yellow was her head than the flower of the broom, and her skin was whiter than the foam of the wave, and fairer were her hands and her fingers than the blossoms of the wood anemone amidst the spray of the meadow fountain. The eye of the trained hawk, the glance of the three-mewed falcon was not brighter than hers. Her bosom was more snowy than the breast of the white swan, her cheek was redder than the reddest roses. Whoso beheld her was filled with her love. Four white trefoils sprung up wherever she trod."[531]

Significantly white trefoils springing up where she trod, combined with the comparative descriptions to flowers and regal birds all suggest her link to the land. And also, when Kilhwch gains her hand he also *"took possession of his castle, and of all his treasures"*,[532] clearly suggesting she is the bestower of sovereignty of the land.

Onirus

Name	Unknown
Known Period of Worship	2nd-5th century CE
Place of Origin	Co. Durham
Place of Worship	Co. Durham

Onirus is an unknown god, to whom an inscription was found at Greta Bridge (Co. Durham).[533]

---

531 Kilhwch and Olwen in the White Book of Rhydderch.
532 Kilhwch and Olwen.
533 RIB 745.

P

Pan

Name	All
Known Period of Worship	1st-3rd century CE
Place of Origin	Greece
Place of Worship	Essex, Kent, Monmouthshire

Pan is the Greek shepherd god who was adopted by the Romans, whose name means *"All"*. Six gems of him have been found in Britain, all dating from 2nd-3rd century CE.[534] Of these three were found in Kent, two in Essex, and one in Caerleon (Monmouthshire). Two are busts, two with a goat, one with Cupid, and one with grapes. There are also thirty-three gems from 1st-2nd century CE with an image described as a satyr, almost always with grapes, of which some or all could also represent Pan.[535]

Panakeia

Name	Cure-all
Known Period of Worship	2nd-5th century CE?
Place of Origin	Greece
Place of Worship	Co. Durham
Other Names	Panacea

Panakeia (or Panacea) is a Greek healing goddess whose name means *"Cure-all"*. She was the daughter of Aesculapius, and is referred to in an inscription with him and Hygiaea.[536]

---

534 A Corpus of Roman Engraved Gemstones from British Sites (vol 2), Henig, 1974, p26.
535 A Corpus of Roman Engraved Gemstones from British Sites (vol 2), Henig, 1974, p27-30, 96.
536 RIB 235.

Pax

Name	Peace
Known Period of Worship	1st-5th century CE
Place of Origin	Rome
Place of Worship	Northumberland

Pax is the Roman goddess of Peace, which is also the meaning of her name. Two inscriptions to her have been found in Britain – one at High Rochester (Northumberland) and one at Carvoran.[537]

Penarddun

Name	Head of Darkness?
Place of Origin	Wales
Place of Worship	Wales
Literary References	Red Book of Hergest, White Book of Rhydderch

Penarddun does not take any role in the stories of the *White Book of Rhydderch*, though she is the sister of Arianrhod, Amaethon, Gilvaethwy, Govannon, Gwydion and Nudd, and wife of Llyr. With Llyr she is the mother of Manawyddan, Bran and Branwen.

Penarddun is also the mother by Eurosswydd of two sons called Nyssien and Evnyssien, the latter of whom is responsible for the war between the Welsh and the Irish in the tale of *Branwen the Daughter of Llyr*.

Her name is probably derived from the Welsh *"pen"* meaning *"head"*, and *"arddu"* meaning *"darkness"*, giving a meaning of *"Head (or Ruler) of Darkness"*. This name might suggest an earlier attribution as an underworld goddess, recalling Pwyll being called the Head (pen) of Annwn.

---

537 RIB 1273, 1791.

Priapus

Name	Unknown
Known Period of Worship	1st-5th century CE
Place of Origin	Rome
Place of Worship	Dumfries & Galloway

Priapus is the phallic Roman god of fertility, originally said to be the son of Dionysus and Aphrodite. The meaning of his name is unknown. A single inscription to him has been found, at Birrens. [538] Two gold rings with phalli (his symbol) on them in relief have been found dating to the first century CE in London and Faversham (Kent).[539]

Pryderi

Name	Relief from Her Anxiety
Place of Origin	Wales
Place of Worship	Wales
Other Names	Gwri Gwallt-Euryn
Literary References	Red Book of Hergest, Stanzas of the Graves, White Book of Rhydderch

Pryderi means *"Relief from her anxiety"*, referring to his birth after concern that Rhiannon would not provide an heir. He was also known as Gwri Gwallt-Euryn, meaning *"Golden Hair"*, the name given to him by his foster parents.

Pryderi is the only character present in all four of the Branches in the *White Book of Rhydderch*. He is born in the first Branch, is one of the seven companions who survive the war with the Irish in the second Branch, is companion to Manawyddan in the third Branch, and is killed by Gwydion in the fourth Branch.

---

538 RIB 2106.
539 A Corpus of Roman Engraved Gemstones from British Sites (vol 2), Henig, 1974, p278.

He does not display any special characteristics apart from good leadership, but if Rhiannon is a goddess then as her son he would be at least semi-divine. Pryderi is named in the *Triads* as one of the *"Three Powerful Swineherds"*.[540]

Pryderi is mentioned in the Stanzas of the Graves, where it says:

> *"In Aber Gewnoli is the grave of Pryderi*
> *Where the waves beat against the land."*[541]

Pwyll

Name	Good Judgement
Place of Origin	Wales
Place of Worship	Wales
Other Names	Head of Annwn
Literary References	Book of Taliesin, Red Book of Hergest, White Book of Rhydderch

Pwyll and meaning *"Good Judgement"* is one of the characters in the *White Book of Rhydderch*. In the tale of *Pwyll Prince of Dyved*, he befriends Arawn and takes his place as Lord of Annwn for a year and a day. During this time he did not abuse the hospitality of Arawn's wife, and after a year he fought Arawn's enemy, Hafgan, mortally wounding him with one blow. He refused to strike a second blow, which would have healed Hafgan, and conquered his lands, uniting the underworld (Annwn). At the end of the year and a day, Arawn was delighted that Pwyll had protected his wife's chastity and the two became friends and allies.

Pwyll was subsequently known as the *"Head of Annwn"*, suggesting an underworld connection. This is reinforced by the reference to him in *Preiddeu Annwn*, where it says *"Complete was the prison of Gweir in Caer Sidi, through the spite of Pwyll and Pryderi."*[542]

---

540 Triad 101.
541 Englynion y Beddau.
542 The Book of Taliesin, ch.30.

Pwyll subsequently married Rhiannon, though he displayed excessive generosity in offering a boon to her suitor, and the situation was only redeemed through the wisdom of Rhiannon. With Rhiannon he fathered Pryderi, who was stolen and found by Teirynon, who became his foster father, and also released Rhiannon from her bondage.

R

Rata

Name	Goddess of the Fortress
Place of Origin	Cumbria or Northumberland?
Place of Worship	Cumbria, Northumberland
Other Names	Ratis

Rata (or Ratis) is an obscure goddess, whose name means *"Goddess of the Fortress"*. She was referred to in inscriptions at Birdoswald and Chesters.[543]

Rhiannon

Name	Great Queen or Maiden of the Otherworld
Place of Origin	Wales
Place of Worship	Wales
Literary References	Red Book of Hergest, White Book of Rhydderch

The name Rhiannon is usually considered as being derived from Rigatona, meaning *"Great Queen"*, which is also one of the translations of Morrígan. It has been suggested however that her name may be derived from the Welsh words *"rhian"* and *"annwn"*, which would give a translation of *"Maiden of the Otherworld"*.[544]

A number of scholars have taken the view that Rhiannon is a counterpart horse goddess of Macha,[545] and also Epona. Rhiannon had a white horse that

---

543 RIB 1454, 1903.
544 See Celtic Gods, Green, 1995, p50.
545 See particularly Epona-Rhiannon-Macha, Jean Gricourt, in Ogam 31:25-40, 137-8; 32:75-86; 34:165-88; 36:269-72, 1954; and Macha and Conall Cernach: A Study of Two Iconographic

could outrun any horse without even breaking sweat, and subsequently had to take the role of a horse carrying people as punishment for the crime of killing her son that she did not commit.[546]

The birds of Rhiannon were able to wake the dead and cause the living to sleep,[547] suggesting she may have been a psychopomp. Rhiannon is also a sovereignty goddess associated with the faery. In the tale *Pwyll Prince of Dyved*[548] her faery association is indicated both by her being initially seen on a mound (faery dwelling) and also riding a pure white horse indicating her divine and regal status. Both these characteristics associate her with the land.

Another association with the land is the bag she gives Pwyll that he fills with food but is never full. This is akin to a reverse cornucopia or horn of plenty. After their union Rhiannon gives away a huge quantity of rich gifts to all who ask, indicating her bountiful nature as a sovereignty goddess.

After Pwyll's death, Rhiannon marries the God of Wisdom and the sea, Manawyddan. She is subsequently turned into an ass by Llwyd to avenge his friend's son for the harm done to him by Pwyll. Manawyddan outwits Llwyd and Rhiannon is restored to human form, but once again we see the horse attribution to her in this story.[549]

Ricagumbeda

Name	Heavenly Battle Grave?
Known Period of Worship	2nd-5th century CE
Place of Origin	Northumberland
Place of Worship	Northumberland

Patterns in Medieval Irish Narratives and Celtic Art, Paula Powers Coe, 1995, p95-99 and 120-33.
546 Pwyll Prince of Dyved in the White Book of Rhydderch.
547 See Branwen the Daughter of Llyr in the White Book of Rhydderch.
548 In the White Book of Rhydderch.
549 See Manawyddan the Son of Llyr in the White Book of Rhydderch.

Ricagumbeda is a goddess whose name may mean *"Heavenly Battle Grave"*. There is an inscription to her at Birrens, but nothing else is known of her.[550]

Rider God

Name	Generic term for Unnamed God
Known Period of Worship	1st-5th century CE?
Place of Origin	Unknown
Place of Worship	Across Britain

The Rider God is a name given to figures of a mounted warrior on horseback. It has been suggested that this was the synthesis of Mars with a native god, whose name was lost. The frequency of horse and rider brooches found in Britain (thirty-five to date) suggests he was a popular figure, probably with the Roman legionnaires.[551] Three engraved gems dating from 1st-3rd century CE also bear the same image.[552]

He did not only occur on brooches, an image, from Kingscote (Oxfordshire), shows a mounted helmeted warrior with shield (the Rider God) with an enthroned goddess, behind who stands an attendant.[553]

Rigisamus

Name	Most Kingly
Known Period of Worship	2nd-5th century CE
Place of Origin	Gaul
Place of Worship	Somerset

Rigisamus is a Gallic war deity whose worship was brought to Britain. His name means *"Most Kingly"*, and he was equated with Mars by the Romans, as

---

550 RIB 2107.
551 The Jewellery of Roman Britain, Jones, 1996, p174.
552 A Corpus of Roman Engraved Gemstones in the British Isles, Henig, p251.
553 Ashmolean Museum Report, 1955, p30 plate iv.

shown by an inscription on a bronze plaque found at West Coker (Somerset).[554]

Rigonemetis

Name	King of the Sacred Grove
Known Period of Worship	2nd-5th century CE
Place of Origin	Lincolnshire?
Place of Worship	Lincolnshire

Rigonemetis means *"King of the Sacred Grove"*. A dedication slab to the god Mars Rigonemetis was found at Nettleham (Lincolnshire), so this may have been a local god conflated with Mars, or a title used for Mars. It is more likely to be the former, as it refers to the sacred grove, a Celtic concept, and is highly reminiscent of the goddess Nemetona.

Roma

Name	Rome
Known Period of Worship	1st-5th century CE
Place of Origin	Rome
Place of Worship	Cumbria, Northumberland
Other Names	Aeternae

Roma is the tutelary goddess of Rome. She was usually depicted as a seated goddess in a short tunic. Her main representation is on coins, though a number of gems depicting her and dating to 1st-3rd century CE have been found in Britain, at York, Colchester (Essex), Cirencester and Silchester (Hampshire).

Four of these depict her, and a fifth shows her as a wolf with the twins Romulus and Remus.[555] An unnamed damaged statue (missing the head)

---

554 RIB 187.
555 A Corpus of Roman Engraved Gemstones from British Sites (vol 2), Henig, 1974, p38, 69.

from Well (Yorkshire) may represent Roma, as she bears a breast (indicating it was not a man) and bears a wreath.

Three other engraved gems of Roma have been found in Britain.[556] In all of them she is seated on a cuirass, with a shield behind her, bearing a patera or sceptre (twice).

Two inscriptions to Roma have been found at Maryport (Cumbria), both with Fortuna,[557] and a third inscription at High Rochester (Northumberland).[558] Another inscription to Aeternae (*"Eternity"*), a common title of Roma, which is also seen in one of the Maryport inscriptions, was found at Old Carlisle.[559]

Rosmerta

Name	Great Provider
Known Period of Worship	BCE-5th century CE?
Place of Origin	Germany
Place of Worship	Somerset, Northumberland, Gloucestershire

Rosmerta is a German deity who was imported into Britain, whose name means *"Great Provider"*. Depictions show her connected with wealth and plentitude, as shown by her cornucopia and bag of coins in the images of her, indicating a fertility or earth goddess. Representations of Rosmerta at Bath and continental healing water sites suggest she may also have been viewed as a healing goddess.

In British images she was commonly paired with Mercury,[560] and also in at least two images with the genii cucullati. Images of her also occur with what look like buckets,[561] which may hint at a water connection, or be symbolic

---

556 A Corpus of Roman Engraved Gemstones from British Sites (vol 2), Henig, 1974, p38.
557 RIB 812, 840.
558 RIB 1270.
559 RIB 886.
560 See e.g. images from Gloucester, Bath and Wellow (in Somerset).
561 At Bath and Gloucester.

cauldrons, or as has been suggested, represent cheese or butter making.[562] An unnamed image from Corbridge (Northumberland) shows a goddess stirring a vat with a ladle. If the symbolism were a dairy one, then this might also represent Rosmerta.

---

[562] By Miranda Green in Celtic Goddesses, 1995; G. Webster in British Gods and Their Worship Under Rome, 1985, and H.R. Davidson in Milk and the Northern Goddess in The Concept of the Goddess, 1993.

S

Sabrina

Name	Fast River?
Known Period of Worship	1st-th century CE
Place of Origin	Severn Estuary
Place of Worship	Severn Estuary
Literary References	Brut, Historia Britonum

Sabrina is a river goddess after whom the river Severn is named in the first century CE by Tacitus in his *Annals* and Ptolemy in his third century CE work *Geography*. Her name is also clearly related to the river name Sabraind as one of the two principal rivers of Britain in the *Historia Britonum* of Nennius.[563]

The name Sabrina is thought to be derived from Habrena, which may come from the roots *abon* meaning *"river"* and *renwo* meaning *"fast"*, giving a meaning of *"Fast River"*. In *Brut* the river is named after the princess who is thrown into the river and drowns with her mother. Another version of the tale says the Severn was named after a Welsh nymph called Hafren (note the similarity of name to Habrena).

Saitada

Name	Saturation? / Goddess of the Throng?
Known Period of Worship	2nd-5th century CE
Place of Origin	Tyne Valley
Place of Worship	Tyne Valley
Other Names	Sattade

---

[563] Historia Britonum, 31.

Saitada (or Sattade) is a goddess mentioned in connection with the Tyne Valley,[564] whose name may be connected with the root *sati* meaning *"throng"*. It has also been suggested her name means *"Saturation"*, suggesting she could be a local water goddess.

Salus

Name	Salvation
Known Period of Worship	BCE?-5th century CE
Place of Origin	Rome
Place of Worship	Co. Durham, Monmouthshire, Northumberland

Salus is a Roman goddess whose name means *"Salvation"*. Altars to her have been at Binchester (Co. Durham), Caerleon (Monmouthshire), Chester, Corbridge (Northumberland), and Ribchester, and five inscriptions have been found. Two of these associate her with Aesculapius, one with Jupiter Dolichenus and the other calls her Regina (*"Queen"*).[565]

Two engraved gems of her, both with a serpent (her cult animal), have been found, at Brecon (Monmouthshire) and Chester.[566] The Brecon image dates to 1st century CE, but interestingly the Chester image of her on a throne dates to 3rd-1st century BCE, so it was either an antique or came with Caesar in his first sally to Britain.

Saturn

Name	Sower
Known Period of Worship	2nd-5th century CE
Place of Origin	Rome
Place of Worship	Northumberland

---

564 RIB 1695.
565 RIB 324, 445, 590, 1028, 1131.
566 A Corpus of Roman Engraved Gemstones in the British Isles, Henig, p220.

Saturn is the Roman god who ruled the Golden Age of Mankind and ruled over seeds sowing, as seen by the meaning of his name as *"Sower"*. He fathered Jupiter and was overthrown by him. He was equated to the Greek Cronos, the associated myths then being transferred to him. Two inscriptions to him have been found in Northumberland[567]

Scáthach

Name	Shadowy One
Place of Origin	Ireland
Place of Worship	Ireland
Literary References	Tochmarc Émire, Verba Scáthaige

Scáthach is an Irish war goddess who trains the hero Cú Chulainn. Her name means *"The Shadowy One"*, and she had a daughter called Úathach, meaning *"spectre"*. Scáthach lived on an otherworldly island called Dún Scaith (the island of Skye) which could only be reached across a bridge called Droichet na ndaltae (*"the Bridge of the Fosterling"*), after a difficult journey.

Scáthach's ability as a warrior and her ability to prophesy are clear indicators of an Irish war goddess. Her prophecy to Cú Chulainn in *Verba Scáthaige* before he leaves is one of the major predictions of the whole myth cycle. Scáthach taught Cú Chulainn the arts of the warrior, including the mighty salmon leap, and the use of the deadly Gae Bolga spear, which was thrown with the feet

The triple motifs which abound in this Cú Chulainn's encounter with her also emphasise her sacred nature. After three days Úathach tells Cú Chulainn the three demands he must make of Scáthach. During his time with Scáthach, Cú Chulainn fights the warrior woman Aífe. He bests her and makes three demands of her: that she gives hostages to Scáthach, that she spend the night with him, and that she bears him a son. She agrees and does all three.[568]

---

567 RIB 1432, 2330.
568 Tochmarc Émire.

Seaxnéat

Name	Sword God or Friend of the Saxons?
Known Period of Worship	Pre-7th century CE
Place of Origin	Unknown
Place of Worship	Essex
Other Names	Saxnot

Seaxnéat is a Saxon god whose name may mean *"Sword God"* or *"Friend of the Saxons"*. Like Woden he was described as being the ancestor of royal lines, in the genealogies of Essex. Little is known about Seaxnéat, apart from the fact that he was one of the gods the continental Saxons were forced to renounce for Christianity.

Segomo

Name	Victor or Mighty One?
Known Period of Worship	2nd-6th century CE
Place of Origin	Gaul
Place of Worship	Co. Waterford, Cumbria

Segomo is a war god connected to horses and associated with Mars, whose name means *"Victor"* or *"Mighty One"*. Two ogham inscriptions in Co. Waterford in Ireland and a statue from Maryport (Cumbria) in northern Britain demonstrate that worship of this Gallic war god spread across the English Channel.[569]

Serapis

Name	Merging of Osiris and Apis
Known Period of Worship	1st-5th century CE
Place of Origin	Greece
Place of Worship	Hampshire, London, Monmouthshire, Yorkshire
Other Names	Sarapis

---

[569] See Pagan Celtic Britain, Anne Ross, 1968, p172-73.

Serapis (or Sarapis) is a Greek god who was formed by merging the Egyptian god Osiris with the divine Apis bull, to form a new and poplar consort for the goddess Isis. His name was also created by the merging of these two gods, the *"sir"* from Osiris being placed before Apis. He would probably have been venerated at the London Iseum, and he had a temple of his own in York.

He was widely worshipped as a god of merchants, and fragments dedicated to him have been found in civilian sites at Silchester (Hampshire) and Caerwent.[570] Six engraved gems to Jupiter Sarapis dating to 2nd-3rd century CE have been found in Britain, three busts, and three bearing a sceptre, and in one instance a patera as well.[571]

Setlocenia

Name	She of the Long Life
Known Period of Worship	2nd-5th century CE
Place of Origin	Cumbria?
Place of Worship	Cumbria

A dedication from Maryport (Cumbria) refers to Setlocenia,[572] whose name means *"She of the Long Life"*. An unnamed relief at the same site shows a goddess bearing a vessel in her hand, which may be her. If so this could suggest a bountiful role, with her carrying a vessel of plenty, which fits with the meaning of her name.

Silvanus

Name	God of the Woods
Known Period of Worship	1st-5th century CE
Place of Origin	Rome
Place of Worship	England

---

570 RIB 658, 762.
571 A Corpus of Roman Engraved Gemstones from British Sites (vol 2), Henig, 1974, p51.
572 RIB 841.

Silvanus is the Roman forest god, derived from the Greek god Silenus. His name means *"God of the Woods"*. Twenty-nine inscriptions to him have been found all over Britain, some in southern England but with the majority in the north around Hadrian's Wall.[573] He was often conflated with indigenous deities, and was also referred to as Invictus (*"Unconquerable"*).

He appears on two engraved gems, found at Corbridge (Northumberland) and Colbin Sands (Morayshire), both of the same design and dating to the second or third century CE, showing him bearded and diademed in a short tunic with hunting boots, with a knife and branch, accompanied by hound.[574]

Six engraved gems to his Greek form of Silenus have also been found dating to the 2nd-3rd century CE. All of these are double-headed, with his head and another god or animal. There are two with Minerva, one with Pan, one duplicate (recalling Janus), one with an elephant and one with a cock.[575]

Sionna

Name	Fox
Place of Origin	Ireland
Place of Worship	Ireland

Sionna was an Irish river goddess, after whom the river Shannon is named. The name Sionna means *"fox"* and has subsequently been Anglicized into this name from the surname O'Sionna. She was a granddaughter of Mannanan, and local folklore tells how she sought to gather hazel nuts from the nine hazel trees of wisdom that surrounded the well of knowledge. As she reached for the nuts she fell into the pool, which rose up and carried her to the sea, giving birth to the river which carries her name.

---

573 RIB 104, 181, 194-95, 303, 659, 732, 763, 796, 798, 923-24, 972, 1136, 1041-42, 1085, 1207, 1271, 1321, 1578, 1696, 1790, 1870, 1905, 2124, 2167, 2178, 2187.
574 A Corpus of Roman Engraved Gemstones from British Sites (vol 2), Henig, 1974, p10-20.
575 A Corpus of Roman Engraved Gemstones in the British Isles, Henig, p232-3.

Sol Invictus

Name	Conquering Sun
Known Period of Worship	1st-5th century CE
Place of Origin	Rome
Place of Worship	London, Northumberland

Sol Invictus, the *"Conquering Sun"*, was established as a major Roman god by the Emperor Aurelian in the mid third century CE. Depictions have been found at Corbridge (Northumberland) and London. On inscriptions he is often linked with Mithras, as seen in six of the thirteen inscriptions found in Britain.[576]

Images on ring gems often show him with a whip in hand (four out of seven intaglios), which was a cult object used to drive his chariot. He is shown mounted once and on a chariot twice. All the gems date to the 1st-3rd century CE[577]

Soter

Name	Saviour
Known Period of Worship	2nd-5th century CE
Place of Origin	Greece
Place of Worship	Cheshire

Soter is a Greek daimon (spirit) associated with the god Zeus. His name means *"Saviour"*, and is often used as a title for Zeus and sometimes for over deities. He is associated with safety and protection from harm. There is an inscription in Greek to him at Chester.[578]

---

[576] RIB 4, 465, 1082, 1101, 1272, 1396-97, 1599-1601, 1992-94.
[577] A Corpus of Roman Engraved Gemstones from British Sites (vol 2), Henig, 1974, p11-13.
[578] RIB 461.

Spes

Name	Hope
Known Period of Worship	1st-2nd century CE?
Place of Origin	Rome

Spes is a Roman goddess of Hope (the meaning of her name), known as *"the last goddess"*, as hope was the last resort of man. Two engraved gems of her have been found dating to 1st-2nd century CE, both showing her holding a fold in her skirt with her left hand and a flower in her right hand. The gems were discovered in Cirencester (Gloucestershire) and Weston-under-Penyard (Hertfordshire).[579]

Sucellos

Name	The Good Striker
Known Period of Worship	BCE-5th century CE
Place of Origin	Gaul
Place of Worship	Across England
Other Names	Sucelus, Sucellus

Sucellos (or Sucelus or Sucellus) is a Gallic hammer god whose name means *"the Good Striker"*. A relief from Thorpe (Nottinghamshire) shows Sucellos and Nantosuelta, and a silver ring from York also bears an inscription to him.

Apart from his hammer, Sucellos was often depicted with a patera, indicating a bountiful aspect as an earth god. He was partnered with Nantosuelta, and the couple were often depicted together in continental images. The Romans equated Sucellos with Silvanus, and in the Moselle region of France he was the god of the vine as well.

Although his worship was an import, there are signs he was worshipped in different parts of Britain. A crude relief of a figure bearing a hammer from

---

[579] A Corpus of Roman Engraved Gemstones in the British Isles, Henig, p227.

Chedworth (Gloucestershire) and a matchstick figure with long-handled hammer on a sceptre binding from Farley Heath (Surrey) may also represent his worship.[580]

Sulis

Name	Eye Goddess or Goddess of the Gap
Known Period of Worship	BCE-5th century CE
Place of Origin	Bath
Place of Worship	Essex, Gloucestershire, Somerset
Other Names	Sul

Sulis is the tutelary goddess of the Bath springs, whose name may be derived from the Irish and Gaelic word *"suil"* meaning *"eye"* or *"hole"*, giving a probable meaning of *"Eye Goddess"* or *"Goddess of the Gap"*. The Romans identified her with Minerva as Sulis Minerva, and named the city after her, calling it Aquae Sulis, referring to the healing hot spa waters there.[581] The large number of votive offerings found at Bath (over twelve thousand coins) attest to the popularity of this cult centre.

There were also one hundred and thirty lead and pewter curse tablets (defixiones) retrieved from the site, showing that Sulis Minerva was being invoked as an avenging goddess to right wrongs as well.

The city of Bath revealed a triple form of Sulis, called the Suleviae, and dedications to them were also found at Cirencester, Colchester (Essex)[582] and in Gaul. The worship of Sulis was very popular and spread as far as Hesse in Germany.

---

580 The Gods of Roman Britain, Green, 1983, p58-9.
581 RIB 141, 143-150, 155.
582 RIB 105-6, 151, 192, 1035.

T

Tailtiu

Name	The Great One of Earth?
Place of Origin	Ireland
Place of Worship	Ireland
Literary References	Banshenchus, Dinshenchas

Tailtiu is the Fomorian foster-mother of Lugh, in whose honour he was said to have founded the feast of Lughnasadh (1st August) after her death, and which was also known as the Fair of Tailtiu.[583] Her husband Eochaid Garb caused the wood of Cuan to be chopped down in her honour, which was done in a month, leaving the plain called Oenach Tailten.[584] It has been suggested that her name may mean *"The Great One of Earth"*, though this is not as yet substantiated.

Taranis

Name	The Thunderer
Known Period of Worship	1st-5th century CE
Place of Origin	Gaul
Place of Worship	Cambridgeshire, Scotland
Other Names	Taramis
Literary References	The Gallic Wars (Caesar), Pharsalia (Lucan)

Taranis (or Taramis) is one of the main Gallic gods, whose name means *"The Thunderer"*. He is one of the three gods referred to by Caesar as being the

---

[583] Rennes Dinshenchas.
[584] Rennes Dinshenchas, Banshenchus.

major gods on the continent,[585] and is also mentioned by Lucan.[586] The Romans equated him primarily with Jupiter, and sometimes with Mars.

There is only one inscription to him in Britain, in Scotland.[587] On the other side of the stone bearing the inscription is a carving of a goose, so this may have been connected with him as a sacred animal. Continental images show the eagle connected with him, which may come from the Roman connection to Jupiter. However this then leads us to believe the sceptre found at Willingham Fen (Cambridgeshire) of a god bearing lightning trampling a figure underfoot with an eagle perched on a wheel may also represent Taranis.

Taranis was often depicted with a wheel, which could indicate that he may be the unnamed Wheel God depicted on many images.

Although there are no traces of Taranis in Wales, we may note that in the tale of Branwen the Daughter of Llyr,[588] one of the seven survivors of the final battle who returned with the head of Bran was Gluneu eil Taran, and Taran is Welsh for *"thunder"* so this could be a faint trace of earlier lost literary references.

Tethys

Name	Grandmother or Nurse
Known Period of Worship	2nd-5th century CE
Place of Origin	Greece
Place of Worship	Yorkshire

Tethys is a Greek Titan sea goddess, a daughter of Gaia and Ouranos, whose name means *"Grandmother"* or *"Nurse"*. With her brother Oceanus she gave

---

585 The Gallic Wars.
586 E.g. Pharsalia 1.444-6.
587 RIB 2335.
588 In the White Book of Rhydderch.

birth to the rivers of the world and the Oceanid nymphs. She is referred to with Oceanus in an inscription in Greek found at York.[589]

Terminus

Name	Boundary or End
Known Period of Worship	2nd-5th century CE?
Place of Origin	Rome
Place of Worship	Monmouthshire

Terminus is the old Roman god of boundaries, celebrated at his festival of Terminalia on February 23rd. His name means *"boundary"* or *"end"*. A boundary stone inscribed to him was found at Caerleon (Monmouthshire).[590]

Teutates

Name	Ruler of the People
Known Period of Worship	1st-5th century CE
Place of Origin	Gaul
Place of Worship	Throughout England
Other Names	Totatis, Toutates
Literary References	Berne Scholiasts on Lucan, Pharsalia (Lucan)

Teutates is a war god whose name means *"Ruler of the People"*. Votive silver plaques and rings have been found in southern and northern England to Teutates,[591] who the Romans equated with Apollo and Mars.[592] Though he was worshipped more prominently in Gaul, his worship was widespread in Britain, as evidenced by inscriptions in Chesterton, plaques at Barkway (Hertfordshire) and silver rings in York.

Variants of his name include Toutates and Totatis. The Roman writer Lucan

---

589 RIB 663.
590 RIB 325.
591 RIB 219, 1017.
592 The Berne Scholiasts on Lucan equate Teutates with Mars as a war god.

describes Teutates as being one of the triumvirate of gods to whom human sacrifice was practiced, along with Esus and Taranis.[593]

Thoth

Name	Leader
Known Period of Worship	2nd-5th century CE?
Place of Origin	Egypt
Place of Worship	Monmouthshire, Surrey
Other Names	Jahuti

Thoth is the Egyptian ibis-headed god of magick and writing, whose name means *"Leader"*. His worship has been suggested by bronze ibis heads at Chiddingfold (Surrey) and Caerwent (Monmouthshire), indicating his worship found its way to Britain, if only in private villas.

Thunor

Name	Thunder
Known Period of Worship	4th-7th century CE?
Place of Origin	Germany
Place of Worship	Throughout Southern England
Other Names	Thor

Thunor is a Saxon thunder god and fertility, and his name means *"Thunder"*. He was the son of Woden and Frigg. He is clearly equated to the Norse Thor, from whom he derives his characteristics. Oak trees were particularly sacred to him, and he was known as the *"Lord of the Blasted Oak"*.

Thunor bore the same characteristics as Thor, a red-bearded giant carrying a hammer, worshipped by farmers and warriors alike. He replaced Tiw as the god of troth, with oaths being sworn on a hammer which symbolised Thunor's famous hammer, Mjollnir. Although it is now a common pendant, the upside-down hammer pendant did not come into use until the tenth

---

593 Lucan I.444-446.

century CE in Scandinavia and there is no evidence to suggest it was worn in Britain during the first millennium.[594]

Thursday takes its name from Thunor, from the Old English Thunres-dæg. Various place names were derived from his name, including Thunderfield and Thunorslege (Sussex), Thundridge (Hertfordshire), Thunoreshlaw (Kent), Thunresfeld (Wiltshire), and Thundersley, or Thunor's sacred grove (Essex).

Tiw

Name	God
Known Period of Worship	2nd-7th century CE?
Place of Origin	Germany
Place of Worship	Southern England
Other Names	Tiwaz, Tyr
Literary References	Rune Poem

Tiw (from the Norse Tyr) is the Saxon god who was protector of judicial assemblies, best known for his courage and honest nature. His name simply means "God". Tuesday is named after him, from the Old English Tiwes-daeg.

There are a number of place names scattered around England which derive from Tiw. These include Tuesley (Surrey) and Tysoe (Warwickshire) and the old place names of Tyesmere (Worcestershire) and Tislea (Hampshire).

He was originally a sky god, as is seen by the stanza dedicated to the rune Tir in the *Rune Poem*, which is his rune:

> "Tiw is a guiding mark. He keeps trust with all men, is ever on his path above the night's mists and never fails."[595]

---

594 See Anglo-Saxon Amulets and Curing Stones, Meaney, 1981.
595 Rune Poem, stanza 17, trans. Tony Linsell in Anglo-Saxon Mythology, Migration and Magic.

Two Roman inscriptions to Mars Thincsus at Hadrian's Wall indicate that the Romans equated Tiw (or Tiwaz) with Mars as a god of battle and law assembly.[596]

Tridamus

Name	Triple Bovine?
Known Period of Worship	2nd-5th century CE?
Place of Origin	Herefordshire?
Place of Worship	Herefordshire

Tridamus is an unknown god referred to in an inscription at Michaelchurch (Herefordshire).[597] The meaning of his name is unknown but may mean *"triple bovine"*, which could refer to the triple-horned bull.

Tyche

Name	Luck or Fortune
Place of Origin	Greece
Place of Worship	Norfolk?

Tyche is a Greek goddess of fortune whose name means *"Luck"* or *"Fortune"*. She was the daughter of Zeus and Hera, equated by the Romans with their goddess Fortuna. A fourth century CE ring with a dark chalcedony gem depicting Tyche was found in the Thetford hoard. This may simply have been an item of personal jewellery, as there is no other evidence for her worship in Britain.

---

596 RIB 1593.
597 RIB 304.

V

Vanuntus

Name	Unknown
Known Period of Worship	2nd-5th century CE?
Place of Origin	Cumbria?
Place of Worship	Cumbria

Vanuntus is an unknown British god to whom an inscription has been found at Castlesteads (Cumbria).[598]

Venus

Name	Love, Beauty or Sexual Desire?
Known Period of Worship	1st-5th century CE
Place of Origin	Rome
Place of Worship	Across England

Venus is the Roman goddess of love and gardens, who became associated with the Greek love goddess Aphrodite. Her name may mean *"love"*, *"beauty"* or *"sexual desire"*. Ten engraved gems of her have been found dating to 1st-3rd century CE, six as Venus Victrix (*"Victorious"*) bearing a shield or helmet (five times).[599]

---

[598] RIB 1991.
[599] A Corpus of Roman Engraved Gemstones from British Sites (vol 2), Henig, 1974, p41-2, 104.

Verbeia

Name	Winding River
Known Period of Worship	BCE-5th century CE
Place of Origin	Yorkshire
Place of Worship	Yorkshire

Verbeia is a goddess from northern England, whose name means *"Winding River"*. She is thought to be connected with the river Wharfe (in Yorkshire) both in the derivation of her name, and as a goddess of the waters. A carving of her shows her with a large head and serpents in both hand, and a single inscription to her.[600]

Vernostonus

Name	Alder's Groan?
Known Period of Worship	3rd-5th century CE?
Place of Origin	Co. Durham
Place of Worship	Co. Durham

Vernostonus is mentioned in one inscription at Ebchester (Co. Durham), which connects this god to another native god, Cocidius.[601] It has been suggested that his name may be derived from the words *werno* meaning *"alder"* and *stono* meaning *"groan"*, thus giving *"alder's groan"*.

Victoria

Name	Victory
Known Period of Worship	1st-5th century CE
Place of Origin	Rome
Place of Worship	Across England

---

600 RIB 635.
601 RIB 1102.

Victoria is the Roman goddess who personifies the meaning of her name, *"Victory"*. She was usually depicted as a winged maiden bearing a palm branch and a wreath. Images of her have been found in reliefs from Maryport (Cumbria) and Risingham (Cambridgeshire), and on a bronze tablet from Colchester (Essex).

Twenty-seven inscriptions have been found in Britain, mainly in the vicinity of Hadrian's Wall, of which eight are with Mars, one with Minerva and two with Brigantia.[602]

Twenty engraved gems have been found depicting her, dating from 1st-4th century CE.[603] In three she drives a chariot, in five she is walking holding a wreath and palm, in five she stands on a globe, and in two on a rudder.

Vinotonus

Name	God of the Vines?
Known Period of Worship	BCE-5th century CE?
Place of Origin	Yorkshire
Place of Worship	Yorkshire

Seven altars to the British god Vinotonus, whose name may mean *"God of the Vines"*, have been found on the Yorkshire Moors.[604] The Romans equated him with Silvanus as a wilderness god.

Viradecthis

Name	She who honours Truth?
Known Period of Worship	2nd-5th century CE
Place of Origin	Germany?
Place of Worship	Northumberland

---

602 RIB 191, 582, 585, 590, 627-28, 779, 842-44, 950, 964b, 1086, 1138, 1273, 1316, 1337, 1595-96, 1731, 1899, 1954, 1995, 2100, 2144, 2176-77.
603 A Corpus of Roman Engraved Gemstones from British Sites (vol 2), Henig, 1974, p43-6.
604 RIB 732, 733, 737 and possibly 734-36.

Viradecthis is an obscure (possibly Germanic) goddess, the meaning of whose name is uncertain. The name may be derived from the words *wiro* meaning *"truth"* and *dekos* meaning *"honour"*, giving a possible meaning of something like *"She who honours truth"*.

An inscription to her was found at Birrens set up by the Condrusi, a Germanic tribe serving in the Roman army.[605]

Viridios

Name	Virile or Manly?
Known Period of Worship	2nd-5th century CE
Place of Origin	Lincolnshire?
Place of Worship	Lincolnshire
Other Names	Viridius

Viridios (or Viridius) is an obscure British god whose name may mean *"Virile"* or *"Manly"*. A head bearing the dedication was found at Ancaster (Lincolnshire).[606]

Vitiris

Name	Shining? / Wise One?
Known Period of Worship	BCE-5th century CE
Place of Origin	Northern England?
Place of Worship	Northern England and Scotland
Other Names	Veter, Veteris, Vetiris, Vetus, Vheteris, Vicres, Viteris, Vitris, Vitires, Votris, Hueteris, Huetiris, Huiteres, Huitires and Huitris

Vitiris is a bull-horned god who was worshipped in northern England and into Scotland. The meaning of the name of this horned god is unknown, and it is spelt in a number of ways.

---

605 RIB 2108.
606 RIB 245.

It has been suggested that the name may stem from the old Nordic root *"hvitr"*, meaning *"shining"* or *"white"*, which might hint at solar connections.[607] Alternatively if it came from the root *witsu* meaning *"knowing"* it could suggest a meaning of something like *"Wise One"*. Another suggestion is that this name refers to a god type, like the Mothers and Nymphs, rather than a specific deity.[608]

Around forty altars to him have been found, showing his significance, and he was invoked both singly and as a triple deity.[609] Among the altars there were a number of phallic representations, indicating fertility, which the Romans equated with Silvanus, and also a number of warrior depictions (i.e. armed) which were equated with Mars.

Some of the altars to him are decorated with serpents and boars, suggesting these may have been cult animals for him. With the bull horns and serpents motifs, it is possible the Meigle relief may be a late representation of Vitiris.

Vulcan

Name	Fire or Fiery Mountain
Known Period of Worship	2nd-5th century CE
Place of Origin	Rome
Place of Worship	Northern England
Other Names	Volcanus

Vulcan (or Volcanus) is the Roman smith god who lived under Mount Etna, celebrated at the festival of Vulcanalia on August 23rd. His name may be translated as *"fire"* or *"fiery mountain"*, appropriate for a god said to live under a volcano (Mount Etna). A number of inscriptions to him have been found, all in the north of England.[610]

---

607 See e.g. The People of Roman Britain, A Birley, 1979, p107-8 and Haverfield in Archaeologia Aeliana 3.15, 1918.
608 Pagan Celtic Britain, Ross, 1967, p375.
609 RIB 660, 727, 925, 971, 973, 1046-8, 1070, 1087, 1088, 1103, 1104, 1139-41, 1335, 1336, 1455-58, 1548, 1549, 1602-07, 1697-99, 1722, 1728-30, 1793-1805, 2068, 2069.
610 RIB 215, 220, 846, 899, 1700.

W

Weland

Known Period of Worship	3rd-7th century CE?
Place of Origin	Germany
Place of Worship	Berkshire, Oxfordshire
Other Names	Volundr, Welund, Weyland, Wieland
Literary References	Beowulf, Deor, Waldere

Weland is the lame Saxon smith god equated with the German Wieland and Norse Volundr. He is also known as Weyland or Welund, and he is now best known for the burial chamber of Weyland's Smithy in Oxfordshire.

Local folklore said that if you left a horse there overnight with a silver coin, Weyland would shoe the horse, and you would find it newly shod in the morning. Sir Walter Scott wrote of this, saying,

"Here lived a supernatural smith, who would shoe a traveller's horse for a 'consideration.' His fee was sixpence, and if more was offered him he was offended."

Weland is mentioned in the Old English tale of *Beowulf* as the smith who makes a magickal coat of chain mail for King Hrethel of the Geats,[611] and in *Waldere* as the maker of Mimming, a special magickal sword.[612] The poem *Deor* refers to Weland as one who understood the meaning of suffering and alienation, indicating the stigma attached to his disability, as a lame god.[613]

---

611 Beowulf, 455.
612 "Surely Welund's work does not betray any man who can hold Mimming hard.", Waldere, 2-3.
613 The Exeter Book, p100a.

"Welund, entramelled, understood wrack. He, stubborn eorl, suffered privation"[614]

He was the son of the giant Wade,[615] and brother of the archer Aegil, and was himself a giant, as indicated by reference to him wading through water nine yards deep. There is also reference to a son of Weland called Widia in Waldere.[616] There is a Wayland Smith's Cave near Lambourn in Berkshire. Weland is depicted on one of the sides of the Franks casket, working in his smithy.

Wheel God

Name	Generic term for Unnamed God
Known Period of Worship	BCE-5th century CE
Place of Worship	Across England

A number of images, sometimes with other deities, show a male figure holding a six-spoked wheel. This figure is known as the Wheel God as there is no specific nomenclature associated with him, though it has been suggested that he is the European god Taranis, who was sometimes depicted with a wheel.[617] Jupiter too was also shown at times depicted with a wheel, and the association of the eagle to a number of the images also supports this possibility.

As well as the wheel, he is also shown at times bearing a cornucopia, or with animals such as the boar or eagle, suggesting fertility. A collection of small bronze boars with small votive wheels was found in Hounslow (Middlesex) further strengthening this association. We should also note that the eagle was a solar symbol, as was the sun disk or wheel itself, indicating the Wheel God may well have been a solar or sky deity.

---

614 Deor, 1-2.
615 Also mentioned in Widsith in the Exeter Book.
616 Waldere, II.8.
617 See The Worship of the Romano-Celtic Wheel God in Britain, M. Green, in *Latomus* 38.2:345-67.

A mould of an armoured wheel god with club was found at Cambridge. Bronzes from Willingham and Cottenham suggest there was a shrine to the wheel god on the edge of the fens in Cambridgeshire.[618]

Woden

Name	See below
Known Period of Worship	4th-7th century CE?
Place of Origin	Germany
Place of Worship	Southern England
Other Names	Wodan, Wotan
Literary References	Maxims I in the Exeter Book, Lacnunga, Rune Poem, The Ecclesiastical History of the English Nation

Woden (or Wodan or Wotan) was the Saxon god of wisdom and the dead derived from the Norse Odin. His name may be derived from the old English word *"Wod"* meaning both *"Fury"*, *"Frenzy"* or *"Intoxication"* or *"Wop"* meaning *"Song"*, *"Voice"* or *"Prophecy"*. In Old English poetry he is associated with Mercury, taking on the guileful qualities linked with that god.[619] Wednesday is named after him, from the Old English Wodnes-dæg.

Woden was associated with the Wild Hunt, or *"loud riders"* as they were known, leading it under his names of Grim and Herian (*"army leader"*). Woden shares most of the characteristics of his Norse alter-ego, so the wolf and raven are both associated with him. Considering the Wild Hunt rode horses, and Woden's own legendary eight-legged horse Sleipnir, it may be suggested that he also had an aspect as a horse god.

Saxon kings claimed direct descent from Woden, emphasising their divine right to be ruler, and he is listed in some early royal genealogies as the progenitor of some of the lines of English kings. Thus we see in Bede,

---

618 Religious Cults at Roman Godmanchester, H.J.M. Green, 1986, in Pagan Gods and Shrines of the Roman Empire, p39.
619 See the poem published in Solomon and Saturn, Kemble.

"Woden, from whose stock the royal race of many provinces deduce their original."[620]

The Anglo-Saxon *Rune Poem* contains reference to Woden. The stanza for the rune Os starts *"A god is the origin of all speech"*, referring to Woden and his gaining the knowledge of the runes.[621]

One of the two references to Woden in old literature outside of royal genealogies and the *Rune Poem* is in the Anglo-Saxon *Nine Herb Charm*.[622] In the charm it says: *"when Woden took nine glory twigs and struck the adder so that it flew into nine pieces."* The glory-twigs seems to be a reference to carved rune staves, which fits with the nine days that Woden (Odin) hung on the world tree Yggdrasill to gain knowledge.

Five lines later there is an ambiguous line, which could refer to Christ or to Woden. Considering the previous reference it seems likely that it is Woden being referred to in the line, *"those herbs the wise Lord created, holy in the heavens, when he was hanging."*

The other literary reference is in the poem *Maxims I*, where he is unfavourably compared to the Christian God: *"Woden made idols, glory made the Almighty."*

The worship of Woden was most prevalent in southern England, as witnessed by place names derived from is name. Thus we see Wansdyke, Woddesgeat, Wodnesbeorg and Wodnesdene in Wiltshire; Wednesbury and Wednesfield in Staffordshire; Wodnesfeld in Essex; Wodneslawe in Bedfordshire, Woodnesborough in Kent, and Wensley in Derbyshire.

---

[620] The Ecclesiastical History of the English Nation, ch. 15.36.
[621] Rune Poem, stanza 4, trans. Tony Linsell in Anglo-Saxon Mythology, Migration and Magic.
[622] Harley MS 585, c. 1000 CE.

Appendix

APPENDIX 1
Genealogies

We have included genealogies for the Welsh gods and the Túatha dé Danann for ease of study. We have also included children who are not referred to as deities in the myths for completion where known.

The following abbreviations are used, which should be noted carefully to avoid confusion:

>F - father
>M - mother
>S - son
>D - daughter

The Welsh Pantheon

The main source of information for the Welsh deities is the *White Book of Rhydderch*, with occasional references in other texts such as the Triads and various Genealogies, which give less well-known connections. Whilst a number of family relationships are given, it is often the case that only a single parent is referred to, hence the number of question marks in this section.

Mathonwy (F) + ? = Math Mathonwy (S) + Don (D)

Don (M) + Beli (F) = Penarddun (D), Arianrhod (D), Amaethon (S), Govannon (S), Gwydion (S), Gilvaethwy (S), Nudd (S) [The Children of Light] [+ Lleu (S)], Aidden (S), Cynan (S), Digant (S), Elawg (S), Elestron (S), Eunydd (S), Hedd (S), Hunawg (S), Idwal (S)

Beli (F) + ? = Ludd (S), Caswallon (S), Nynyaw (S), Llevelys (S), Rhun (S), Jago (S)

Penarddun (M) + Llyr (F) = Manawyddan (S), Bran (S, Branwen (D) [The Children of Darkness]
Penarddun (M) + Eurosswydd (F) = Nyssien (S), Evnyssien (S)

Bran (F) + ? = Caradawc (S)

Arianrhod (M) + Gwydion? (F) = Dylan (S), Lleu Llaw Gytfes (S)
Arianrhod (M) + Lliaws mab Nwyfre (F) = Gwenwynwyn (S), Gwanar (S)

Nudd (F) + ? = Gwyn ap Nudd (S), Edeyrn (S), Dryan (S)

Gilvaethwy (F) + Gwydion (M) = Hydwn (S), Hychdwn the Tall (S), Bleiddwn (S)

Ludd (F) + ? = Mandubratius (S), Tavlogan (S), Creiddylad (D)

Rhiannon (M) + Pwyll (F) = Pryderi (S)

Separate from the main family line there is also:

Arawn (F) + ? = Modron (D)

Modron (M) + ? = Mabon (S)

Modron (M) + Urien (F) = Owein (S), Morfydd (S)

The Irish Pantheon

The gods of the Túatha dé Danann are referred to in a number of texts, some of which give conflicting familial relationships. We have presented the main relationships with their variations.

Delbaeth (M) + Néit? (F) = Elatha (S)

Elatha (F) + Eri (M) = Bres (S)

Bres (F) + Bride (M) = Ruadán (S)
Balor (F) + ? = Ethne (D), Fea (D)
Ethne (M) + Cian (F) = Lugh (S)

? + ? = Daghda (S), Ogma (S), Nuada (S), Bres (S)

Ernmas (M) + ? = Badb (D), Macha (D), Danu (D) and/or the Morrígan (D), Ériu (D), Banba (D), Fotla (D), Glon (S), Gaim (S), Coscar (S)

Or Fiachra (M) + ? = Ériu (D), Banba (D), Fotla (D)

Morrígan (M) + ? = Mechti (S)

Danu (M) + Bilé (F) = Daghda (S), Brian (S), Iuchar (S), Iucharba (S)

Lir (F) + ? = Manannan (S)

Manannan (F) + ? = Áine (D), Grián (D)
Manannan (F) + Fand (M) = Niamh (D), Clíodna (D)
Manannan (F) + wife of Fiachna Finn (M) = Mongán (S)

Daghda (F) + Boann (M) = Angus Mac Og (S)
Daghda (F) + ? = Tethor MacCecht (S), Cethor MacGreine (S), Sethor MacCuill (S), Brigid (D), Áine (D), Echtgi (D), Aedh (S), Cermait (S), Dian Cecht (S)

Banba (M) + Tethor MacCecht (F) = Cesair (S)

Dian Cecht (F) + ? = Miach (S), Cu (S), Cethen (S), Cian (S), Airmed (D), Etan (D)

Daghda (F) + ? = Lugh (S), Ogma (S)

Flidais (M) + ? = Argoen (D), Dinand (D) (Danu?), Be Theite (D), Bé Chuille (D)

APPENDIX 2
Timelines

To give an idea of the events that shaped the worship of the gods and goddesses discussed, we have included a timeline of major events for a clearer perspective.

Historical Timeline

Time (CE)	Events
8th-5th century BCE	Celts settle in Britain, inter-marrying with the existing tribes
3rd century BCE	Creation of the Elder Futhark
120 BCE	First wave of Belgae migrate to Britain.
80-75 BCE	Second wave of Belgae Celts (from Gaul) settle in the South and East of England
55-54 BCE	Caesar makes two excursions to Britain
43	Romans land in Kent and start taking over
60	Boudicca's revolt and destruction of Camulodunum, Londinium and Verulamium.
61	Romans destroy Druid base on Anglesey
77	Romans conquer Mona (Anglesey) and parts of Caledonia (Scotland)
84	Agricola defeats the Caledonians at Mons Graupius
122	Construction of Hadrian's Wall begins
136	Hadrian's Wall completed
142	Antonine Wall built north of Hadrian's Wall
163/4	Following years of revolts and attacks by the Brigantes and Selgovae the Romans retreat south to Hadrian's Wall
200	Roman Christianity arrives in Britain, the long process of Christianization begins
202	Edict issued in Rome prohibiting Christian and Jewish proselytism

250	Emperor Decius orders that all citizens of the Empire should sacrifice to the gods
257	Emperor Valerian bans the Christian cult
259-273	Britain becomes part of the Gallic Empire of the rebel Postumus until his death when Rome re-asserts control
286-296	Britain ruled as separate province by the usurper governor Carausius, murdered by Allectus in 293 who ruled until his death in 296
c. 300	Angles, Saxons & Jutes marauding Britain's coasts
300	First recorded Ogham in Ireland
4th-6th century	British migration to Gaul to form Brittany.
313	Emperor Constantine issues the Edict of Milan giving Christianity freedom of worship in the Roman Empire
325	The First Council of Nicaea effectively lays the foundations of the Catholic Church
341	Emperor Constans decrees all pagan religions illegal
362	Emperor Julian reverses earlier decrees and makes the pagan religions legal again
391-393	Emperor Theodosius declares paganism illegal
392	Eugenius declares himself Emperor and splits the Empire, with him representing the last stand of paganism against Christianity, Theodosius encourages the destruction of the Great Library of Alexandria
394	Eugenius is killed in battle, Christianity is enforced as the religion of the Empire
410	Roman legions pull out of Britain
431	St Palladius travels to Ireland and establishes churches there.
450	St Patrick travels to Ireland
c. 450	Creation of the Anglo-Saxon Futhark from the Elder Futhark
c.450	Angles, Saxons & Jutes start settling
516	Battle of Mount Badon halts Saxons and preserves integrity of Wales.
577	Battle of Deorham results in a Saxon victory with subsequent conquest of much of Gloucestershire
597	Augustine arrives in Britain to Christianise the Pagans.

	Aethelbert becomes the first Christian Anglo-Saxon king
633	The term Cymru used in a poem identifying Wales as a nation.
655	Penda of Mercia, the last Anglo-Saxon king, dies
664	Synod of Whitby, England is now largely (nominally) Christian.
c. 720	Last links between Wales and Brittany severed.
738	Celtic Church in Wales reunites with Church of Rome.
784	Offa's Dyke built, separating Wales and England
793	Viking raiders destroy the monastery of Lindisfarne
851	Vikings settling on the English coastline
878	Alfred the Great defeats the Vikings at the Battle of Edington, preserving Wessex, and has the Viking king Guthrum baptized. He also encouraged Church schools.
10th century	Uneasy period of minor wars and division of kingdoms with increased Viking influence
1014	High King Brian Boru dies defeating a Viking invasion of Ireland, breaking the Viking threat.
1066	William the Conqueror defeats King Harold at the Battle of Hastings and establishes a new Norman Royal dynasty in Britain.
1170	Anglo-Norman invasion of Ireland begins.
1337	Hundred Years War between England and France begins.
1348	Black Death arrives in Britain from Europe. In three years a third of Europe is wiped out.
1376	John Wycliffe translates the Bible into English from Latin, creating uproar in the church.
1453	Hundred Years War ends.
1455	War of the Roses for the English crown begins.
1476	William Caxton sets up a printing press in Westminster.
1485	War of the Roses ends. Sir Thomas Mallory's Le Morte d'Arthur printed.
1534	England breaks from the Roman Catholic Church with the King the Supreme Head of the new church (The Act of Royal Supremacy 1534).
1536	Henry VIII begins the Dissolution of the Monasteries. The Act of Union unites England and Wales formerly.

APPENDIX 3

The Return of the Pagan Gods

After nearly a thousand years of Christian dominance, the nineteenth century saw a revival of interest in the old gods. This had been subtly increasing for the previous two centuries in Britain, and can be seen in literary references, such as those found in the work of Shakespeare, or allegorical works using pagan imagery, such as Spenser's *Fairy Queen*, through to authors such as Byron, Keats, Shelley and Wordsworth.

The return of the classical Romano-Greek gods can be seen from the late fifteenth century in Italy, through the works of such figures as Marsilo Ficino and Pico della Mirandola, and of course in their ongoing popularity in art. The availability of such material as the *Corpus Hermtica* and Neoplatonic philosophies, together with the emergence of Kabbalah into the European world all heralded a subtle return to ancient pagan images and ideas.

From the beginning of the eighteenth century there was a revival of interest in Druidry. From early attempts at reconstruction, these groups seem to have been largely Christian, until the mid-twentieth century with the introduction of much more Celtic imagery and symbolism, resulting in a whole plethora of Druid groups, both Christian and pagan.[623]

The eighteenth century also saw the gradual British colonialisation of India. From this a slow trickle of Hindu ideas, which began to blossom in the late nineteenth century through such organisations as the Theosophical Society, resulted in the inclusion of a whole range of Indian concepts into modern paganism, such as karma and chakras. The culmination of this influence has been the widespread increase in Hindu temples since the early 1970s, catering for the large number of Hindus now living in Britain.

---

[623] For more detail of this development see The New Druidry, in Witches, Druids and King Arthur, Hutton, 2003, p239-58.

In 1887 CE the Hermetic Order of the Golden Dawn, the most significant magickal order of recent ages, marked a further change in the spiritual landscape. The Golden Dawn was in many ways the midwife for the later pagan revival, with equality of the sexes, and teaching an amalgam of magickal ideas including the Egyptian deities, Indian concepts and Kabbalah. Despite its Christian core in the inner order, the arrival of the Golden Dawn nonetheless heralded the beginning of a new wave of pagan worship.

Since the 1950s with large numbers of people arriving from the Commonwealth, followed by more recent tides from the European Union, Britain has become an increasingly multi-cultural society. As a result the number of deities from around the world worshipped in Britain is nigh-on impossible to determine, and indeed could even be described as a *"global pantheon of worship"*.

The development of subsequent traditions like Wicca and its neo-pagan offshoots is well documented and needs no further comment, except to say that the old pagan gods are more in our midst than they have been for many centuries.

Bibliography

Abbot, T.K., *Catalogue of the Manuscripts in the Library of Trinity College, Dublin*, 1900, Hodges Figgis & Co, Dublin

Alcock, Joan P., *The Concept of Genius in Roman Britain*, 1986, in *Pagan Gods and Shrines of the Roman Empire*, Oxford University Committee for Archaeology No. 8, 113-34

Allason-Jones, Lindsay, *Coventina's Well*, 1996, in *The Concept of the Goddess*, p107-119

Allen, D.F., *The Coins of the Ancient Celts*, 1980, Edinburgh University Press, Edinburgh

Allen, R. (trans), *Brut*, 1992, Dent, London

Ando, Clifford (ed), *Roman Religion*, 2003, Edinburgh University Press Ltd, Edinburgh

d'Arbois de Jubainville, H., *Étude sur le Táin Bó Cúalnge autrement dit "Enlèvement des vaches de Cooley"*, 1907, in *Revue Celtique* 28:17-40

---------, *Enlèvement du taureau divin et des vaches de Cooley*, 1908, trans, in *Revue Celtique* 28:145-77, 28:241-61; 29:153-201; 30:78-88, 30:156-85

Arthurs, M.J.B., *Macha and Armagh*, in *Bulletin of the Ulster Place Name Society* 1:25-9

Ashe, Geoffrey, *Mythology of the British Isles*, 1990, Methuen, London

Bader, Françoise, *Rhapsodies Homériques et Irlandaises*, 1980, in *Recherches sur les religions de l'antiquité classique*, Librairie Champion, Paris

Barnard, S., *The Matres of Roman Britain*, 1985, in *Archaeological Journal* 142:237-43

Bartrum, P.C., *Early Welsh Genealogical Texts*, 1964, University of Wales Press, Cardiff

Bates, Brian, *The Wisdom of the Wyrd*, 1996, Rider, London

Bellows, Henry A. (trans), *The Poetic Edda*, 1936, Princeton University Press, Princeton

Beresford Ellis, P., *A Dictionary of Irish Mythology*, 1987, Constable, London

Best, R.I. & Bergin, Osborn (eds), *Lebor na huidre: Book of the Dun Cow*, 1929, Royal Irish Academy, Dublin

Best, R.I. & O'Brien, M.A. (eds), *The Book of Leinster* (Volume 2), 1956, Dublin Institute for Advanced Studies, Dublin

---------, *The Book of Leinster* (Volume 4), 1965, Dublin Institute for Advanced Studies, Dublin

---------, *The Book of Leinster* (Volume 5), 1967, Dublin Institute for Advanced Studies, Dublin

Bhreathnach, M., *The Sovereignty Goddess as Goddess of Death?*, 1982, in *Zeitschrift für Celtische Philologie* 39:243-60

Billington, Sandra, and Green, Miranda (eds), *The Concept of the Goddess*, 1999, Routledge, London

Billson, Charles James, *County Folk-Lore Printed Extracts No.3: Leicestershire & Rutland*, 1895, David Nutt, London

Binchy, D.A., *Celtic and Anglo-Saxon Kingship*, 1970, Clarendon Press, Oxford

-----------, *Bretha Déin Chécht*, 1966 in *Ériu* 20:1-66

Boece, Hector, *The Chronicles of Scotland*, 1936, The Scottish Texts Society, Edinburgh

Boon, George C., *A Coin with the Head of the Cernunnos*, September 1982, in *Seaby Coin & Medal Bulletin*, p276-282

-----------, *Some Romano-British Domestic Shrines and Their Inhabitants*, 1983, in *Rome and Her Northern Provinces*, ed. B Hartley, Alan Sutton Publishing Ltd, Gloucester, p33-55

Borsje, Jacqueline, *The Evil Eye in Early Irish Literature and Law*, 2003, in *Celtica* 24:1-39

Bowen, Charles, *Great-Bladdered Medb: Mythology and Invention in the Táin Bó Cúailnge*, 1975, in *Eire-Ireland* 10:14-34

---------, *A Historical Inventory of the Dinshenchas*, 1975/6, in *Studia Celtica* 10-11:113-37

Bradley, S.A.J. (trans), *Anglo-Saxon Poetry*, 1982, Dent, London

Branston, Brian, *The Lost Gods of England*, 1957, Thames & Hudson, London

Briggs, Katherine, *A Dictionary of Fairies*, 1976, Penguin Books, London

British Museum, *British Museum Guide to the Antiquities of Roman Britain*, 1958, British Museum Press, London

Bromwich, R. (ed), *Trioedd Ynys Prydein: The Welsh Triads*, 1978, University of Wales Press, Cardiff

Burl, Aubrey, *Rites of the Gods*, 1981, J.M. Dent & Sons Ltd, London

Bushe-Fox, J.P., *Third Report on the Excavations of the Roman Fort at Richborough, Kent*, 1932, Oxford

Caesar, Caius Julius, *The Gallic War*, 1917, William Heinemann, London

Cameron, Kenneth, *Place-Name evidence for the Anglo-Saxon Invasion and Scandinavian Settlements*, 1975, English Place Name Society, Nottingham

Campbell, J.F., *Popular Tales of the West Highlands* (4 volumes), 1860, Alexander Gardner, London

---------, *The Scottish Historical Review* Volume 12, 1915, 4:413

Campbell, John G., *Superstitions of the Highlands & Islands of Scotland*, 1900, MacLehose & Sons, Glasgow

---------, *Witchcraft and Second Sight in the Highlands & Islands of Scotland*, 1902, MacLehose & Sons, Glasgow

Carey, John, *The Name Túatha dé Danann*, 1980-1, in *Éigse* 18:291-94

---------, *Notes on the Irish War Goddess*, 1982-3, in *Éigse* 19:263-75

Cassius, Dio, *Dio's Roman History* (9 volumes), 1924, William Heinemann, London

Cathain, Seamas O, *The Festival of Brigit*, 1995, DBA Publications Ltd, Dublin

Chadwick, N.K., *Imbas Forosnai*, 1935, in *Scottish Gaelic Studies* IV 2:97-135

Clark, Rosalind, *The Great Queens: Irish Goddesses from the Morrigan to Cathleen Ní Houlihan*, 1991, Irish Literary Studies 34, Colin Smythe, Gerrards Cross

Clarke, David & Roberts, Andy, *Twilight of the Celtic Gods*, 1996, Blandford, London

Clauss, Manfred, *The Roman Cult of Mithras*, 2000, Edinburgh University Press, Edinburgh

Coe, Paula Powers, *Macha and Conall Cernach: A Study of Two Iconographic Patterns in Medieval Irish Narratives and Celtic Art*, 1995, Dissertation, UCLA, Los Angeles

Collingwood, R.G. & Wright, P.G. (eds), *The Roman Inscriptions of Britain*, 1965, Clarendon Press, Oxford

Condren, Mary, *The Serpent and the Goddess: Women, Religion, and Power in Celtic Ireland*, 1989, Harper Collins Publishers, New York

Cross, Tom Peete, & Slover, Clark Harris, *Ancient Irish Tales*, 1936, Barnes & Noble, New York

Cunliffe, Barry, *The Ancient Celts*, 1997, Oxford University Press, Oxford

-----------, *The Celtic World*, 1979, Constable & Co., London

Curry, Eugene, *Cath Mhuighe Léana, or The Battle of Magh Leana*, 1855, Celtic Society, Dublin

-----------, *Lectures on the Manuscript Materials of Ancient Irish History*, 1861, Celtic Society, Dublin

Daniels, C.M., *Mithras and His Temples on the Wall*, 1989, Museum of Antiquities, Newcastle-upon-Tyne

Davidson, H.R. Ellis, *The Lost Beliefs of Northern Europe*, 1993, Routledge, London

----------, *Myths and Symbols in Pagan Europe: Early Scandinavian and Celtic Religions*, 1988, Syracuse University Press, Syracuse

----------, *Milk and the Northern Goddess*, in *The Concept of the Goddess*, 1996, Routledge, p91-106

Davies, Wendy, *Celtic Women in the Early Middle Ages*, 1983, in *Images of Women in Antiquity*, Croom Helm, London, p145-66

Dillon, Myles, *The Cycles of the Kings*, 1946, G. Cumberledge, London

---------, *Early Irish Literature*, 1948, University of Chicago Press, Chicago

Dineen, Rev. Patrick S., *Foclóir Gaedhilge agus Béarla*, 1927, Irish Texts Society, Dublin

Doan, James E., *Women and Goddesses in Early Celtic History, Myth and Legend*, 1987, North-eastern University, Boston

---------, *Sovereignty Aspects in the Roles of Women in Medieval Irish and Welsh Society*, 1984, North-eastern University, Boston

Dobbs, Margaret C., *The Battle of Findchorad*, 1923, in *Zeitschrift für Celtische Philologie* 14:395-420

---------, *The Ban-shenchus*, 1930-2, in *Revue Celtique* 47:238-339; 48:161-234; 49:437-489

Donahue, C., *The Valkyries and the Irish War-Goddesses*, 1941, in *Publications of the Modern Language Association of America* 56:1-12

Dudley, D.R., & Webster, G., *The Rebellion of Boudicca*, 1962, Routledge & Kegan Paul, London

Dumézil, Georges, *Le trio de Macha*, 1954, in *Revue de l'histoire des religions* 146:5-17

Dunn, Vincent A., *Cattle Raids and Courtships: Medieval Narrative Genres in a Traditional Context*, 1989, in *Garland Monographs in Medieval Literature* 2, Garland, London

Duvau, Louis, *La Legende de la Conception de Cuchulainn*, 1888, in *Revue Celtique* 29:1-13

Ekwall, Eilert, *English River-Names*, 1928, Clarendon Press, Oxford

Fairless, Kenneth J., *Three Religious Cults from the Northern Frontier Region*, p224-42, in *Between and Beyond the Walls*, 1984, John Donald Publishers, Edinburgh

Ellis, Peter Berresford, *Chronicles of the Celts*, 1999, Robinson, London

Enright, Michael J., *Lady with a Mead Cup: ritual, prophecy, and lordship in the European warband from LaTene to the Viking Age*, 1996, Four Courts, Dublin

Epstein, Angelique G., *War Goddess: The Morrígan and her Germano-Celtic Counterparts*, 1998, UCLA

---------, *Divine Devouring: Further Notes on the Morrígan and the Valkyries*, 1998, in *Journal of Indo-European Studies Monograph* 27:86-104

---------, *The Morrígan and the Valkyries*, 1997, in *Journal of Indo-European Studies Monograph* 21:119-50

---------, *Woman's Words: Threats and Prophecies, Lies and Revelations in Arthurian Romance and Medieval Irish Literature*, 1992, in *Proceedings of the Harvard Celtic Colloquium* 12:184-195

Evans, D. Ellis, *Irish Folk Ways*, 1957, Routledge & Kegan Paul, London

Evans, J. Gwenogvryn, *Report on Manuscripts in the Welsh Language*, Volume 1 Part 2 – Peniarth, 1899, Stationery Office, London

-----------, *The White Book Mabinogion: Welsh tales & romances reproduced from the Peniarth manuscripts*, 1907, Pwllheli

Evans-Wentz, W.Y., *The Fairy Faith in Celtic Countries*, 2003, Dover Publications Inc., New York

Fee, Christopher R., *Gods Heroes & Kings: The Battle for Mythic Britain*, 2001, Oxford University Press, Oxford

Findon, Joanne, *A Woman's Words: Emer and Female Speech in the Ulster Cycle*, 1997, University of Toronto Press, Toronto

Fitzgerald, D., *Popular Tales of Ireland VI: Gearóid Iarla and Áine N'Chliar*, 1879, in *Revue Celtique* 4:185-99

Flint, Valerie I.J., *The Rise of Magic in Early Medieval Europe*, 1991, Princeton University Press, New Jersey

Ford, Patrick K., *Celtic Women: the Opposing Sex*, 1988, in *Viator* 19:417-38

Foster, Jennifer, *Bronze Boar Figurines in Iron Age and Roman Britain*, 1977, British Archaeological Reports 39

Fraser, J. (ed, trans), *The First Battle of Moytura*, 1916, in *Ériu* 8:1-63

Freeman, Philip Mitchell, *The earliest classical sources on the Celts: A linguistic and historical study*, 1994, Dissertation, Harvard

Fries, Maureen, *Shape-shifting Women in the Old Irish Sagas*, 1991, in *Bestia: Yearbook of the Beast Fable Society*, 3:15-21

Gantz, Jeffrey (trans), *Early Irish Myths and Sagas*, 1981, Penguin Books, London

Geoffrey of Monmouth, *The History of the Kings of England*, 1977, Penguin, London

Gerald of Wales, *The History and Topography of Ireland*, 1982, Penguin, London

Giles, J.A., *Six Old English Chronicles*, 1848, H.G. Bohn, London

-----------, *Works: Bede*, 1843, Oxford

Gillies, W., *The Craftsman in early Celitc literature*, 1981 in *Early Technology in Northern Britain*, p70-85, Scottish Archaeological Forum 11

Glick, Andrew S., *A Comprehensive Dictionary of Gods, Goddesses, Demigods, and Other Subjects in Greek and Roman Mythology*, 2004, The Edwin Mellen Press, New York

Goedheer, A.J., *Irish and Norse Traditions about the Battle of Clontarf*, 1938, Haarlem

Goodburn, Roger & Waugh, Helen, *The Roman Inscriptions of Britain* [RIB], 1983, Alan Sutton Publishing Ltd, Gloucester

Gordon, E.O., *Prehistoric London: Its Mounds and Circles*, 1932, The Covenant Publishing Co Ltd, London

Grant, Katherine Whyte, *Myth, Tradition and Story from Western Argyll*, 1925, Oban Times Press, Oban

Gray, Elizabeth A. (ed, trs), *Cath Maige Tuired*, 1982, Irish Texts Society 52

-----------, *Cath Maige Tuired: Myth and Structure*, 1982, in *Éigse* 19:230-62

Green, H.J.M., *Religious Cults at Roman Godmanchester*, 1986, in *Pagan Gods and Shrines of the Roman Empire*, Oxford University Committee for Archaeology No. 8, 29-56

Green, Miranda, *The Gods of the Celts*, 1986, Sutton Publishing Ltd, Stroud

-----------, *Dictionary of Celtic Myth and Legend*, 1992, Thames & Hudson, London

-----------, *Celtic Goddesses*, 1997, British Museum Press, London

-----------, *The Celtic Goddess as Healer*, 1996, in *The Concept of the Goddess*, p26-40

-----------, *The Gods of Roman Britain*, 2003, Shire Publications Ltd, Princes Risborough

-----------, *The Religions of Civilian Roman Britain*, 1976, British Archaeological Reports 24, Oxford

----------, *The Worship of the Romano-Celtic Wheel God in Britain*, 1979, in *Latomus* 38.2, p345-67

----------, *The Wheel as a Cult-Symbol in the Romano-Celtic World*, 1984, in *Collection Latomus 183*, Brussels

---------- (ed), *The Celtic World*, 1995, Routledge, London

----------, *Any Old Iron! Symbolism and Ironworking in Iron Age Europe*, 2002, in *Artefacts and Archaeology: Aspects of the Celtic and Roman World*, p8-19

----------, *The Gods and the Supernatural*, 1995, in *The Celtic World*, Routledge, London, p465-88

Green, Miranda & Webster, Peter, *Artefacts and Archaeology: Aspects of the Celtic and Roman World*, 2002, University of Wales Press, Cardiff

Greene, David & O'Connor, Frank, *A Golden Treasury of Irish Poetry AD 600 to 1200*, 1967, Macmillan, London

Gregory, Lady A. (trans), *Cuchulainn of Muirthemne: The Story of the Men of The Red Branch of Ulster*, 1902, John Murray, London

---------, *Irish Myths and Legends*, 1998, Courage Books, Pennsylvania

Gricourt, Jean, *Epona-Rhiannon-Macha*, 1954, in *Ogam* 31:25-40, 137-8; 32:75-86; 34:165-88; 36:269-72

Griffiths, Bill, *Aspects of Anglo-Saxon Magic*, 1996, Anglo-Saxon Books, Norfolk

Grinsell, L.V., *Folklore of Prehistoric Sites in Britain*, 1976, Newton Abbot

Gruffydd, W.J., *Rhiannon: An Inquiry into the Origins of the First and Third Branches of the Mabinogi*, 1953, University of Wales Press, Cardiff

----------, W.J., *Mabon ap Modron*, 1912, in *Revue Celtique* 33:452-461

Guest, Lady Charlotte E., *The Mabinogion*, 1997, Dover Publications Inc., New York

Gwynn, Edward (ed, trans), *The Metrical Dinshenchas* (Vol 2), 1906, Royal Irish Academy, Dublin

---------, *The Metrical Dinshenchas* (Vol 3), 1913, Royal Irish Academy, Dublin

---------, *The Metrical Dinshenchas* (Vol 4), 1924, Royal Irish Academy, Dublin

---------, *The Metrical Dinshenchas* (Vol 5), 1935, Royal Irish Academy, Dublin

---------, *On the Idea of Fate in Irish Literature*, 1910, in Journal of the Ivernian Society 2:152-65

Halle, A.S. & Niemeyer, Max, *Anecdota* (Vol. 1), 1907, Oxford Univeristy Press, Oxford

Hamel, Anton Gerard van, *Lebor Bretnach. The Irish version of the Historia Britonum ascribed to Nennius*, 1932, Irish Manuscripts Commission, Dublin

----------, *On Lebor Gabála*, 1915, in *Zeitschrift für Celtische Philologie* 10:97-197

Hanley, W., *Tales and Legends of the Banshee*, 1908, in *Ireland's Own* XII no. 312

Harris, E. & J., *The Oriental Cults in Roman Britain*, 1963, E.J. Brill, Leiden

Hartley, B. (ed), *Rome and Her Northern Provinces*, 1983, Alan Sutton Publishing Ltd, Gloucester

Henderson, G (ed, trans), *Fled Bricrend, The Feast of Bricriu*, 1899, David Nutt, London

---------, *Survivals in Beliefs among the Celts*, 1911, Glasgow

Henig, Martin, *Religion in Roman Britain*, 1986, B.T. Batsford, London

----------, *A Corpus of Roman Engraved Gemstones from British Sites* (2 volumes), 1974, British Archeaological Reports 8(ii), Oxford

Henig, Martin & King, Anthony (eds), *Pagan Gods and Shrines of the Roman Empire*, 1986, Oxford University Committee for Archaeology Monograph No. 8

Hennessy, W.M., *The Ancient Irish Goddess of War*, 1870, in *Revue Celtique* 1:32-55

Herbert, Kathleen, *Looking for the Lost Gods of England*, 2002, Anglo-Saxon Books, Norfolk

---------, *Transmutation of an Irish Goddess*, 1996, in *The Concept of the Goddess*, Routledge, London

Herodian, *History of the Empire after Marcus*, 1969, LOEB, London

Hogan, E., *Onomasticon Goedelicum*, 1910, Dublin

Holder, A., *Le soi-disant mot gaulois Louyos*, 1905, in *Revue Celtique* 26:129

Horsley, J., *Romania Britannia*, 1732, London

Howe, Nicholas, *Migration and Mythmaking in Anglo-Saxon England*, 2001, University of Notre Dame Press, Indiana

Howey, M. Oldfield, *The Horse in Magic and Myth*, 1923, William Rider & Son Ltd, London

Hull, Eleanor, *The Cuchullin Saga in Irish Literature*, 1898, David Nutt, London

---------, *Folklore of the British Isles*, 1928, Methuen & Co. Ltd, London

Hull, Vernam, *Noínden Ulad: The Debility of the Ulidians*, 1968, in *Celtica* 8:1-42

----------, *Ces Ulad*, 1962, in *Zeitschrift für Celtische Philologie* 29:305-14

Hutchinson, Valerie J., *The Cult of Bacchus in Roman Britain*, 1986, in *Pagan Gods and Shrines of the Roman Empire*, Oxford University Committee for Archaeology No. 8, p135-46

Hutton, Ronald, *The Pagan Religions of the Ancient British Isles*, 1991, Basil Blackwell Ltd, Oxford
----------, *Witches, Druids and King Arthur*, 2003, Hambledon & London, London
Huw, Daniel, *Medieval Welsh Manuscripts*, 2000, University of Wales Press, Cardiff
Jackson, Kenneth (ed), *Cath Maighe Léna*, 1938, Dublin Institute for Advanced Studies, Dublin
Jams, S., *Exploring the World of the Celts*, 2005, Thames & Hudson, London
Johns, Catherine, *The Jewellery of Roman Britain*, 1996, UCL Press Ltd, London
----------, *Faunus at Thetford*, 1986, in *Pagan Gods and Shrines of the Roman Empire*, Oxford University Committee for Archaeology No. 8, 93-102
Jolif, Thierry, *The Cernunnos Mystery*, 2004, in *Runa* 15:2-6
Jones, John, *Welsh Place Names*, 2003, John Jones Publishing Ltd, Ruthin
Jones, T. Gwynn, *Welsh Folklore and Custom*, 1930, Methuen & Co, London
Jordan, Michael, *Encyclopedia of Gods*, 1992, Kyle Cathie Ltd, London
Keegan, John, *Legends and Tales of the Queen's County Peasantry*, 1839, in *The Dublin University Magazine* 14:366-74
Keppie, L.J.F., *Roman Inscriptions from Scotland: some additions and corrections to RIB I*, 1983, in *Proc Soc Antiq Scot* 113:391-404
Kinsella, Thomas (trans), *The Tain*, 1970, Oxford University Press, Oxford
Knott, Eleanor (ed), *Togail Bruidne Da Derga*, 1936, Dublin Institute for Advanced Studies, Dublin
Knott, Eleanor & Murphy, Gerard, *Early Irish Literature*, 1966, Barnes & Noble Inc, New York
Krappe, A.H., *Nuada à la main d'argent*, 1932, in *Revue Celtique* 49:91-95
Leahy, A.H., *Heroic Romances of Ireland* (2 volumes), 1906, David Nutt, London
Lejeune, M. & Marichal, R., *Textes gaulois et gallo-romains en cursive latine*, II: Chamalières, 1976-77, in *Études Celtiques* 15:151-68
LeRoux, Francoise, *Morrígan-Bodb-Macha, la souveraineté guerrière de l'Irelande*, 1983, in *Celticum* 25
----------, *Cernunnos*, 1953, in *Ogam* 25-6:324-9
Lewis, Samuel, *A Topographical Dictionary of Wales*, 1849, S. Lewis & Co, London

Lindahl, Carl, McNamara, John & Lindow, John, *Medieval Folklore, An Encyclopedia of Myths, Legends, Tales, Beliefs, and Customs*, 2002, Oxford University Press, Oxford

Linsell, Tony, *Anglo-Saxon Mythology, Migration & Magic*, 1994, Anglo-Saxon Books, Pinner

Lloyd, J.H., Bergin, O.J. & Schoepperle, G., *The Reproach of Diarmaid*, 1912, in *Revue Celtique* 33:41-57

-----------, *The Death of Diarmaid*, 1913, in *Revue Celtique* 33:157-79

Lloyd-Morgan, Glenys, *Nemesis and Bellona: a preliminary study of two neglected goddesses*, 1996, in *The Concept of the Goddess*, p120-8

Loomis, Roger S., *Morgan le Fee and Celtic Goddesses*, 1940, in *Speculum* 20:183-203

Lottner, C., *Response to Hennessy, "The Ancient Irish Goddess of War"*, 1870, in *Revue Celtique* 1:55-57

Lysaght, Patricia, *Aspects of the Earth Goddess in Traditions of the Banshee in Ireland*, 1996, in *Concepts of the Goddess*, p152-65

MacAlister, S., *Lebor Gabála Érenn*, (5 volumes), 1941, Irish Texts Society, Dublin

MacCana, Poinsias, *Celtic Goddesses of Sovereignty*, in *Goddesses Who Rule*, 2000, Oxford University Press, Oxford

-----------, *The Learned Tales of Medieval Ireland*, Dublin Institute for Advanced Studies, Dublin 1980

-----------, *Aspects of the Theme of King and Goddess in Irish Literature*, 1955-59, in *Études Celtiques* 7:76-114, 356-413; 8:59-65

-----------, *Celtic Mythology*, 1970, Hamlyn, London

-----------, *Branwen Daughter of Llyr: A Study of the Irish Affinities and of the Composition of the second Branch of the Mabinogi*, 1958, University of Wales Press, Cardiff

MacCulloch, J.A., *Religion of the Ancient Celts*, 1911, T & T Clark, Edinburgh

-----------, *The Mythology of All Races*, 1918, in *Celtica* 3:30.

-----------, *The Celtic and Scandinavian Religions*, 1948, Hutchinson's University Library, London

MacKenzie, Donald A., *Scottish Folk Lore and Folk Life*, 1935, Blackie, London

Mackinnon, D., *Fulacht na Morrígna*, 1912, in *The Celtic Review* 8:74-6

MacMullen, Ramsay, *Christianity and Paganism in the Fourth to Eighth Centuries*, 1997, Yale University Press, New Haven

MacNeill, Eoin, *Duanaire Finn I*, 1904, Irish Texts Society, Dublin
MacNiocaill, Gearóid, *Ireland before the Vikings*, 1972, Gill, Dublin
Magrath, John Mac Rory, *Caithréimm Thoirdhealbhaigh (The Triumphs of Turlough)*, 1929, Simpkin Marshall Limited, London
Maier, Berhard, *Dictionary of Celtic Religion and Culture*, 1997, Boydell, New York
Mallory, J.P. (ed), *Aspects of the Táin*, 1992, December Publications, Belfast
Mancoff, Debra (ed), *The Arthurian Revival: Essays on Form, Tradition, and Transformation*, 1992, Garland Publishing Inc., London
Marcellus, Ammianus, *Roman History*, 1940, William Heinemann, London
Marstrander, Carl, *A New Version of the Battle of Mag Rath*, 1911, in *Ériu* 5:226-47
McAnally, D.R., *Irish Wonders*, 1888, London
McGrath, Sheena, *The Sun Goddess: Myth, Legend and History*, 1997, Blandford, London
McKenna, Lambert S.J., *The Book of Maguaran*, 1947, The Dublin Institute for Advanced Studies, Dublin
Meaney, Audrey L., *Anglo-Saxon Amulets and Curing Stones*, 1981, BAR British Series 96, Oxford
Mee, Arthur, *Leicestershire and Rutland*, 1937, Hodder & Stoughton, London
Meyer, Kuno, (ed, trans) *Cáin Adamnán*, 1905, Clarendon Press, Oxford
---------, *The Wooing of Emer*, 1888, in *The Archaeological Review* 1:68-75, 151-55, 231-35, 298-307
---------, *The Oldest Version of Tochmarc Émire*, 1890, in *Revue Celtique* 11:424-55
---------, *Sanas Cormaic: An Old-Irish Glossary*, 1912, Hodges Figgis & Co Ltd, Dublin
Miller, Arthur W.K. (ed), *O'Clery's Irish Glossary*, 1879-83, in *Revue Celtique* 4:349-428; 5:1-69
Miller, Hugh, *Scenes and Legends of the North of Scotland*, 1835, A & C Black, Edinburgh
Morganwg, Iolo, & Smith, Malcolm, *The Triads of Britain*, 1977, Wildwood House Ltd, London
Murphy, Gerard, *Notes on Cath Maige Tuired*, 1956, in *Éigse* 8:191-98
Myvyrian Archaeology, 1870, Denbigh
Näsström, Britt-Mari, *Freyja - the Great Goddess of the North*, 1995, Lund studies in History of Religions Vol. 5, Sweden

Nettlau, Max, *The Fragment of the Táin Bó Cúailnge in MSS Egerton 93*, 1894, in *Revue Celtique* 15:62-78, 198-208

Ní Bhrolcháin, M., *Women in Early Irish Myths and Sagas*, 1980, in *The Crane Bag* 4:1, 12-19

North, Richard, *Heathen Gods in Old English Literature*, 1997, Cambridge University Press, Cambridge.

O'Brien, M.A., *Second Battle of Moytura*, 1938, in *Ériu* 12:239-240

Ó'Cathasaigh, T., *Táin Bó Cúailnge*, 1993, in *Studien zur Táin Bó Cúailnge*, Tübingen, p114-132

----------, *The Cult of Brigid: A Study of Pagan-Christian Syncretism in Ireland*, 1982, in *Mother Worship*, University of North Carolina Press, p53-74

Ó Cuív, Brian (ed), *Cath Muighe Tuireadh*, 1945, Dublin Institute for Advanced Studies, Dublin

O Donovan, John (ed), *The Banquet of Dun na n-Gedh and The Battle of Magh Rath*, 1842, Irish Archaeological Society, Dublin

---------, *Supplement to O'Reilly's Irish-English Dictionary*, 1864, James Duffy & Co, Dublin

---------, *Sanas Chormaic: Cormac's Glossary*, 1868, Whitley Stokes, Dublin

O'Grady, S.H., *Silva Gadelica*, 1892, London

O'Grady, Standish, *The Triumph and Passing of Cú Chulainn*, 1920, The Talbot Press, Dublin

---------, *Caithréim Thoirdhealbhaigh*, 1929, Irish Texts Society, London

Ó hÓgáin, D., *Myth, Legend and Romance: An Encyclopaedia of Irish Folklore Tradition*, 1990, Prentice Hall, London

Olmsted, Garret S., *The Gods of the Celts and the Indo-Europeans*, 1994, Archaeolingua, Budapest

----------, *The Gundestrup Cauldron*, 1979, in *Collection Latomus* 162, Brussels

Opland, Jeff, *Anglo-Saxon Oral Poetry*, 1980, Yale University Press, New Haven

O'Rahilly. Cecile (ed), *The Stowe Version of the Táin Bó Cúailnge*, 1961, Dublin Institute for Advanced Studies, Dublin

---------, (ed), *Táin Bó Cúailnge from the Book of Leinster*, 1967, Dublin Institute for Advanced Studies, Dublin

---------, (ed), *Táin Bó Cúailnge Recension I*, 1976, Dublin Institute for Advanced Studies, Dublin

O'Rahilly, Thomas F., *Early Irish History and Mythology*, 1946, Dublin Institute for Advanced Studies, Dublin

Ó Riain, Pádraig (ed), *Cath Almaine*, 1978, Dublin Institute for Advanced Studies, Dublin

Owen, Gale R., *Rites and Religions of the Anglo-Saxons*, 1981, David & Charles, Newton Abbot

Owen, Hywel Wyn, *The Place Names of Wales*, 1998, University of Wales Press, Cardiff

Pollington, Stephen, *Leechcraft: Early English Charms Plantlore and Healing*, 2003, Anglo-Saxon Books, Norfolk

Porter, E., *Cambridgeshire Customs and Folklore*, 1969, Routledge & Kegan Paul, London

Ptolemy, Claudius, *The Geography*, 1991, Dover Publications, London

Pudill, Rainer & Eyre, Clive, *The Tribes & Coins of Celtic Britain*, 2005, Greenlight Publishing, Essex

Puttock, Sonia, *Ritual Significance of Personal Ornament in Roman Britain*, 2002, BAR British Series 327, Archaeopress, Oxford

Radner, Joan N. (ed, trans), *Fragmentary Annals of Ireland*, 1978, Dublin Institute for Advanced Studies, Dublin

Rankin, H.D., *Celts and the Classical World*, 1987, Croom Helm, London

Rankine, David, *Heka - The Practices of Ancient Egyptian Ritual & Magic*, 2005, Avalonia, London

Rankine, David & D'Este, Sorita, *The Guises of the Morrígan*, 2005, Avalonia, London

Rees, Alwyn & Brinley, *Celtic Heritage: Ancient Tradition in Ireland and Wales*, 1961, Thames & Hudson, New York

Rhys, John, *Celtic Folk-Lore, Welsh and Manx* (2 volumes), 1901, Oxford University Press, Oxford

Roberts, Alexander & Donaldson, James (ed), *The Anti-Nicene Fathers* (vol 3), 1992, Eerdmans Publishing Company, Michigan

Roberts, Brynley F. (ed), *Early Welsh Poetry*, 1988, National Library of Wales, Aberystwyth

Rodrigues, Louis J., *Anglo-Saxon Verse Charms, Maxims & Heroic Legends*, 1993, Anglo-Saxon Books, Pinner

Rolleston, T.W., *Myths and Legends of the Celtic Race*, 1911, G.G. Harrap & Co, London

Ross, Anne, *Pagan Celtic Britain*, 1967, Routledge & Kegan Paul Ltd, London

----------, *The Divine Hag of the Pagan Celts*, in *The Witch Figure*, Venetia Newell (ed), 1973, Routledge & Kegan Paul, London

---------, *The Folklore of the Scottish Highlands*, 1976, B.T. Batsford, London

---------, *Folklore of Wales*, 2001, Tempus Publishing Ltd, Stroud

Royal Irish Academy, *Dictionary of the Irish Language* (DIL), 1983, Dublin University Press, Dublin

Russell, Paul, *The Sounds of a Silence: The Growth of Cormac's Glossary*, 1988, in *Cambridge Medieval Celtic Studies* 15:1-30

Sayers, William, *Airdrech, Sirite and Other Early Irish Battlefield Spirits*, 1991, in *Éigse* 25:45-55

----------, *Bargaining for the Life of Bres in Cath Maige Tuired*, 1987 in *Bulletin of the Board of Celtic Studies* 34:26-40

Scheid, John, *An Introduction to Roman Religion*, 2003, Edinburgh University Press, Edinburgh

Scott, Sir Walter, *Minstrelsy of the Scottish Border*, 1802, Edinburgh

---------, *Letters on Demonology and Witchcraft*, 1831, London

Scowcroft, R. Mark, *Leabhar Gabhála Part I: The Growth of the Text*, 1987, in *Ériu* 38:81-142

---------, *Leabhar Gabhála Part II: The Growth of the Tradition*, 1988, in *Ériu* 39:1-66

Siculus, Diodorus, *The Library of History*, 1933, William Heinemann, London

Skene, William F., *The Four Ancient Books of Wales* (2 volumes), 1868, Edmonston and Douglas, Edinburgh

Smith, D.J., *The Shrine of the Nymphs and the Genius Loci at Carrawburgh*, 1962, in *Archaeologia Aeliana* 40:59-81

Smith, John Holland, *The Death of Classical Paganism*, 1976, Geoffrey Chapman Publishers, London

Spaeth, Barbette Stanley, *The Roman Goddess Ceres*, 1996, University of Texas Press, Austin

Stanley, E.G., *The Search for Anglo-Saxon Paganism*, 1975, Goldcrest Press, Wiltshire

Stevenson, Rev. Joseph, *The Historical Works of the Venerable Bede*, 1853, Seeleys, London

Stevenson, W.H. (ed), *Asser's Life of King Alfred*, 1904, Oxford University Press, Oxford

Stewart, Bob, *The Waters of the Gap: The Mythology of Aquae Sulis*, 1981, Bath City Council, Bath

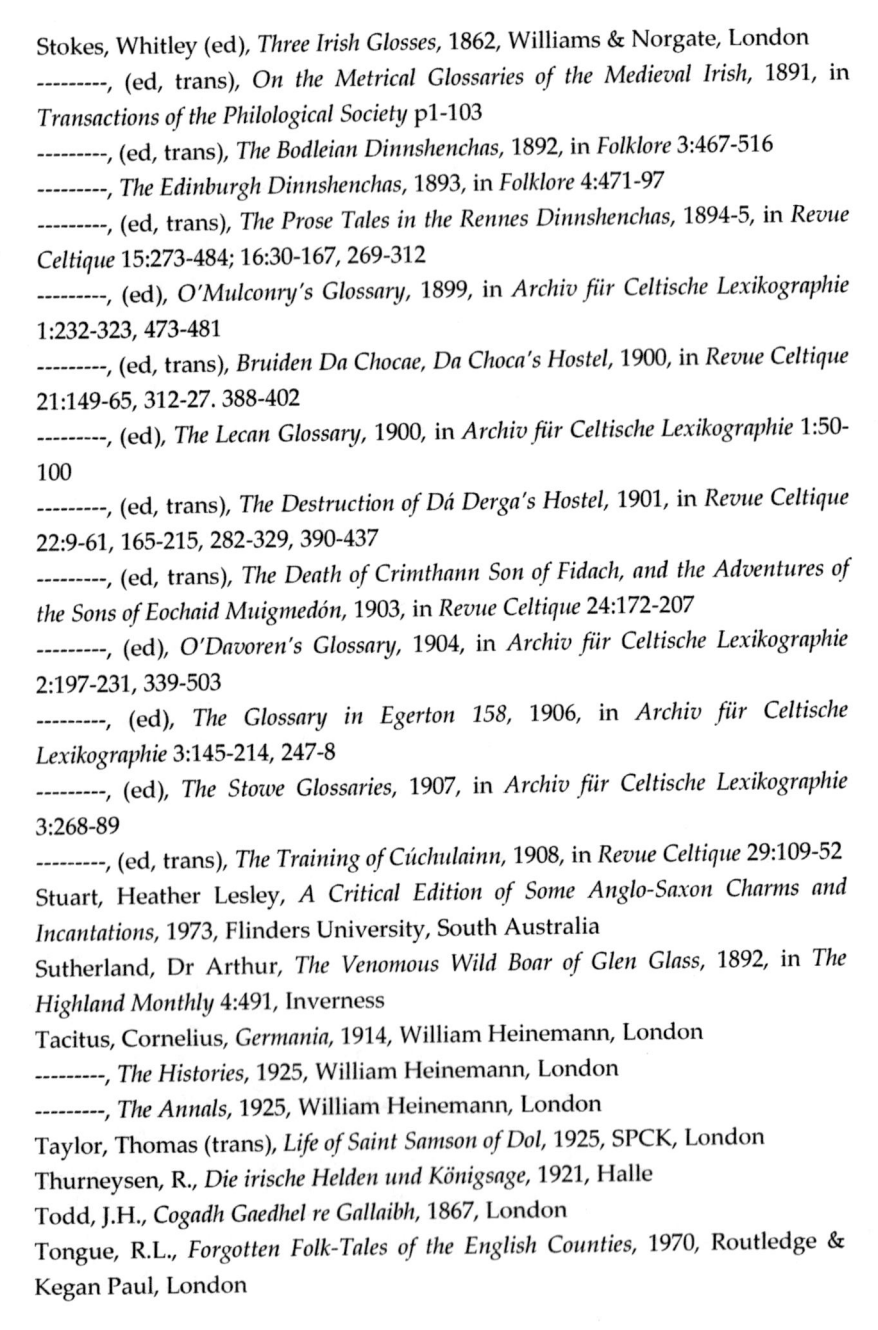

Stokes, Whitley (ed), *Three Irish Glosses*, 1862, Williams & Norgate, London

---------, (ed, trans), *On the Metrical Glossaries of the Medieval Irish*, 1891, in *Transactions of the Philological Society* p1-103

---------, (ed, trans), *The Bodleian Dinnshenchas*, 1892, in *Folklore* 3:467-516

---------, *The Edinburgh Dinnshenchas*, 1893, in *Folklore* 4:471-97

---------, (ed, trans), *The Prose Tales in the Rennes Dinnshenchas*, 1894-5, in *Revue Celtique* 15:273-484; 16:30-167, 269-312

---------, (ed), *O'Mulconry's Glossary*, 1899, in *Archiv für Celtische Lexikographie* 1:232-323, 473-481

---------, (ed, trans), *Bruiden Da Chocae, Da Choca's Hostel*, 1900, in *Revue Celtique* 21:149-65, 312-27. 388-402

---------, (ed), *The Lecan Glossary*, 1900, in *Archiv für Celtische Lexikographie* 1:50-100

---------, (ed, trans), *The Destruction of Dá Derga's Hostel*, 1901, in *Revue Celtique* 22:9-61, 165-215, 282-329, 390-437

---------, (ed, trans), *The Death of Crimthann Son of Fidach, and the Adventures of the Sons of Eochaid Muigmedón*, 1903, in *Revue Celtique* 24:172-207

---------, (ed), *O'Davoren's Glossary*, 1904, in *Archiv für Celtische Lexikographie* 2:197-231, 339-503

---------, (ed), *The Glossary in Egerton 158*, 1906, in *Archiv für Celtische Lexikographie* 3:145-214, 247-8

---------, (ed), *The Stowe Glossaries*, 1907, in *Archiv für Celtische Lexikographie* 3:268-89

---------, (ed, trans), *The Training of Cúchulainn*, 1908, in *Revue Celtique* 29:109-52

Stuart, Heather Lesley, *A Critical Edition of Some Anglo-Saxon Charms and Incantations*, 1973, Flinders University, South Australia

Sutherland, Dr Arthur, *The Venomous Wild Boar of Glen Glass*, 1892, in *The Highland Monthly* 4:491, Inverness

Tacitus, Cornelius, *Germania*, 1914, William Heinemann, London

---------, *The Histories*, 1925, William Heinemann, London

---------, *The Annals*, 1925, William Heinemann, London

Taylor, Thomas (trans), *Life of Saint Samson of Dol*, 1925, SPCK, London

Thurneysen, R., *Die irische Helden und Königsage*, 1921, Halle

Todd, J.H., *Cogadh Gaedhel re Gallaibh*, 1867, London

Tongue, R.L., *Forgotten Folk-Tales of the English Counties*, 1970, Routledge & Kegan Paul, London

Ua Duinním, An tAth P., *Amhráin Sheagháin Chláraigh Mhic Dhomhnaill*, 1902, Dublin

Wait, G.A., *Ritual and Religion in Iron Age Britain*, 1985, B.A.R., Oxford

Watson, E.C., *Highland Mythology*, 1908, in *The Celtic Review* 5:48-70

Watts, Dorothy, *Christians and Pagans in Roman Britain*, 1991, Routledge, London

Webster, Graham, *The British Celts and their Gods under Rome*, 1986, B.T. Batsford Ltd, London

Wilde, Sir William R., *On the Battle of Moytura*, 1866, Proceedings of the Royal Irish Academy 9

Williams, J.E. Caerwyn, & Ford, Patrick K., *The Irish Literary Tradition*, 1992, University of Wales Press, Cardiff

Wissowa, Georg, *The Development of Roman Religion: An Overview*, 2003, in *Roman Religion*, p330-57

Wood-Martin, W.G., *Traces of the Elder Faiths of Ireland*, 1902, Longmans Green & Co, London

Index

Abandinus 51
Aber Alaw
   Anglesey 91
Aberaeron
   Cardiganshire 53
Abergavenny
   Monmouthshire 149
Abona
   river 51
Abraxas 51
Adammair 141
Æcerbot 37, 131, 132
Aedh 119, 261
Aegil 52, 253
Aeron 52
   river 54
Aesculapius 53, 164, 221, 233
Aethelbert 264
   King 46
Against All Heresies 36, 52
Agroná 52, 54
Ahriman 68, 200
Ahura Mazda 200
Aidden 126, 259
Aífe 234
Ailill Finn 141
Ailill mac Mata 194
Áine 54, 55, 110, 119, 149, 261
Airmed 123, 262
Aislinge Oenguso 36, 60
Aithbe Dam Bés Mora 37, 98
Aithed Gráinne re Diarmait ua
   nDuibne 39, 149, 150
Alaisagae 30, 56
Alator 56, 57, 192
Alder 89, 90, 248
Alecto 204

Alfred the Great 47, 145, 265
All Hallows Eve 101
Almondbury
   Yorkshire 104
Altrier
   France 131
Amaethon 57, 65, 66, 79, 89, 90, 125, 148, 153, 222, 259
Amergin 127, 133
Ammon 30, 58, 170
Amon 100
Anand 121
Anann 121
Ancasta 58
Ancaster
   Lincolnshire 250
Anchors 214
Andarta 59
Andescociuoucus 59, 197
Andraste 59
Andreas 34
Anextiomarus 60, 64
Angles 35, 264
Anglo-Saxon Futhark 264
Angus Mac Og 60, 61, 85, 100, 118, 119, 120, 124, 198, 261
Anicestus 61
Aniseed 82
Annals of Lough Cé 39, 209
Annwn 57, 65, 154, 202, 224
Antaeus 158
Antenocitus 62
Antocidicus 62
Antonine Wall 211
Anu 71, 75, 79, 82, 97, 100, 121, 134, 142, 184
Anubis 62

Aobh 174
Aodh 174
Aoibheall 63, 110
Aoife 174, 188
Aonbharr 188
Aphrodite 69, 223, 247
Apis 236
Apollo 25, 30, 53, 60, 62, 64, 66, 78, 122, 149, 190, 243
Apollo Grannus 64, 149
Apollo Maponos 64
Apologeticum 36, 78
Apotheosis 20
Arawn 57, 65, 89, 153, 224, 260
Arecurius 66
Argoen 141, 262
Arianrhod 57, 66, 67, 79, 83, 125, 127, 148, 151, 152, 174, 175, 176, 222, 259
Ariarcon 66
Arimanius 68
Armagh 187
Arnemetia 68
Arnomectae 68
Asklepios 53
Asser 31, 37, 145, 146
Astarte 68, 69
Atanta 131
Atargatis 69
Attis 69, 70, 117, 178
Auchendavy
    East Dunbartonshire 41, 131
Ausecus 136, 137
Ausonius 78
Autumn Equinox 106
Avagddu 107
Avon
    river 52
Bacchus 72, 73
Backworth
    Northumberland 42, 43

Badb 71, 72, 75, 80, 121, 134, 142, 184, 185, 203, 204, 207, 209, 261
Badbh Catha 71
Baile in Scáile 37, 180, 182
Bald 34, 37
Baldur 73
Balor 74, 123, 137, 180, 181, 186, 207, 215, 261
Banba 71, 75, 119, 121, 132, 134, 142, 143, 182, 184, 209, 261, 262
Banshee 55, 63, 135, 138, 209
Banshenchus 38, 74, 75, 76, 110, 119, 132, 135, 142, 143, 198, 199, 206, 207, 208, 241
Bar Hill
    Dunbartonshire 104
Barkway
    Hertfordshire 57, 243
Barrecis 76, 192
Bastet 76
Bath
    Somerset 41, 44, 78, 114, 156, 178, 197, 199, 210, 230, 240
Battle of Clontarf 63, 209
Battle of Deorham 264
Battle of Edington 47, 265
Battle of Hastings 265
Battle of Magh Mór an Aonaigh 93
Battle of Maige Mucrima 75
Battle of Mount Badon 31, 264
Battle of Tailtiu 133
Bé Chuille 76, 141, 262
Bé Néit 71, 80, 81, 208
Be Theite 141, 262
Bean Sìdhe 209
Bear 27, 193, 211
Beara Peninsula 99
Bed of the Couple 204
Beda 56
Bede 31, 36, 130, 161, 254
Befind 85

Beinn Chailleach Bheur
  Argyllshire 103
Beinn na Caillich
  Islay 103
Bel 78
Belatucadros 77, 111, 192
Belenus 78, 79, 80, 116
Belgae
  tribe 24
Belgium 104, 105, 219
Beli 57, 66, 78, 79, 125, 148, 151, 179, 259
Beli Mawr 79
Belisama 79
Bellona 72, 80
Beltane 27, 78, 101, 154, 180
Beluctadros 80
Ben Nevis 100
Ben Vaichaird 102, 103
Benwell
  Northumberland 62, 174, 203
Beowulf 34, 37, 146, 165, 166, 252
Berne Scholiasts 37, 243
Berne Zinc Tablet 147
Bes 81, 167
Bevis Marks
  London 178
Bewcastle
  Cumbria 111, 125
Bilé 78, 79, 81, 82, 121, 146
Binchester
  Co. Durham 41, 233
Bird 102, 204
Birdoswald
  Cumbria 41, 173, 226
Birds of Rhiannon 89, 110, 227
Birrens
  Dumfries & Galloway 156, 223, 228, 250
Bitterne
  Hampshire 58
Black Agnes 82

Black Annis 32, 82, 83, 160
Black Book of Carmarthen 32, 34, 39, 107, 108, 150, 153, 154, 179, 180, 183, 189
Black Monday 82
Blackfriars
  London 43, 167
Bleiddwn 146, 259
Blodeuwedd 67, 83, 84, 152, 175, 193
Blood .. 71, 72, 83, 158, 195, 200, 203, 218
Blotugus 136, 137
Boand 119
Boann 60, 85, 86, 120, 206, 261
Boar 27, 102, 104, 105, 111, 146, 150, 165, 166, 183, 190, 212, 251, 253
Bodedern
  Anglesey 129
Bona Dea 86, 98
Bonedd yr Arwyr 39, 125, 126
Bonus Eventus 87
Book of Armagh 37
Book of Ballymote 39
Book of Durrow 36
Book of Fermoy 33, 39
Book of Hy Many 39
Book of Invasions 33, 38, 54, 71, 75, 82, 93, 119, 121, 133, 134, 167, 168, 174, 182, 184, 189, 203, 207, 209
Book of Lecan 33, 39, 93, 121, 168, 204, 205
Book of Leinster 33, 38, 121, 134, 138, 195
Book of Lismore 33, 39
Book of Magauran 39
Book of Taliesin 34, 39, 65, 66, 67, 78, 79, 84, 107, 109, 126, 127, 152, 154, 162, 163, 224
Book of the Dun Cow 33, 38
Borough Green
  Kent 58
Boudicca 59
Boudihillia 56
Bovinda 86

Bow 116, 117, 158
Bow and Arrow 116, 122
Boyne
   river 85
Braciaca 88, 192
Braint
   river 94
Bran 57, 88, 89, 90, 91, 153, 171, 172, 177, 189, 222, 242, 259
Branwen 90, 91, 177, 189, 222, 259
Branwen the Daughter of Llyr 88, 90, 171, 189, 222, 227, 242
Braughing
   Hertfordshire 210
Bread 42
Brechin
   river 94
Brecon
   Monmouthshire 233
Bregans 91
Brennus 26
Brent
   river 94
Bres 92, 95, 132, 181, 215, 261
Bretha Déin Chécht 36, 123, 124
Bri Bruachbrec 199
Brian 63, 75, 93, 121, 167, 168, 204, 261, 265
Brian Bóru 63, 265
Bride 95, 100, 102, 261
Bride's Day 102
Brigantes
   tribe 91, 94, 263
Brigantia 44, 91, 94, 96, 98, 125, 249
Brigid 95, 96, 119, 261
Brigindo 94
Brigit 92, 94, 95, 96
Britannia 96
Brittany 264, 265
Broom 83, 220
Brough-on-Noe

Derbyshire 68
Brown Bull of Cúailnge 194, 204
Brugh na Boinne 61
Bruiden Da Chocae 39, 71, 72
Brut 143
Bryn Gwydion
   Gwynedd 153
Búan 96, 97
Búan's Well 97
Búanann 96, 97
Bull 27, 109, 110, 154, 200, 201, 236, 250, 251
Bull Horned 109, 250
Buonia's Well 97
Butterfly 117
Buxton
   Derbyshire 68
Cad Goddeu 39, 57, 65, 83, 84, 88, 90, 127, 150, 151, 152, 153, 154, 201
Caduceus 196, 197
Caelestis 30, 87, 98, 125
Caerleon
   Monmouthshire 210, 221, 233, 243
Caernarvon
   Anglesey 201
Caerwent
   Monmouthshire 44, 173, 197, 217, 236, 244
Caesar 17, 27, 33, 36, 110, 180, 181, 211, 233, 241, 263
Caicher 75, 207
Cailitín 194
Caillagh ny Gromagh 98, 102
Cailleach 72, 98, 99, 100, 101, 102, 204
Cailleach Beara 98, 99, 103
Cailleach Bheur 82, 98, 100, 101, 102, 103
Cailleach Bolus 99
Cailleach Corca Duibune 99
Cairpre 207

Caithréimm Thoirdhealbhaigh 71, 72, 278
Callirius 104
Camóg river 55
Campestres 43
Camulodunum 104, 263
Camulos 104, 192
Canterbury Kent 58, 147
Caradawc 259
Carlisle Cumbria 40, 41, 76, 106, 112, 169, 182, 230
Carman 105
Carnelian 62, 70, 156
Carpre 135
Carrawburgh Northumberland 41, 43, 44, 114, 201
Carriag Chlíona Co. Cork 110
Carvetii tribe 77
Carvoran Northumberland 69, 131, 222
Castlesteads Cumbria 41, 43, 247
Caswallan 259
Caswallon 79, 179
Cat 76, 82
Cat Anna 82
Cath Magh Mucrama 38, 54, 55
Cath Maige Tuired 37, 60, 61, 74, 76, 85, 92, 93, 95, 115, 118, 119, 123, 124, 135, 147, 148, 167, 168, 178, 179, 180, 181, 184, 186, 187, 188, 202, 203, 204, 207, 215, 216, 218
Cath Muighe Rath 38
Cath Muighe Tuireadh 37, 71, 76, 77, 92, 118, 123, 140, 141, 184, 198, 202, 203, 207, 215, 218

Catona 131
Catterick Yorkshire 69, 122
Cattle 85, 102, 140, 158
Catuvellauni tribe 116
Cauldron 65, 102, 107, 108, 109, 118, 147, 171, 172, 175, 205, 231
Cautes 105, 106
Cave 61, 82, 83
Celts 33, 42, 59, 77, 101, 120, 173, 176, 263
Cerberus 158
Cerealia 106
Ceres 106, 213
Ceridwen 19, 107, 108, 126
Cermait 119, 218, 261
Cerne Abbas 157
Cernunnos 109, 110, 158
Ces Noinden 186
Cesair 75, 262
Cethen 123, 262
Cethor MacGreine 119, 132
Cethor MacGriene 261
Chair of Ceridwen 67
Chariot 80, 138, 140, 181, 188, 214, 238, 249
Chedworth Gloucestershire 240
Cheese 231
Chess 201
Chester Cheshire 164, 210, 233, 238
Chesterford Essex 211
Chesterholm Northumberland 41, 157, 214
Chesters Northumberland 62, 86, 226
Chicken 108
Chiddingfold

Surrey 244
Children of Darkness 177, 259
Children of Light 79, 177, 259
Chilgrove
   Sussex 142
Chiron 53
Christ 73, 255
Cian 93, 123, 180, 181, 261, 262
Cirencester
   Gloucestershire 115, 229, 239, 240
Cirencester Relief
   Gloucestershire 42
Clídna 110
Cliodna 187
Clíodna 261
Cliona's Wave 110
Cloak 194
Club 103, 116, 119, 157, 158, 160, 161, 199, 254
Clynnog Fawr
   Gwynedd 153
Cocidius 111, 192, 248
Cock 117, 196, 237
Cockersand Moss
   Lancashire 214
Codex of St Gall 37, 148
Cogadh Gaedhel re Gallaibh 38, 208, 209
Cóir Anman 38, 140
Colbin Sands
   Morayshire 237
Colchester
   Essex 40, 59, 104, 131, 156, 196, 229, 240, 249
Comb 135, 183
Compert Mongán 187
Conch Shells 214
Conchobar 194
Concordia 112
Condatis 112, 192
Condrusi

tribe 250
Conn 174
Conn of the Hundred Battles 182
Connacht 194, 209
Connaught 138
Conservatores 40
Contrebis 113, 165
Coranians 179
Corbridge
   Northumberland 66, 69, 112, 117, 125, 158, 199, 231, 233, 237, 238
Cormac's Glossary 37, 80, 81, 95, 96, 97, 184, 185, 186, 208
Cormorant 101
Corn 87, 105, 106, 107, 170
Cornucopia 41, 44, 142, 206, 219, 227, 230, 253
Coronis 53
Corotiacus 113, 192
Corrgenn 119
Corrguinecht 181
Corryvreckan 102, 205
Coscar 134, 261
Cottenham
   Cambridgeshire 254
Council of Arles 45
Coventina 44, 114
Cow 85, 86, 99, 140, 160, 204
Cramond
   Lothian 112
Crane 188, 199
Creiddylad 154, 180, 259
Creidhne 115, 147, 179
Creirwy 20, 107
Cridenbel 61
Crone 98, 99, 101
Cronos 234
Crow 71, 101, 133, 185, 204, 209
Cruinn 185
Crunnchu 185
Cu 123, 262

289

Cú Chulainn 20, 86, 96, 97, 99, 138, 139, 175, 182, 186, 187, 194, 203, 204, 209, 234
Cuda 115
Cuirass 230
Cultores 40
Cunobelin 116
Cunobelinus 116
Cup 140, 182, 197
Cupid 116, 221
Curse 185, 186
Custodes 40
Custom Scrubs
  Gloucestershire 219
Cwmbran
  Monmouthshire 90
Cwn Annwn 99, 154
Cybele 69, 87, 117
Cynan 126, 259
Daghda 60, 61, 75, 85, 92, 95, 118, 119, 120, 121, 123, 140, 143, 202, 203, 204, 218, 261, 262
Daglingworth
  Gloucestershire 115
Daigh Bhride
  Co. Clare 96
Danand 121
Dane Hills
  Leicestershire 82
Danu 79, 93, 120, 121, 125, 167, 168, 204, 205, 209, 218, 261
Danube
  river 120
De Gabáil in t-Sída 38, 60, 61
Dea Nutrix 43, 44
Dea Syria 69
Deer 102, 140, 146, 151, 159, 160, 192
Defixiones 17, 197, 210, 240
Delbaeth 261
Demeter 106
Demon 107

Dendrophori 70
Deo Qui Vias et Semitas Commentus Est 122
Deor 252
Derby
  Derbyshire 88
Detar 143
Devil 161
Diadem 169, 197
Dian 105
Dian Cecht 115, 119, 123, 148, 180, 215, 261, 262
Diana 28, 122
Diarmaid 150
Diarmuid 61, 150
Digant 126, 259
Digenis 19
Dinand 141, 262
Dinshenchas 33, 38, 85, 86, 105, 119, 123, 184, 186, 187, 202, 203, 204, 241
Dio Cassius 33, 59
Diodorus Siculus 27, 33
Dionysiaca 73
Dionysus 223
Dis Pater 79, 110
Disciplina 124
Dithorba 186
Divination 59
Dobar 181
Dobunni
  tribe 115
Dog 93, 103, 151, 183, 191, 201, 214
Doliche 124
Dolichenus 30, 98, 124, 170, 233
Dolphin 111, 117, 211
Don 57, 66, 79, 109, 125, 126, 146, 148, 151, 152, 176, 177, 259
Donn 82, 126, 133, 207
Donn Cúlainge 204
Dothur 105
Dove 69

Dovecote 206
Dragon 179
Dream of Rhonabwy. 107, 129, 183, 201
Droichet na ndaltae 234
Drudwyn 183
Druid 263
Dryan 216, 259
Dub 105
Dún Scaith 234
Dunaire Finn 38, 150
Dylan 66, 67, 127, 148, 174, 176, 259
Eagle 84, 101, 152, 170, 175, 242, 253
East Stoke
   Nottinghamshire 206
Ebchester
   Co. Durham 248
Ecclesiastical History of the English
   Nation 36, 254
Echtgi 119, 261
Echtra Mac Echach Muigmeddóin .. 39, 135
Eddas 18, 31, 34
Edeyrn 129, 153, 216, 259
   Gwynedd 129
Edict of Milan 45, 264
Eel 204
Egg 115, 201
Eggs 42
Elatha 92, 261
Elawg 126, 259
Elcmar 61, 85, 120
Elder Edda 34
Elder Futhark 263, 264
Elene 34
Elephant 237
Elestron 126, 259
Emain Macha 139, 186
Emer 139
Emhain Abhlach 188
Emperor Aurelian 238
Emperor Constans 264

Emperor Constantine 264
Emperor Decius 264
Emperor Eugenius 264
Emperor Julian 264
Emperor Theodosius 264
Emperor Valerian 264
England 41, 43, 53, 64, 72, 82, 87, 94, 96, 104, 111, 112, 122, 130, 190, 202, 211, 212, 213, 236, 237, 239, 243, 244, 245, 247, 248, 250, 251, 253, 254, 255, 263, 265
Englynion y Beddau 39, 184, 201
Enid 129
Eochaid 121, 123, 194, 198, 199, 215
Eochaid Airem 198
Eochaid Dala 194
Eochaid Garb 241
Eochaid Ollathair 118
Eogonacht 55
Eolgarg Mór 99
Eostra 130, 165
Epona 30, 130, 131, 184, 226
Erce 131
Eri 92, 132, 261
Ériu 71, 75, 119, 121, 126, 132, 133, 134, 142, 184, 261
Ernmas 71, 75, 121, 132, 134, 143, 204, 261
Esarg 123
Esus 244
Étaín 135, 187, 198, 199
Etan 123, 262
Etar 75
Ethlinn 181
Ethne 74, 93, 123, 180, 261
Eunydd 126, 259
Eurosswydd 177, 222, 259
Evnyssien 172, 222, 259
Exeter Book 34, 37, 252, 253, 254
Exodus to the Ingefolc 166
Eye 83, 86, 101, 186

Faery 55, 60, 100, 138, 153, 154, 213, 227
Faery Queen 54, 63, 194, 202
Fail-Inis 181
Fallsteads
    Cumbria 173
Fand 187, 261
Fanum Cocidi 111
Farley Heath
    Surrey 161, 240
Fates 42, 136, 138
Fauna 86
Faunalia 136
Fauni 136
Faunus 86, 136, 137, 195
Fea 137, 209, 261
Fedelm 137, 138, 139
Fer Diad 175, 194
Fergus 139, 140, 141, 194, 195
Fiachna 99, 139, 187, 188
Fiachna Finn 99, 187, 188, 261
Fiachra 75, 132, 143, 174, 261
Fidchell 181
Fimmilena 56
Finn 33, 38, 149, 150, 187, 188, 199
Fionn Cycle 33
Fionnula 174
Fir 123
Fir Bolgs 32, 71, 92, 121, 123, 134, 171,
    184, 198, 203, 215
Fire 71, 78, 96, 203, 251
First Battle of Moytura 115, 121, 186, 215
First Council of Nicaea 264
Firth of Cromarty 83
Fish 69, 108, 117, 127, 188, 214
Fled Bicrenn 194
Flidais 139, 140, 141, 194, 262
Fomorians 32, 74, 76, 85, 92, 93, 95, 105,
    119, 121, 123, 135, 137, 168, 188, 203,
    204, 207, 218, 241
Fortuna 87, 141, 142, 230, 246

Fotla 71, 75, 119, 121, 132, 134, 142, 143,
    184, 209, 261
Fraech 85
Fragarach 187
Frampton
    Gloucestershire 211
France .... See Gaul
Franks Casket 52, 253
Freefolk
    Hampshire 144
Fretherne
    Gloucestershire 144
Frey 166
Freya 143, 144
Friagabis 56
Fridaythorpe
    Yorkshire 144
Friden
    Derbyshire 144
Frigg 143, 144, 244
Frobury
    Hampshire 144
Froxfield
    Wiltshire 117
Froyle
    Hampshire 144
Fruit 84, 87, 107
Fryup
    Yorkshire 144
Fuamnach 187
Fury 204
Gae Bolga 175, 234
Gaia 242
Gaim 134, 261
Garmangabi 145
Gaul 43, 44, 60, 79, 80, 105, 109, 110,
    130, 147, 149, 173, 178, 193, 202, 206,
    228, 235, 239, 240, 241, 243, 263, 264
Gavenny
    river 149
Geat 31, 145

Geats
  tribe 146, 252
Geis 150
Genii Cucullati 41, 42, 115, 230
Genius 40, 41
Genius Centuriae 40
Genius Cohortis 40
Genius Collegi 40
Genius Cucullatus 41
Genius Loci 40, 41, 44
Genius Praetori 40
Genius Terrae Britannicae 41
Gentle Annie 83
Gen-traiges 86
Geography
  Ptolemy 17, 36, 79, 158, 218, 232
  Strabo 36
Geraint 129
Geraint the Son of Erbin 129, 153
Gerald Fitzgerald 55
Germania 36, 212
Gilvaethwy 57, 66, 79, 125, 146, 148, 151, 192, 222, 259
Glastonbury Tor 154
Globe 94, 142, 249
Glon 134, 261
Gloucester
  Gloucestershire ... 40, 76, 81, 117, 208
Gluneu eil Taran 242
Goat 102, 117, 170, 221
Gobannos 30, 147
Godmanchester
  Cambridgeshire 51
Gododin Poems 36, 52
Goewin 146, 151, 192
Goibniu .95, 115, 147, 148, 179, 180, 188
Golden Fleece 53
Goldsmiths
  London 178
Gol-traiges 85
Goose 55, 117, 173, 242

Gorse 102
Gorsedd Bran
  Denbighshire 90
Gort na Morrígna
  Co. Louth 205
Govannon 57, 66, 79, 125, 126, 127, 147, 148, 149, 222, 259
Grainne 61, 101
Grannos 149
Grapes 87, 117, 221
Grawl 190
Greta Bridge
  Co. Durham 220
Greyhound 108
Grián 149, 186, 261
Grianaig 101
Grianan 101
Griánne 150
Grim 254
Gronw 84, 152, 175
Gull 101
Gundestrup Cauldron 109
Gwanar 67, 151, 259
Gweirydd 116
Gwenwynwyn 67, 259
Gwern 90
Gwion Bach 20, 107, 108
Gwri Gwallt-Euryn 223
Gwydion 57, 66, 67, 79, 83, 84, 89, 125, 126, 146, 148, 151, 152, 175, 176, 192, 222, 223, 259
Gwyn ap Nudd 129, 153, 154, 155, 180, 216, 259
Gwythyr ap Greidal 154, 180
Gyre Carling 101, 103
Hadrian's Wall 44, 56, 117, 124, 125, 210, 237, 246, 249, 263
Hafgan 65, 224
Hafren 232
Hag 71, 83, 101, 150
Hallstatt Culture 25

Hammer 131, 239, 240, 244
Hare 59, 82, 87, 108, 111, 117
Harimella 156
Harlow
   Essex 116
Harold
   King 265
Harpocrates 156, 161, 166
Harpokrates 29
Hartland Point
   Devon 158
Hawk 108, 161, 220
Hazel 206, 237
Head of Annwn 224
Hebe 61, 169
Hecataeus 25
Hector 207
Hedd 126, 259
Helios 157
Helioserapis 157
Helis .... *See* Helith
Helith 157
Helmet 131, 188, 196, 200, 247
Hera 157, 246
Herakles 157
Hercules 19, 28, 30, 61, 157, 158, 199
Hercules Promontory 158
Herian 158, 254
Herne 158, 159
Herodian 36, 78
Herodotus 25
Heron 101
Hesperides 93, 181
Hiccafrith 32, 160
High Rochester
   Northumberland 40, 44, 202, 222, 230
Hippocamp 117
Historia Britonum 37, 126, 127, 137, 232
Histories 25
History of Rome 36, 59

History of the Empire after Marcus. 36, 78
Hoe 117
Holly 102, 124
Horned Goose 131
Horse 27, 55, 83, 117, 126, 129, 130, 131, 135, 138, 139, 151, 154, 160, 175, 176, 181, 184, 185, 187, 188, 194, 214, 226, 227, 228, 235, 252, 254
Horus 29, 156, 161, 166
Hospitales 40
Hot Springs 195
Hounslow
   Middlesex 253
House of Don 125
Housesteads
   Northumberland. 41, 42, 56, 200, 201
Hreda 161
Hu Gadarn 162, 163
Huan 176
Hunawg 126, 259
Hychdwn the Tall 146, 259
Hydwn 146, 259
Hygiaea 164, 221
Ialona 165
Ialonus 113, 165
IAO 52
Iceni
   tribe 59
Idath 85
Idwal 126, 259
Imbass Forosna 138
Imbolc 95
Indech 85
Ing 165, 166
Ingaevones
   tribe 146, 166
Ireland 54, 55, 57, 60, 71, 74, 75, 76, 80, 81, 85, 88, 92, 93, 94, 95, 96, 98, 101, 103, 105, 110, 115, 118, 119, 120, 123, 126, 127, 132, 133, 134, 135, 137, 139,

140, 141, 142, 147, 149, 150, 167, 168, 171, 174, 178, 180, 182, 184, 186, 187, 188, 189, 193, 195, 198, 202, 203, 204, 205, 206, 207, 208, 215, 218, 234, 235, 237, 241, 264, 265
Iron.82, 103, 124, 125, 148, 171, 212, 213
Isaiah 203
Isis 29, 30, 156, 166, 167, 236
Isle of Man 98, 187, 188
Isle of Thanet 180
Itchen
river 58
Iuchar 93, 167, 168, 204
Iucharba 93, 121, 167, 168, 204
Iveragh
Co. Kerry 96
Jago 79, 259
Janus 116, 237
Jasper 52, 157
Javelin 147, 161
Jesus 100
Jet 129, 193
John O'Donovan 97
Judith 34
Junius Manuscript 34
Juno 28, 87, 169, 199
Jupiter 28, 29, 58, 98, 106, 124, 157, 169, 170, 191, 196, 199, 233, 234, 236, 242, 253
Jutes 35, 264
Kettering
Northamptonshire 73
Kicva 189
Kilhwch 154, 183
Kilhwch and Olwen 34, 37, 57, 67, 107, 148, 154, 180, 183, 190, 216, 219, 220
King Arthur 65, 89, 129, 154, 183, 201, 219
King Richard II 159
King Richard III 82
Kingscote

Oxfordshire 142, 228
Knife 188, 237
Knockainey
Munster Plain 54
Kymideu Kymeinvoll 171
La Tene Culture 26
Labrad Lesbric 207
Lacnunga 34, 37, 254
Ladle 231
Lagobolon 87
Lair Derg 55
Lament of the Old Woman of Beara 37, 99
Lamia 203
Lamiae 203
Lancaster
Lancashire 165
Lance 129, 170
Lanchester
Co. Durham 40, 41, 106, 145
Lares 43, 44
Latis 173
Laymon 144
Leabhar Bhaile an Mhóta 39
Leabhar Buidhe Lecain 33, 39, 98, 118
Leabhar Méig Shamhradháin 39, 75, 142, 143, 198
Leabhar Mór Leacain 33, 39, 93, 120, 167, 168, 202
Leabhar na h-Uidhri 33, 38, 120, 134, 137, 193
Leanan Sídhe 55
Lebar na nUidre 33, 38
Lebor Gabála Érenn 33, 38, 54, 71, 75, 81, 82, 92, 93, 119, 120, 121, 123, 126, 127, 132, 133, 134, 137, 142, 143, 147, 167, 168, 174, 180, 182, 184, 187, 189, 202, 203, 206, 207, 208, 209, 215, 216
Leechbook 34, 37
Leicestershire 82
Leinster 101

Lenumius 174
Lenus 173, 192, 217
Life of King Arthur 37, 145
Life of Saint Samson of Dol 37, 99
Lightning 159, 242
Lir 120, 174, 177, 187, 261
Llantwit Major
   Glamorgan 142
Llassar Llaesgyvnewid 171
Lleu 67, 83, 84, 127, 152, 174, 175, 176, 182
Lleu Llaw Gyffes 66, 67, 174, 259
Llevelys 179, 259
Lliaws mab Nwyfre 67, 151, 259
Lludd Llaw Ereint 179
Llwyd 190, 227
Llyfr Coch Hergest See Red Book of Hergest
Llyfr Du Caerfyrddin See Black Book of Carmarthen
Llyfyr Gwyn Rhydderch See White Book of Rhydderch
Llyn Bran
   Denbighshire 90
Llyn Llion
   lake 163
Llyr 177, 190, 222, 259
Lochmaben
   Dumfriesshire 191
Lockleys
   Hertfordshire 167
Loki 73, 177
London 43, 44, 69, 70, 73, 89, 117, 156, 179, 189, 201, 217, 236, 238
London Hunter God 70, 178
Longes mac nUsnig 38, 139, 140
Lotus 156
Loucetius 178, 192
Lower Slaughter
   Gloucestershire 41
Lucan 27, 33, 36, 241, 242, 243, 244

Luchar 121, 261
Luchta 115, 147, 178, 179
Ludd 179, 180, 216, 259
Ludd and Llevelys 179
Lugh 20, 61, 74, 92, 93, 99, 119, 120, 121, 123, 132, 141, 175, 176, 180, 181, 182, 188, 241, 261, 262
Lugh Lamfada 180
Lughnasadh 27, 241
Lugus 175, 182
Luin Spear 181
Lune
   river 165
Lydney
   Gloucestershire 73, 214
Mabinogion 33, 39, 216
Mabon 60, 70, 183, 184, 190, 260
Mac Cecht 205
Macha 71, 75, 121, 130, 134, 142, 184, 185, 186, 187, 203, 204, 226, 261
Macha Mongruad 186
Macha's Acorn Crop 184
Macha's Mast 185
Maeve 194
Magh Mechi 205
Magh Mell 188
Magick Staff 101, 102
Magick Wand 67, 175, 192
Magna Mater 117
Maia 196
Maiden 100, 101, 138, 139, 150
Manannan 261
Manannán 54, 99, 120, 187, 188, 189
Manawyddan 90, 177, 189, 190, 222, 223, 227, 259
Manawyddan the Son of Llyr .. 189, 227
Mandubratius 180, 259
Mani 72
Mannanan 61, 174, 237
Mantle 100, 197
Maol Flidais 140

Maponos 60, 70, 190
Maponus 190
Mars25, 28, 56, 57, 62, 76, 77, 80, 88,
    105, 111, 112, 113, 130, 169, 173, 178,
    191, 192, 196, 210, 214, 217, 219, 228,
    229, 235, 242, 243, 246, 249, 251
Mars Corotiacus 113
MarsThincsus 246
Martlesham
    Suffolk 113
Maryport
    Cumbria 41, 230, 235, 236, 249
Math67, 83, 84, 125, 146, 151, 152, 175,
    192, 193
Math Mathonwy 259
Math the Son of Mathonwy65, 66, 83,
    84, 127, 146, 151, 175, 192
Matholwch 90
Mathonwy 125, 192
Matres 42, 43, 136
Matres Brittiae 43
Matres Coccae 42
Matres Domesticae 43
Matres Germaniae 42
Matres Ollototae 43
Matres Omnium Gentium 43
Matres Tramarinae 42
Matrona 201
Matunus 193
Maurice Fitzgerald 55
Maxims I 254, 255
Mechi 205
Mechti 261
Medb 72, 138, 193, 194, 195
Medicina de Quadrupedibus 37, 53
Medigenus 136, 137, 195
Medocius 192, 196
Meduana 195
Meigle
    Perthshire 251
Menstrual Blood 195

Mercury28, 59, 110, 173, 181, 196, 197,
    230, 254
Mermaid 69
Mesca Ulad 36
Mesrad Machae 185
Methe 197
Metrical Dinshenchas 186
Miach 123, 262
Michaelchurch
    Herefordshire 246
Midir 124, 135, 198, 199
Milesians 32, 75, 120, 126, 133
Milidh 82
Milk 92
Mimir 89
Mimming 252
Minerva28, 73, 80, 94, 96, 97, 158, 199,
    237, 240, 249
Mistletoe 73
Mithraea 200, 201, 217
Mithraeum 69, 73, 201
Mithras 29, 30, 62, 105, 106, 200, 238
Mjollnir 244
Modron 65, 183, 184, 201, 260
Mogons 202
Mongán 99, 187, 188, 261
Morda 107
Morfydd 201, 202, 260
Morrígan54, 59, 71, 81, 85, 86, 93, 97,
    99, 100, 119, 121, 125, 134, 140, 167,
    168, 184, 185, 194, 202, 203, 204, 205,
    208, 226, 261
Morrígna 185
Morrigu 54, 139, 204
Morvran 107
Mount Etna 251
MSS Bannatyne 103
MSS Harley 3859 .... 78, 79
MSS Peniarth 127 39
MSS Peniarth 98b 39
MSS Regina 215 203

MSS Trinity H.3.18 184
Munster 209
Musselborough
   Midlothian 149
Mynogen 79
Mythological Cycle 33
Nama 207
Nant y Llew
   Gwynedd 176
Nantosuelta 30, 206, 239
Narius 136, 137
Nechtan 86, 206, 207
Neit 74, 80, 92
Néit 71, 81, 123, 125, 207, 208, 261
Neith 208
Nemain 81, 137, 204, 207, 208, 209
Nemean Lion 158
Nemedh 185
Nemesis 30, 209
Nemetate
   tribe 211
Nemetes
   tribe 211
Nemetius 192, 210
Nemetona 114, 178, 209, 210, 229
Nennius 37, 232
Neptunalia 211
Neptune 211, 214, 217
Nerthus 131, 165, 212, 213
Nettleham
   Lincolnshire 229
Nettleton
   Lincolnshire 60
Newcastle-upon-Tyne
   Tyne & Wear 40, 217
Niall of the Nine Hostages ... 36
Niamh 187, 261
Nike 59
Nimes
   Gaul 80
Nine 100

Nine Herb Charm 255
Nodens 73, 192, 211, 213, 214
Noe
   river 68
Noínden Ulad 7 Emuin Macha37, 184, 185
Norici
   tribe 78
Norns 138
North Tawton
   Devon 211
Northwich
   Cheshire 112
Notre Dame 109
Nuada 92, 115, 118, 123, 186, 214, 215, 216, 261
Nudd 57, 66, 79, 125, 129, 148, 150, 153, 180, 214, 215, 216, 222, 259
Nun 98, 208
Nymph 44, 114, 196, 197, 243
Nynyaw 179, 259
Nyssien 222, 259
Nyx 216
O'Davoren's Glossary 39
Oak 82, 83, 158, 159, 244
Oceanus 217, 242
Ocelius Promontory 218
Ocelos 173, 217
Ocelus 192, 217
Odin 31, 158, 254, 255
Oenach Tailten 241
Offa's Dyke 265
Ogham 57, 162, 218, 235, 264
Ogma 61, 92, 93, 118, 119, 120, 218, 261, 262
Ogma Grianainech 218
Ogma Trenfher 218
Ogmia 218
Ogmios 218
Ogniad 199
Oidhe Chloinne Lir 39, 174

Oidheadh Chloinne Tuireann 38, 92, 93, 94, 140, 141, 167, 168, 180, 181, 187, 188
Old Carlisle
   Cumbria 80
Old English Herbarium 34, 37
Old Penrith
   Northumberland 125
Oll 123
Olloudius 192, 219
Olwen 154, 219, 220
Onirus 220
Onyx 167, 170
Orbsen 189
Orpheus 89
Osiris 29, 166, 236
Ostara 130
Oswyo
   King 46
Otherworld 99, 103, 110, 133, 135, 141, 148, 154, 182, 187, 188, 198
Otter 108
Ouranos 242
Ouroboros 167
Overborough
   Lancashire 113, 164
Owein 201, 202, 260
Owl 84, 152
Pagan Celtic Britain 105, 235, 251
Palm 249
Pan 221, 237
Panakeia 221
Panther 73
Paps of Ana 121
Paps of Anu 121, 134
Parcae 42, 136
Pasture 184
Patera 41, 64, 87, 142, 169, 170, 196, 200, 210, 230, 236, 239
Pax 222

Penarddun 57, 66, 79, 125, 148, 177, 222, 259
Penates 40
Persephone 106
Pharsalia 36, 241, 242, 243
Philip Urswick 159
Phrygian Soft Cap 70, 178
Pig 65, 93, 102, 103, 140, 151, 152, 181, 188, 192
Pine Cone 70
Plough 132
Poetic Edda 34
Porridge 85, 119
Poseidon 211
Preiddeu Annwn 39, 65, 224
Priapus 223
Prophecy 138, 209, 234
Prophetess 185
Prose Edda 34, 39
Prosperina 106
Pryderi 65, 151, 152, 189, 190, 192, 223, 224, 225, 259
Psychopomp 62, 227
Ptolemy 17, 36, 79, 158, 211, 218, 232
Pwyll 65, 190, 222, 224, 225, 227, 259
Pwyll Prince of Dyved 224, 227
Queen Mab 194
Queen Medb 194
Queen of Summer 100
Queen of Winter 100
Quirinus 28
Ram 41, 58, 77, 104, 196, 210
Ram Horned 77, 104
Ram-headed Serpent 192
Rata 226
Rattle 196
Raven 27, 41, 42, 71, 88, 90, 101, 107, 131, 185, 201, 206, 209, 254
Red 100
Red Book of Hergest 34, 39, 57, 65, 66, 78, 83, 88, 90, 107, 125, 127, 129, 146,

148, 150, 151, 153, 162, 163, 171, 174, 177, 179, 183, 189, 192, 201, 216, 219, 222, 223, 224, 226
Red Mare 55
Regina 87, 131, 169, 233
Reicne Fothaid Canainne 37
Rhea 87
Rhiannon130, 184, 189, 190, 223, 224, 225, 226, 227, 259
Rhine
  river 44, 145, 210, 211
Rhun 79, 259
Ribble
  river 79
Ribchester
  Lancashire 233
Ricagumbeda 227, 228
Richborough
  Kent 218
Rider God 192, 228
Rigatona 226
Rigisamus 192, 228
Rigonemetis 229
Rigonemetos 192
Risingham
  Cambridgeshire 40, 193, 249
River 120
Ro-ech 139
Rokeby
  Yorkshire 210
Roma 229, 230
Romulus and Remus 229
Rosmerta 182, 230, 231
Roussas
  Drôme 131
Ruabon
  Denbighshire 184
Ruadán 95, 148, 261
Ruadh Rofhessa 118
Rudchester
  Northumberland 64, 201

Rudder 142, 249
Rudston
  Yorkshire 142
Rune Poem143, 144, 165, 166, 245, 254, 255
Ruxox
  Bedfordshire 73
Sabert
  King 46
Sabraind
  river 232
Sabrina 232
Saint Albanus 45
Saint Augustine 46
Saint Columba 45
Saint Martin of Tours 53
Saint Mellitus 46
Saint Palladius 45
Saint Samson 100
Saitada 232, 233
Salmon 138, 206
Salmon Leap 234
Salmon of Llyn Llyw 183
Salus 98, 233
Samhain 60, 101, 203
Saternius 136, 137
Saturn 106, 233, 234
Saxons 35, 166, 235, 264
Scandinavia 35, 73, 143, 177, 245
Scáthach 96, 234
Scéla Conchobair maic Nessa38, 139, 140
Sceptre .169, 170, 210, 230, 236, 240, 242
Scorpions 200
Scotland64, 83, 94, 98, 102, 103, 104, 111, 130, 188, 190, 191, 202, 241, 242, 250, 263
Scuabtuinne 187
Sea Mills
  Somerset 197
Seaxnéat 31, 235

Second Battle of Moytura 74, 92, 119, 132, 181, 186, 203, 216
Sedulius 146
Segomo 192, 235
Selgovae
   tribe 263
Serapis 29, 30, 157, 166, 235, 236
Serglige Con Culainn 38, 187
Serpent 27, 167, 170, 200, 205, 233, 248, 251
Sethor MacCuill 118, 143, 261
Setlocenia 236
Severn
   river 178, 214, 232
Severn Estuary 178
Sgrìoh na Caillich 103
Shakespeare 154, 158, 180
Shannon
   river 237
Shape-shifting 101, 204
Shears 188
Sheep 83
Shield 52, 89, 111, 161, 192, 200, 228, 230, 247
Sidhe 55
Sigmall 207
Silchester
   Hampshire 52, 229, 236
Silenus 237
Silures
   tribe 217
Silva Gadelica 110
Silvanus 25, 28, 104, 111, 214, 236, 237, 239, 249, 251
Silver 100, 101
Silver Hand 115, 215
Sionna 237
Sir Walter Scott 103
Sir Yder 129
Sirona 149
Sistrum 167

Skaldic Verses 31, 34, 35
Skye 234
Slack
   Yorkshire 91, 104
Sleipnir 254
Sliab na Caillighe 103
Sling 74
Snorri Sturluson 34
Sol 62
Sol Invictus 200, 218, 238
Song of Fothad Canainne 37
Sorcery 203
Soter 238
South Shields
   Co. Durham 40, 57, 60, 64, 211
Southbroom
   Wiltshire 63, 192, 196
Southbroom Hoard 63
Southwark
   London 166, 178
Sovereignty 63, 132, 194, 227
Sow 101
Spear 73, 88, 94, 111, 140, 147, 148, 175, 179, 182, 192, 194, 200, 234
Spear of Lugh 181
Spears 52, 115, 147
Spes 239
Spindle 117
Spring Equinox 105
Springs 211, 240
Spurn Head
   Humberside 218
Sreng 92
St Albans
   Hertfordshire 196, 201
St Albans Abbey
   Hertfordshire 170
St Bride 96
St Brigid's Well
   Co. Galway 96
St Collen and Gwyn ap Nudd 154

St Patrick 264
Stag 62, 107, 109, 111, 146, 159
Stag-Horned 109
Stanzas of the Graves 127, 128, 174, 176, 179, 183, 201, 223, 224
Starling 91
Stone 204
Stonesfield Oxfordshire 142
Strabo 33, 36
Strathlachlan 103
Suan-traiges 86
Sucellos 30, 206, 239
Suevi tribe 145
Suleviae 240
Sulis 62, 78, 114, 199, 240
Sulis Minerva 240
Summer 82, 102
Sun ... 64, 85, 101, 157, 181, 188, 214, 253
Swan 60, 198, 220
Sword .. 123, 147, 187, 188, 200, 215, 252
Synod of Whitby 46, 265
Syrinx Pipes 70
Tacitus 33, 36, 211, 212, 213, 232
Tadhg mac Céin 110
Tailtiu 241
Táin 185, 194
Táin Bó Cúailnge 33, 35, 37, 134, 137, 138, 139, 193, 194, 202, 204, 208, 209
Táin Bó Flidais 38, 140, 141, 195
Táin Bó Fraích 38, 85
Taliesin 19, 20, 107, 108, 125
Tanith 98
Taranis 241, 242, 244, 253
Tavlogan 180, 259
Tech Duinn 126
Tegid Voel 19, 107
Teirynon 225
Terminalia 243
Terminus 243

Tertullian 36, 52, 78
Tesiphone 72
Tethor MacCecht 75, 118, 261, 262
Tethys 217, 242
Teutates 111, 192, 243, 244
Thames river 89
The Adventure of the Sons of Eochaid Muigmedón 39, 135
The Anglo Saxon Chronicles 160
The Annals 36, 211, 232
The Battle of the Trees 39, 152
The Book of Taliesin 39
The Chair of Ceridwen 109, 125, 126, 151, 152
The Conception of Mongán . 38, 99, 188
The Courtship of Ferb 38
The Death-song of Dylan, son of the Wave 127
The Destruction of Da Derga's Hostel 38, 126, 135
The Dialogue of Gwyddno Garanhir and Gwyn ap Nudd 150, 153
The Dream of the Rood 34, 37, 73
The Elegy of Aeddon 163
The Exile of the Sons of Usnech 38, 139, 140
The Fate of the Children of Tuirenn 38, 93, 188
The Ford of Barking 65, 201
The Frenzy of the Phantom 37, 182
The Gallic Wars 17, 36, 211, 241, 242
The Hawk of Achill 36
The Histories 36
The Intoxication of the Ulstermen 36
The Library of History 36
The Merry Wives of Windsor .. 158, 159
The Ode of Ceridwen 108
The Second Battle of Moytura 37
The Stanzas of the Graves 39, 180
The Taking of the Fairy Mound 38, 120

The Thebaid of Statius 72
The Tidings of Conchobar son of Ness
.... 38, 139
The Venomous Wild Boar of Glen Glass
.... 101, 149, 150
The Voyage of Bran 36, 188
The War of the Gaedhil with the Gaill
.... 38, 209
The Wasting Sickness of Cú Chulainn
.... 38
The Wooing of Emer 37, 96
The Wooing of Étaín ... 36, 135, 187, 198
Thetford
  Norfolk 52, 137, 195, 246
Thor 31, 244
Thorpe
  Nottinghamshire 239
Thoth 244
Three 100
Three Gods of Danu 121
Thunderfield
  Sussex 245
Thundersley
  Essex 245
Thundridge
  Hertfordshire 245
Thunor 31, 244, 245
Thunoreshlaw
  Kent 245
Thunorslege
  Sussex 245
Thunresfeld
  Wiltshire 245
Tinne 194
Tír fo Thonn 188
Tír na mBean 188
Tír na nOg 188
Tír Tairnigir 188
Tislea
  Hampshire 245
Titan 242

Titans 217
Tiw 192, 244, 245, 246
Tiwaz 246
Tobar Áine
  well 54
Tobar Bhride
  Co. Roscommon 96
Tobar na Baidhbe
  Co. Waterford 72
Tochmarc Émire 37, 71, 80, 96, 137, 139,
  234
Tochmarc Étaíne 36, 85, 135, 187, 198
Tochmarch Ferbae 38, 71, 72
Togail Bruidne Da Derga 38, 71, 126
Tom Hickathrift .... See Hiccafrith
Torc 62, 196
Torch 80, 105, 106, 116, 117
Traprain Law
  East Lothian 64
Triads 39, 65, 79, 89, 116, 162, 163, 176,
  177, 179, 216, 224, 259
Tridamus 246
Trioedd Ynys Prydein 39, 65, 107, 116,
  151
Triple-horned Bull 246
Tritons 214
Túatha dé Danann 32, 74, 75, 92, 93, 94,
  95, 105, 115, 118, 119, 120, 121, 123,
  126, 133, 168, 174, 179, 181, 186, 188,
  198, 203, 204, 215
Tuesley
  Surrey 245
Tuirenn 93
Tuis 181
Turenn 167, 168, 181
Twrch Trwyth 183, 190
Tyche 246
Tyesmere
  Worcestershire 245
Tyr 245
Tysoe

Warwickshire 245
Uaithne 86
Uath Beinne Etair 37, 39, 60, 61
Úathach 234
Ulster 185, 194
Ulster Cycle 33
Ulstermen 185, 186, 209
Underworld 62, 68, 154, 202, 224
Uni 169
Urien 201, 260
Urine 195
Vanuntus 247
Vellaunes 173
Vellaunus 217
Venus 69, 116, 247
Venus Victrix 247
Verba Scáthaige 234
Verbeia 248
Vercelli Book 34, 37, 73
Vernostonus 248
Verulamium 263
Vesta 87, 106
Victoria 94, 200, 248, 249
Viking 265
Vikings 35, 209, 265
Vindolanda
  Northumberland 40, 191
Vinotonus 249
Viradecthis 249, 250
Virgo 98
Viridios 250
Vitiris 25, 250, 251
Volcanus 251
Volundr 252
Votive Offerings 17, 27, 114, 240
Vulcan 169, 251
Vulcanalia 251
Wade 253
Wagon 160, 166, 212, 213
Waldere 36, 37, 252, 253

Wales 52, 57, 65, 66, 78, 83, 88, 90, 91, 107, 125, 127, 129, 146, 148, 150, 151, 153, 162, 171, 173, 174, 177, 179, 183, 189, 192, 201, 216, 219, 222, 223, 224, 226, 264, 265, 280
Walter Scott 101, 252
Wansdyke
Wiltshire 255
Warlingham
  Surrey 157
Washer at the Ford 63, 202
Water 51, 54, 84, 94, 111, 114, 127, 149, 154, 173, 188, 195, 203, 206, 213, 214, 230, 233, 253
Wayland Smith's Cave
  Berkshire 253
Weaver 138
Wednesbury
  Staffordshire 255
Wednesfield
  Staffordshire 255
Weland 52, 252, 253
Well
  Yorkshire 230
Well of Youth 100
Wells 96
Wensley
  Derbyshire 255
West Coker
  Somerset 229
Weston-under-Penyard
  Hertfordshire 239
Westwood
  Essex 216
Weyland's Smithy
  Oxfordshire 252
Wharfe
  river 248
Whatley
  Somerset 117
Wheel God 32, 160, 242, 253

Whip 52, 80, 214, 218, 238
*White Book of Rhydderch*19, 32, 34, 39, 57, 65, 66, 78, 83, 88, 90, 107, 125, 127, 129, 146, 148, 150, 151, 153, 154, 163, 171, 174, 175, 177, 179, 183, 189, 190, 192, 201, 216, 219, 220, 222, 223, 224, 226, 227, 242, 259
White Horse 226, 227
White Ravens 198
Whitley Castle
   Northumberland 64
Widsith.. 36, 253
Wieland 252
Wild Hunt... 153, 154, 158, 159, 160, 254
William Hutchinson.......................... 213
William the Conqueror
   King 265
Willingham
   Cambridgeshire............................ 254
Willingham Fen
   Cambridgeshire............................ 242
Willoughby
   Nottinghamshire 211
Wiltshire.. 131
Windsor Forest 158, 159
Winter.......................... 100, 101, 102, 103
Woddesgeat
   Wiltshire 255

Woden31, 73, 143, 144, 178, 235, 244, 254, 255
Wodnesbeorg
   Wiltshire.. 255
Wodnesdene
   Wiltshire.. 255
Wodnesfeld
   Essex 255
Wodneslawe
   Bedfordsire 255
Wolf 102, 146, 151, 193, 204, 229, 254
Wood Anemone 220
Woodeaton
   Oxfordshire.................................. 211
Woodnesborough
   Kent.. 255
Woodpecker 137
Wreath...230, 249
Wroxeter
   Shropshire.................................... 167
Yellow Book of Lecan..33, 39, 99, 118, 198
Yggdrasill.................................... 73, 255
York
   Yorkshire40, 41, 43, 66, 68, 217, 229, 236, 239, 243
Yspaddaden................................ 154, 219
Zeus 238, 246
Zodiac 201